NAVAL AIR

NAVAL AIR

CELEBRATING A CENTURY OF NAVAL FLYING

PHILIP KAPLAN

Pen & Sword
AVIATION

First published in Great Britain in 2013 by
PEN & SWORD AVIATION
An imprint of
Pen & Sword Books Ltd
47 Church Street
Barnsley
South Yorkshire
S70 2AS

ISBN 978 1 78159 241 0

Printed and bound in England
By CPI Group (UK) Ltd, Croydon, CR0 4YY

Pen & Sword Books Ltd incorporates the Imprints of Pen & Sword Aviation,
Pen & Sword Family History, Pen & Sword Maritime, Pen & Sword Military,
Pen & Sword Discovery, Pen & Sword Politics, Pen & Sword Atlas,
Pen & Sword Archaeology, Wharncliffe Local History, Wharncliffe True Crime,
Wharncliffe Transport, Pen & Sword Select, Pen & Sword Military Classics,
Leo Cooper, The Praetorian Press, Claymore Press, Remember When,
Seaforth Publishing and Frontline Publishing

For a complete list of Pen & Sword titles please contact
PEN & SWORD BOOKS LIMITED
47 Church Street, Barnsley, South Yorkshire, S70 2AS, England
E-mail: enquiries@pen-and-sword.co.uk
Website: www.pen-and-sword.co.uk

CONTENTS

INTRODUCTION

When air power became a major factor in modern warfare during the Second World War, the role of the battleship as the primary capital ship of the world's most powerful navies was taken over by the aircraft carrier. The carrier has enabled such a navy to project its nation's influence through the capabilities of naval aviation, anywhere in the world where that nation's vital interests may be threatened. The head of the Royal Navy, Admiral Sir Mark Stanhope, has said: "To put it simply, countries that aspire to strategic international influence have aircraft carriers."

2011 marked the 100th anniversary of naval aviation. From its awkward beginnings, to the present power projection of the American supercarrier strike groups around the world, naval air has evolved into the most significant and imposing fighting force in history. These strike groups, each comprised of a supercarrier and several warships in her support, are able to bring nearly unimaginable military force to wherever it may be needed. While not entirely invulnerable to attack, the strike groups carry a threat that cannot be ignored or dismissed. The United States, the principal operator of such supercarrier strike groups, has never been an expansionist nation, but has always recognised the need to protect and defend her interests at home and abroad. The focus of that requirement is her technologically advanced, rapidly mobile and highly effective naval air force.

Naval aviation arrived in the First World War with balloons and airships employed by the British Royal Navy for reconnaissance. Interest then was growing in the possibility of a greater aeronautical capability for the service. Britain's tradition of projecting her global reach through sea power would, in the view of many, be considerably enhanced through such a capability. Among the most influential British advocates of such military aircraft development was the Naval Minister Winston Churchill. The Royal Naval Air Service was established in 1914 and would come out of the war with 67,000 officers and men, nearly 3,000 aircraft, more than 100 airships, and 126 coastal air stations. The British government then decided to merge it with the Royal Flying Corps to form the Royal Air Force. It was the end of the Fleet Air Arm, as it had been known, until 1938 and the threat of a second world war.

NAVAL AIR explores the most significant aspects in the development of naval aviation in the past century. It looks at the evolution of the first aircraft carriers and the impact of the 1922 Washington naval disarmament conference. The great British raid on the Italian fleet in the harbour of Taranto and the carrier-launched Japanese surprise attack on Pearl Harbor which drew the United States into the Second World War and inspired the first American retaliatory bombing attack on Japan by bomber aircraft from the carrier *Hornet* are are examined. A chapter called Fighting Lady offers brief descriptions of some of the movies that have featured naval aviation. Action in the Coral Sea and Midway campaigns of World War Two is recalled, as are the achievements of some of history's greatest naval air aces. Compelling incidents of the Korean, Vietnam, and Falklands wars are revisited. Many of the most important naval aircraft are described, as is the role and structure of the carrier strike group. A chapter called Women On Board considers the impact and effects of the female presence aboard aircraft carriers in recent decades. The roles and contributions of the helicopter in naval aviation are the basis of another chapter, and the book concludes with some perspectives on the long, difficult, and rewarding journey of the fledgling naval aviator candidate to the fleet.

THE FIRST CARRIERS

It was on the recommendation of Rear Admiral W. S. Cowles, Chief of the United States Navy Bureau of Equipment, to the American Secretary of the Navy, on December 2, 1908, that "a number of aeroplanes be purchased to operate from a ship's deck, carry a wireless telegraph, operate in weather other than a dead calm, maintain a high rate of speed, and be of such design as to permit convenient stowage on board ship." Thus began the history of the aircraft carrier and naval aviation, more than five years prior to the start of the First World War.

Before the coming of the aircraft carrier the great navies of the world were essentially battleship forces, operating the largest, most heavily armed and armoured warships afloat. So intimidating were these vessels that their very presence had on some occasions seen them prevail without even engaging the enemy. Why then did the aircraft carrier virtually scuttle the venerable battlewagon as the new capital ship of the world sea powers? Versatility. The aircraft carrier is both a self-sufficient, self-propelled mobile air base, and a wholly effective servicing facility. In the 21st century, the modern nuclear-powered U.S. supercarrier (CVN) operates as the spearhead of an awesome carrier strike group force in which the carrier is supported by destroyers, frigates, cruisers, replenishment tankers, and fast attack submarines.

In a further advantage over the its battleship predecessor, the carrier gives the fleet the ability to fight and win a naval battle at arm's length— out of sight of the enemy. By the year 2000, the eleven operational aircraft carrier strike groups of the U.S. Navy, and its assault carriers, had become capable of covering immense areas of ocean, sending massive air strikes at inshore as well as ocean targets, providing air support for amphibious landings, helicopter troop ferrying, search-and-rescue, and conducting highly sophisticated anti-submarine warfare.

Though less than entirely invulnerable to enemy attack, the CVN, within the protective shelter of her strike group, is the biggest, widest-ranging, most powerful and fearsome threat that has ever put to sea; her capabilities utterly eclipsing those of the battleship she succeeded. The late U.S. Senator John C. Stennis, after whom one of America's great carriers is named, said, "The best way to avoid war is to be fully prepared, have the tools of war in abundance, and have them ready." Referring to the CVN, he said "It carries everything and goes full strength and is ready to fight or go into action within minutes after it arrives at its destination . . . there is nothing that compares with it when it comes to deterrence."

A less than successful early French aviator, Clement Ader, made the world's first flight in a powered aeroplane from level ground on 9 October 1890, doing the brief hop in a large, bat-like monoplane, the *Eole*. The French Minister of War then asked Ader to design, build and test a two-seat version of the plane to carry a light bomb load for the military. The result crashed at Satorg in October 1891. Ader's government contract was cancelled, but his interest in aviation persisted and he accurately predicted that land warfare would be transformed by reconnaissance from aircraft and that aircraft would also revolutionise the operational methods of naval fleets, which would carry their aircraft to sea. He coined the term *porte avions* (aircraft carrier) and, with amazing foresight, wrote that such ships would be unlike any other, with clear, unimpeded flight decks, and elevators to take aircraft (with their wings folded) from the flight deck to stowage below for servicing and repairs and bring them back again. He predicted that the carriers would be able to operate at a high rate of speed.

The first relatively successful take-off by a fixed-wing aircraft from the deck of a ship was achieved by Eugene Ely, an exhibition pilot for aircraft designer and builder Glenn Curtiss, in a Curtiss Pusher. In November 1910 Ely flew the craft down a gently sloping wooden platform on the forecastle of the U.S. light cruiser *Birmingham* as the ship steamed slowly in Chesapeake Bay near Washington, DC.

In the attempt, the aircraft actually hit the water once, but Ely retained control and managed to land safely on the nearby shore. In an equally significant trial held in San Francisco Bay in January 1911, Ely successfully landed a Curtiss aircraft on a specially-built platform over the quarter deck of the cruiser *Pennsylvania*. He used undercarriage hooks to engage one of twenty-two transverse wires that were stretched across the platform and anchored at the sides with sandbags. Nine months later Ely was dead, killed in the crash of a plane he was displaying at Macon, Georgia.

A month prior to Ely's landing demonstration in San Francisco, Glenn Curtiss offered to instruct an officer of the U.S. Navy in the operation and construction of a Curtiss aeroplane. Four months later, Lt. T. G. Ellyson was graduated by Curtiss, who wrote to the Secretary of the Navy "Lt. Ellyson is now competent to care for and operate Curtiss aeroplanes." Ellyson became the world's first navy aviator.

Within eight years of Wilbur and Orville Wright's initial powered flight at Kitty Hawk on the North Carolina coast, the capability to take off and recover an aircraft to a carrier deck (using arresting wires) was proven. Gradually, the American Navy became convinced of the value and importance of aviation for patrol and reconnaissance in its future, concluding that floating airports—aircraft carriers—would have to be developed and acquired to support and exploit its combat aeroplanes.

But it was the British who, by the time of the Royal Navy's 1913 Naval

Manoeuvres, had identified and defined nearly all the fundamental requirements for carrier-borne operation, aircraft and equipment. Wing-folding to facilitate the improved stowage of otherwise bulky aircraft on the limited space of a ship deck, the testing and evaluation of bomb dropping, gun mounting and firing, and the successful launch of a 14-inch torpedo from an early British-built carrier-borne aircraft, propelled the Royal Navy to the forefront of such development. They also concluded that the purpose-built aircraft carrier must be developed and, by the end of World War One, had achieved that goal.

The way to this achievement led to the 1914 conversions of the bulk carrier *Ark Royal* and the large light cruiser *Furious* to aircraft carriers, *Ark Royal* being designed almost from scratch to meet the needs of naval air operations as they were then perceived. Both France and Japan had begun work in 1912 on the conversion of a torpedo depot ship and a merchant ship respectively, to be operational seaplane carriers. Britain's first sea-plane carrier, however, resulted from the conversion of the light cruiser HMS *Hermes*, which was equipped with a hangar that could house three seaplanes.

With the coming of the First World War, HMS *Ark Royal* was not yet operational and the Royal Navy took over three South East and Chatham Railway Company cross-channel ferries, the *Riviera*, *Empress*, and *Engadine*, for conversion to seaplane carriers. By 1915, the British had additionally converted three Isle of Man steamers, the *Vindex*, *Manxman*, and *Ben-My-Chee*, as well as two captured German ships, the *Anne*, and *Raven II*, all to seaplane carriers. But it had already become clear to the admirals of the Royal Navy that they needed carriers with larger flight decks capable of launching and recovering both land and seaplanes. The first of these would be HMS *Campania*, a converted ocean liner with a 200-foot flight deck. *Campania* became operational in August 1915, and her design was repeated two years later in HMS *Nairana* and HMS *Pegasus*. After much trial and error, the first British ship to eventually evolve into a recognisable modern aircraft carrier design was HMS *Furious*, with a full-length flight deck and an island command structure. Two further refinements in carrier design followed in the form of HMS *Argus* and HMS *Vindictive*, both entering Royal Navy service in 1918. In 1922, the next advance in British carriers appeared in HMS *Eagle* which, in 1924, led to the completion of Britain's first wholly purpose-built aircraft carrier, also named HMS *Hermes*.

Aboard HMS *Furious* in the summer of 1917, Royal Navy aviator E.H. Dunning was among the first of his squadron pilots to realise that the speed of *Furious* was key to devising a safe and routine landing procedure. The squadron was flying Sopwith Pups, a relatively slow and forgiving aeroplane that most of the pilots found fairly easy to bring aboard for a reasonable landing. *Furious* had no arrestor wires rigged, so Dunning decided to have rope handles fitted to his plane and told the deck hands to grip the handles as soon as he had landed and hold the little aircraft firmly to the deck. The technique enabled him to make the first successful carrier deck landing on a ship that was steaming into the wind. Two days later, Dunning made a similar attempt, but a tyre on the Sopwith burst causing the plane to cartwheel over the edge of the flight deck into the sea. Dunning drowned in the incident which, along with some others, led to the realisation that a far larger hull and flight deck was needed for pilots and air crew to operate with acceptable safety. It would mean acceptance by aircraft carrier designers that the placement of the bridge, funnel and other structures was critical and a full-length, full-width flight deck, free of obstructions, was essential to safe aircraft launch and recovery operation. The ultimate concept required that take-offs be made from the forward end of the ship, with landings onto the aft end. When working out placement of the ship's funnel, the designers also had to contend with the hazard of the ship's boiler gases reducing visibility over the deck for the fliers. The problem was never really resolved until the advent of the nuclear (smokeless) powerplant for aircraft carriers in the 1960s.

The initial American effort was the conversion of a collier, the *Jupiter*, to be an experimental aircraft carrier, renamed the USS *Langley* and recommissioned in March 1922. Japan entered the carrier race in December of that year with the commissioning of her first carrier, the *Hosho*, one of the most significant aircraft carriers ever built. *Hosho* was diminutive as carriers go, with a mere 7,470-ton displacement. But she was so cleverly designed that she could accommodate an air wing of twenty-six aircraft. Her most remarkable feature, however, was her innovative, pioneering experimental light-and-mirror landing system to assist pilots in their approaches to the deck. In a final irony of her career, *Hosho* was the only one of Japan's ten principal aircraft carriers of World War Two to survive the war.

An American contribution to the advancement of carrier design arrived in 1927 when two new ships, the *Lexington* and *Saratoga*, employed the transverse arrestor wire landing system. The carrier was finally starting to fulfill Clement Ader's predictions.

In 1930s Britain, government ministers were beginning to take seriously the threat of German re-armament, and were re-evaluating the requirements of the British armed forces. Mismanagement of the Fleet Air Arm under the control of the Air Ministry had led to a lack of state-of-the-art aircraft and the loss of many Royal Naval Air Service pilots through absorption into the fledgling Royal Air Force. By 1937 the government had

had a bellyfull of interservice rivalry between the navy and the air force, and handed the responsibility for British naval aviation back to the Royal Navy.

WASHINGTON

A major factor in the development of naval aviation and the aircraft carrier during the 1930s was the Washington Naval Treaty of 1922. The Washington Naval Conference, which was also known as the Washington Arms Conference, was called by U.S. President Warren G. Harding to convene on November 12, 1921 through February 6, 1922. The five principal naval powers invited to attend were Japan, the United States, France, Great Britain, and Italy. The conference was by no means the end of the debate. Further naval arms limitation conferences followed, to tighten or extend the limitations on warship construction. In 1930, the London Naval Treaty, and another in 1936, were convened to modify the terms of the Washington agreement.

Britain, the U.S. and Japan had been allies during the First World War, but with the war behind them, they found themselves competing in a naval arms race which none of them wanted or could afford. The race had begun in the United States when President Wilson announced plans for the expansion of the U.S. Navy in 1916 and again in 1919, with the goal of a fifty-battleship fleet. The Japanese Parliament then authorised construction of eight new battleships and eight battlecruisers, all of a larger, more powerful class than that which it would replace. In America, the isolationist Congress voted down the 1919 plan, and Senator William E. Borah of Idaho championed a congressional campaign demanding that the United States engage its two main naval arms race competitors, Britain and Japan, in negotiations toward disarmament. Late in 1921, the Harding administration learned that Britain was planning to call a conference on the strategic situation in the Pacific and Far East. President Harding acted to forestall the British meeting, and in response to substantial pressure in the U.S., to call a global disarmament conference.

The U.S. invited Britain, France, Japan, and Italy to participate in discussions on the reduction of naval force capacity, and China, Belgium, the Netherlands, and Portugal were asked to take part in talks on the situation in the Far East.

Each nation's delegation arrived in the American capital with its own agenda. In the aftermath of the First World War, "the war to end all wars," most people just wanted peace and disarmament. In much of the world women had recently won the right to vote and were already flexing their newfound political muscle, influencing their government representatives about the importance of saving money, avoiding future wars, and winning votes through an urgent campaign to halt the arms race. On Armistice Day, the day before the start of the Naval Arms Limitation conference, thousands of American women marched down Pennsylvania Avenue in Washington with placards stating SCRAP THE BATTLESHIP AND THE PACIFIC PROBLEMS WILL SETTLE THEMSELVES.

With the end of the war, both the United States and Japan were deeply involved in expensive programmes of warship construction. Britain, while still the biggest naval power in the world, presided over many largely obsolescent capital ships. She was then in a treaty, the Anglo-Japanese Alliance of 1902, that was due to expire in 1922, and the British were concerned about the American-Japanese rivalry in the Pacific region. The Americans were looking for a new naval disarmament agreement to curb Japanese expansion in the Far East and they hoped to reduce tensions between Japan and the U.S. that could lead to another war. U.S. planners were determined to maintain naval supremacy over the Japanese, while Japan was equally set against any attempt to reduce her fleet, interpreting that as a primary threat to her national security.

Historically, the Americans had been relatively tolerant of Japan's expansionist policies in the Far East, but with the startling defeat of the Russian fleet by Japan in 1905, American attitudes towards the Japanese government began to harden, with concerns that the Japanese Empire now posed a serious threat to U.S. possessions in the region, principally the Philippines and Guam, where the Americans were planning development of major new naval bases. In their view the Japanese threat made the U.S. position in the Far East extremely difficult, with their only advantage then being the superior American Pacific fleet. The acquisition, maintenance and operation of that fleet was hugely expensive and did not have the unqualified support of many in the U.S. Congress.

Thus the Washington Naval Conference began with intrigue and murky motivations. The gathering was immediately startled by the opening remarks of the American Secretary of State, Charles Evans Hughes, who declared that the United States was prepared to scrap nearly thirty capital ships and accept a ten-year moratorium on capital ship construction. The Hughes proposal required the following total tonnage limitations on the five naval powers: Britain—capital ships=525,000 tons, aircraft carriers=135,000 tons; United States—capital ships=525,000 tons, aircraft carriers=135,000 tons; Japan—capital ships=325,000 tons, aircraft carriers=81,000 tons; France—capital ships= 175,000 tons, aircraft carriers=60,000 tons; Italy—capital ships= 175,000 tons, aircraft carriers= 60,000 tons. The actual size limits imposed were: battleships and battlecruisers=35,000 tons displacement with guns no larger than 16-inch calibre; aircraft carriers=27,000 tons displacement with no more than ten guns of a maximum 8-inch calibre. Each signatory was permitted to use two existing capital ship hulls for aircraft carriers with a displacement limit of 33,000 tons each. All other warships were limited to a maximum displacement of 10,000 tons and a maximum gun calibre of 8-inches.

Essentially, the Hughes proposal, if implemented, would spell the end to British domination of the seas and, in particular, its ability to provide an adequate naval presence simultaneously in the Mediterranean, the North Sea, and the Far East—a realisation that did not sit well with the Royal Navy. But Britain was under considerable pressure to accept the proposal because of the 1902 Anglo-Japanese Alliance, an agreement of great concern to the United States.

Since the end of the First World War, American leaders increasingly viewed Japan as a significant military threat; an expansionist power out to extend its territory and influence in the Pacific and Far East. The Americans were disturbed by a threat they perceived to their Pacific possessions—the Philippines, Guam, and Hawaii—and to their trade with China. They feared that if the U.S. and Japan were to become involved in a war, Britain might be obliged to join with Japan against the Americans. They believed it vital to both end that Anglo-Japanese Alliance, and create a new Four-Power Agreement to ensure that none of the nations involved would ever be obligated to enter a future conflict; an agreement that would provide a framework for discussion if such a conflict arose. After three days of discussion, both the Japanese and British delegations agreed in principle to the American proposal. The Japanese, however, did not agree to the exact ship limitation ratio proposed by the Americans, leading to several more days debate.

The primary aim of the Americans in the conference was to restrain the expansion of Japanese naval forces in the western Pacific, mainly in relation to fortifications on strategically important islands. Additionally, they were concerned about possible Anglo-American tension over the Anglo-Japanese Alliance; they wanted agreement on a favourable naval warship ratio vis-à-vis Japan; and they wanted Japanese acceptance of a continuation of the Open Door (trade) Policy with China.

The British came to Washington with a less specific, more general wish list. Beginning with a desire for peace in the Pacific, the hope of avoiding a naval arms race with the United States, and the intention of preventing the Japanese from incursions into Pacific areas under British influence; they were determined to preserve the security of Singapore, Hong Kong, and the Dominion countries. But these were all more in the nature of desirable outcomes than demands.

The Japanese turned up with two specific goals to be achieved: 1) The signing of a new naval treaty with Britain and the United States, and 2) Official recognition by the conference of Japan's special interests in Mongolia and Manchuria. Along with these items, they wanted consideration of their general concerns over the continuing and growing presence of

American warships in the Pacific, and other concerns.

Behind the scenes of the conference, an intrigue developed that would dramatically influence the course of the negotiations. Under the direction of Herbert Yardley, a U.S. government intelligence service department known as the Cypher Bureau was conducting espionage operations on the communications of the various delegations with their home capitals. The Japanese delegation was soon singled out for special attention by the Cypher Bureau spies, whose penetration, interception and decryption of the coded Japanese messaging was most productive. It resulted in the American negotiators achieving the best possible deal with the Japanese, by virtue of having advance knowledge of Japan's minimum negotiating position.

Like the Royal Navy, many command officers of the Imperial Japanese Navy were highly suspicious and outspokenly opposed to the terms of the agreement then being hammered out in Washington.

The Americans and the British believed that the 5:5:3 (U.S., Britain, Japan) warship limitation ratio was justifiable by the fact that Japan's concentration of naval force was based on a one-ocean navy, whereas the U.S. required a two-ocean navy, and Britain a three-ocean navy. The developing agreement was driving a wedge between the Japanese naval commanders who supported the new treaty and those who sided with Japan's ultra-nationalists in opposition to it. The latter viewed the treaty as one of the main factors that contributed to the worsening of relations between Japan and the United States, and would lead to Japan renouncing the Naval Limitation Treaties in 1936.

The man who in 1941 would mastermind Japan's surprise attack on U.S. Navy capital ships and facilities at Pearl Harbor, Hawaii, drawing the United States into the Second World War, Admiral Isoroku Yamamoto, supported the treaty. His experience of having served in the Japanese Embassy in Washington led him to believe the U.S.had a huge advantage in its ability to substantially out-produce Japan in war materials and equipment, and that other means would be needed to even the odds in a conflict. This undoubtedly influenced his advocacy of the Pearl Harbor attack plan.

Meanwhile, back at the conference table, the delegation from France was expressing outrage over the part of the Hughes proposal that reduced French capital ship tonnage to 175,000, insisting on a figure of 350,000, slightly higher than that of Japan. The delegates reached a stumbling block when Britain demanded the complete abolition of submarines, weapons which had nearly defeated her in World War I. The French were adamantly opposed to this British position, demanding an allowance of 90,000 tons in submarines. The conference would end with no agreement on the limitation of submarines. Ultimately, concessions to France on cruisers and submarines contributed to French agreement on the limitation of capital warships.

When the attention of the conference turned to the important matter of limiting the construction of "secondary" warships (cruisers and destroyers), it was unacceptable to the British and French to apply limits in the same proportions as those on capital ships. Britain offered a counter-proposal in which it would be allowed cruiser tonnage totaling 450,000, due to her larger commitment, with the U.S. and Japan allowed 300,000 and 250,000 respectively. This too was rejected and the focus then shifted to a new British proposal with a qualitative limit on new cruisers of a 10,000-ton maximum displacement and 8-inch calibre guns, on which the three nations agreed. At various points in the deliberations, the parties became bogged down in detail and the seemingly endless talks appeared to be going nowhere. As the American and Japanese delegates argued the precise definition of "existing strength", the Americans insisted that warships then under construction be counted, while the Japanese demanded that only vessels already in service qualify.

The Japanese, motivated by their anguish at involvement in an arms race with the United States, eventually came up with a compromise proposal which the other delegates found acceptable. It tied Japanese acceptance of the U.S.-proposed tonnage ratio to a new provision that banned any expansion of American fortifications in the Philippines and Guam, which Japan saw as a threat to her lines of communication. The American delegates had previously been briefed not to discuss the U.S. naval bases in the Pacific, but as the talks went on, the American representatives chose to include the subject of the fortifications in the conversation, believing that doing so might help allay some Japanese mistrust and possibly lead to the desired agreement.

The issue of the American fortifications in the Philippines and Guam remained firmly in the forefront of the Japanese agenda for the conference. They doggedly pursued two related proposals they had brought, the first requiring the total disarmament of the Philippines, Guam, and Hawaii, in return for the Japanese disarmament of Formosa, the Bonins, and the Ryukyus. Their second proposal was for partial disarmament of Guam and either the Philippines or Hawaii, in exchange for the Japanese disarmament of either Formosa, the Bonins, or the Ryukyus. The American response was basically that any proposal to limit the fortification of Hawaii was unacceptable, but proposals to limit the fortifications on Guam and in the Philippines were negotiable—if the Japanese agreed to the naval arms limitation.

In another development, a discussion arose about construction of Japan's newest and most advanced battleship, *Mutsu*, a project the Japanese were anxious to retain. It was being funded through contributions from the general public as well as through donations from schoolchildren. Agreement was reached allowing construction of *Mutsu* to continue and in return and the United States were each allowed to build a comparable vessel.

The American response to the *Mutsu* matter also included acceptance of the Japanese proposal (with certain modifications) about U.S. fortifications in the Pacific. The modifications specifically excluded Hawaii and provided a distinct separation between offensive and defensive base facilities. It further provided that Britain, France, and the Netherlands must also be signatories on any fortification agreement.

Importantly, the Americans made it clear to the Japanese that a fortification agreement was contingent upon a general agreement on naval disarmament. After a delay allowing the Japanese a consultation with their government, a fortification agreement was reached and announced by Japan, Britain, and the U.S. Non-fortification of the Pacific islands would continue, except for Hawaii, Australia, New Zealand, and Japan proper, as well as the coasts of the United States and Canada.

The resulting five-power naval treaty limited the construction of battleships, battlecruisers, and aircraft carriers by the signatories. While the numbers of the various other types of warships—cruisers, destroyers, and submarines—were not limited by the new treaty, their tonnage per vessel was limited to 10,000 tons displacement. But what really resulted from the conference agreements?

Superficially, it seemed that the United States achieved its aims and preserved the balance of power in the Far East. The delegations had put into effect a qualitative standard based on tonnage displacement. They created a ten-year agreement during which a fixed battleship ratio of 5:5:3 would prevail: United States—525,000; Britain—525,000; and Japan—315,000, with smaller limits for France and Italy. Battleships were limited to a displacement of 35,000 tons. For aircraft carriers, the tonnage limits established were: U.S.—135,000; Britain—135,000; and Japan—81,000. The conference agreements appeared to head off the sort of naval arms race that the world feared and the major powers could not afford. Under the agreements the United States and Britain had to scrap many of their older battleships, for a total of capital ships scrapped greater than that of those lost in any sea battle in history.

For more than a decade, the United States would lack the naval power it had before the Washington treaties were enacted, and was heavily dependent upon the new naval treaty to curb Japanese expansion in the Pacific. In their treaty negotiations the Americans seemed to have overlooked, or underestimated the worth of their Far Eastern bases in future negotiations with Japan. And while Japan's fleet was within easy steaming reach of any area of possible conflict in the region, the American Navy would have to support such an effort from the end of a long supply line at San Diego on the U.S. west coast. Thus, the American need for its outposts in the Pacific was far greater than that of Japan for hers.

Initially it appeared that Japan had been forced into a reluctant accept-ance of some unfavourable warship ratios, with little of advantage to her. But when considering other factors, including the relative obsolescence of the British fleet by the time of the conference, the virtual elimination of the British Asiatic Fleet as a fighting force, the moratorium on battleship construction and the scrapping by the U.S. of twenty-eight warships including eleven capital ships, a U.S. commitment to a two-ocean navy which substantially reduced the number of warships it could commit to the Pacific Fleet, and the base-building and fortification restrictions of the Four-Power Treaty, Japan actually benefited considerably from the effects of the Washington treaties. In fact, she was left in a locally superior and relatively dominant position. In a final achievement, the Nine-Power Treaty of the Washington conference affirmed the internationalisa-tion of the U.S. Open Door Policy in China, ensuring that all of the signatories would respect the territorial integrity of China and equal opportunity for all the nations trading with China, who agreed not to discriminate against any nation attempting to do business in China. Like the Four-Power Treaty, it provided a mechanism for consultations should a violation occur.

The Washington conference treaties effectively ended a long era of battle-ship construction and caused the scrapping of many such vessels then under construction and the conversion of some new hulls into aircraft carriers. It identified every warship to be retained by the navies of each of the major sea powers, and the measures to be taken to put various warships beyond military use. In addition to scrapping, provision was made for some of the vessels to be employed as target ships or training vessels with the complete removal of their armament, armour and other combat-related equipment. Some of these ships were also allowed to be converted into aircraft carriers. The treaties also spec-ified which warships were to be scrapped and when the remaining ships in each of the navies could be replaced. The United States was required to scrap 28 existing or planned capital ships; Britain 23, and Japan 16.

For several years the treaty limitations were adhered to and then extended by the London Naval Treaty of 1930. On 29 December 1934, the Empire of Japan announced its intention to terminate the Washington Naval Treaty of 1922, with Japan leaving the treaty during 1936. By the mid-1930s the major navies had begun building battleships again.

The existence of the Washington Naval Treaty limitations did little to stem the suspicions the major naval powers had of each other, and another arms race of sorts occurred as they engaged in a competition from 1927-1930 to design and build new heavy cruisers which, in a war situation, could be con-verted to mount larger guns. This matter was resolved in the 1930 conference leading to the London Naval Treaty of that year, which also set limits on sub-marines; the U.S., Britain, and Japan, each permitted a total tonnage of 53,000. The naval arms limitation agreements reached in Washington in 1922 remained in effect for fourteen years until Japan withdrew from them.

TARANTO

Two waves of Swordfish biplanes took off from the Royal Navy carrier HMS *Illustrious* in the evening of 11 November 1940. Their mission: to attack the warships of the Italian Navy anchored in Taranto harbour, a main seaport in the arch of the Italian boot, about 250 miles southeast of Rome. During the Roman Empire, it was called Tarantum.

Early in the Second World War, the Royal Navy was trying to protect the Allied merchant ship convoys from the continuing threat of U-boats, land-based attacks, and from sorties by the capital ships of the Italian fleet. The convoys were bringing vitally needed supplies to Malta, whose survival was crucial in the effort to defeat Italian and German forces in North Africa.

The British planned to ease pressure on the forces of Admiral Sir Andrew Cunningham, the Royal Navy Commander-in-Chief in the Mediterranean. As they escorted and protected the convoys, a strike was organised in the autumn of 1940 on the key Italian capital ships in Taranto harbour. The aircraft carriers HMS *Eagle* and *Illustrious* were to carry out the attack, but *Eagle* had to be withdrawn when a major problem with her fuel system developed. Five of her Swordfish aircraft and eight Swordfish crews were then transferred to HMS *Illustrious* for the raid.

Earlier in the day of the eleventh, an R.A.F. reconnaissance flight over Taranto identified six Italian battleships, and the attack was scheduled for that evening. In the late afternoon, the twelve Swordfish planes of the first wave attack were being armed. Six would carry torpedoes, four carried bombs, and two were bringing bombs and flares. The crews were briefed that they would be facing twenty-two anti-aircraft guns, barrage balloons, and torpedo nets guarding the harbour.

The plan required the torpedo-armed aircraft to launch their weapons at the battleships anchored in the outer harbour. As they did so, the other Swordfish aircraft would create a synchronised diversion, attacking the cruisers and destroyers moored along the harbour quay. It was believed that the small-warhead 18-inch British torpedoes could be launched at low level into the shallow waters of the harbour with good effect against the Italian warships. The intent was for the bomb and flare-dropping Swordfish planes to distract the local defences, enabling the torpedo planes to weave at a 75-knot cruising speed around and between the barrage balloon cables towards their targets.

The British aircraft strike force assembled near *Illustrious* and headed off on the 170-mile flight to Taranto harbour by 8:57 p.m. with Lt Cdr K. Williamson in command. Within thirty minutes, however, the weather conditions deteriorated and the strike force became separated in thick cloud cover. The aircraft would have to make their attacks independently.

The bomb and flare-carrying aircraft dropped an illuminating pattern of flares along the eastern edge of the harbour at 10:56 p.m. and proceeded to drop their bombs on a nearby oil tank farm, setting it ablaze. As they did this, Lt Cdr Williamson led three of the torpedo-armed Swordfish in a diving run on the battleship *Cavour*. Their attack left the warship beyond repair, though Williamson's plane was hit by return fire from the *Cavour*, and came down near the battleship. He and his observer survived to become prisoners of war.

As the second lot of torpedo-armed Swordfish attacked the battleship *Littorio*, the balance of the other aircraft dropped their bombs on the cruisers and destroyers, and the seaplane base in the harbour.

The second wave of Swordfish planes began taking off from *Illustrious* at 11:23 p.m. under the command of Lt Cdr J. W. Hale. This force included five torpedo planes, two bombers, and two aircraft carrying bombs and flares. The bomber-flare aircraft made additional strikes on the oil storage facility, while the torpedo planes formed a line-astern approach towards the battleships. Now the Italians were putting up a massive box barrage of anti-aircraft fire from their shore batteries and ship guns. Hale's planes were forced to fly through the worst of the flak and one of them was shot down.

The striking force lost two Swordfish in the raid, but managed to score four hits on *Littorio* and one each on the battleships *Cavour* and *Duilio*, leaving *Littorio* listing heavily, and *Duilio* run aground. *Cavour* was left listing to port with her stern awash. The next day she settled on the shallow harbour bottom. Only two of the Italian battleships were left operational after the raid.

John W.G. Wellham, Fleet Air Arm Swordfish pilot, Royal Navy: "I was serving in HMS *Eagle*, a very old carrier which had been in the fleet for some years. We came to the Mediterranean at a time when it was obvious that Mussolini was going to come into the war on the side of the Germans. He'd been sitting on the sidelines, waiting to see which side was likely to produce the most glory for him. As the Germans were sweeping through Europe, it was clearly going to be their side that he wanted to join. We, therefore, were sent to join the Mediterranean fleet, which we did but a few weeks before Mussolini came into the war.

"Led by Sir Andrew Cunningham, a wildly enthusiastic chap, we tore around the Med looking for someone with whom to be hostile, and actually only found the Italian fleet at sea once. We attacked them twice in four hours with our Swordfish torpedo bombers. Unfortunately, there were only nine of us making the attacks, quite inadequate against a fast-moving fleet. So it was necessary for us to catch them in harbour. Our admiral did his homework and found that attacking enemy ships in harbour had been quite successful right back to 300 bc.

"The R.A.F. had a squadron of Bristol Blenheims in the area which they were using for reconnaissance of the various North African harbours, including Bomba. One day they told us about a submarine depot ship at Bomba with a submarine alongside it. They did a recce for us the next morning and discovered another submarine coming into the harbour, so the three of us went off in our Swordfish and, at Bomba, spotted the large submarine on the surface, obviously recharging its batteries. Our leader put his torpedo into it and the sub blew up and sank very satisfactorily. The other chap and I went on and as we got closer we found that, not only was there a depot ship and a submarine, there was a destroyer between the two of them. I let my torpedo go towards the depot ship. My colleague dropped his from the other side and it went underneath the submarine and hit the destroyer. I was very excited and was shouting. Things were going up in the air that all four ships had sunk, which was confirmed later by aerial reconnaissance. That night the Italians admitted on the radio that they had lost four ships in the harbour. However, they said that the loss was due to an overwhelming force of motor torpedo boats and torpedo bombers which had attacked them during the night. If I had been commanding officer of that base, I would have reported something along those same lines. I certainly wouldn't have been prepared to admit that three elderly biplanes had sunk four of my ships.

"The attack on the ships in harbour at Bomba had confirmed for us, and for Cunningham, that the best way to attack ships was when they were in harbour. He then decided that an attack on the main Italian fleet in their base at Taranto was imperative. This was all very well, but we in *Eagle* had a limited number of aircraft and no long-range fuel tanks to get us there and back. We also needed absolutely up-to-date reconnaissance to do an attack like that. Then the new carrier *Illustrious* came to join us, bringing us the long-range tanks we needed. The Royal Air Force provided a flight of three Martin Maryland bombers for the reconnaissance work, and they were very good for that. They had the speed, the training, and the ability, and each day at dawn and dusk they gave us reports on the positions of ships in Taranto. We couldn't have done the job without them.

The go-ahead was given for the raid because both *Illustrious* and *Eagle* were fully prepared to do it—but then complications arose. *Illustrious* had a fire in the hangar deck which caused a delay. Meanwhile, *Eagle*, which had been bombed repeatedly by the aircraft of the Reggia Aeronautica, had developed plumbing problems. When we tried to put fuel in our aircraft we really weren't quite sure what we were fueling them with, and so *Eagle* was scrubbed from the operation. We went on with the plan, however, and transferred five aircraft and eight crews over to *Illustrious*.

"The attack was called Operation Judgement and it was set for 11 November 1940. Diversionary actions involving merchant navy convoys elsewhere in the Med were organised and worked well, disguising the fact that we were going to hit Taranto.

"We went off in two waves, some of us with bombs, some with torpedoes. The Martin recce flights had shown us that the Italian battleships were in the Mar Grande, the largest part of Taranto harbour, while destroyers, cruisers, submarines and various auxiliary vessels were in the inner harbour, Mar Piccolo.

"At Taranto, I had to dodge a barrage balloon and in doing so I was hit by flak which broke the aileron control spar, and I couldn't move the control column, which is very embarrassing in the middle of a dive. So, using brute force and ignorance, I cleared the column enough to get it fully over to the right. While this was going on and I was trying to get the thing to fly properly, I suddenly appreciated that I was diving right into the middle of Taranto City, which was obviously not a good thing. So I hauled the plane out of the dive, found the target and attacked it. But when you drop 2,000 pounds off an aircraft of that weight, it rises. There is nothing you can do about it, and it rose into the flak from the battleship I was attacking. I was hit again and got a hole about a metre long by at least a half-metre wide. The Swordfish still flew and we got back 200 miles over the sea with the aircraft in that condition. It was very painful because, to fly straight, I had to keep left rudder on all the time, which is bad for your ankle, but we got home."

It may be that no one was more interested in the method and results of the British attack on Taranto harbour than the Japanese. Thirteen months after the raid, the Japanese mounted their own attack on the battleships of the great American fleet in Pearl Harbor, Hawaii, and, while they had already planned their raid on Pearl before the Taranto raid, what the British did, and what they achieved, at Taranto undoubtedly influenced and helped motivate the Japanese forces in the execution of theirs.

PEARL

"Yesterday, December 7th 1941—a date which will live in infamy—the United States of America was suddenly and deliberately attacked by naval and air forces of the Empire of Japan.

"The United States was at peace with that nation, and, at the solicitation of Japan, was still in conversation with its government and its Emperor looking toward the maintenance of peace in the Pacific.

"Indeed, one hour after Japanese air squadrons had commenced bombing in the American island of Oahu, the Japanese Ambassador to the United States and his colleague delivered to our Secretary of State a formal reply to a recent American message. And, while this reply stated that it seemed useless to continue the existing diplomatic negotiations, it contained no threat or hint of war or of armed attack.

"It will be recorded that the distance of Hawaii from Japan makes it obvious that the attack was deliberately planned many days or even weeks ago. During the intervening time the Japanese government has deliberately sought to deceive the United States by false statements and expressions of hope for continued peace.

"The attack yesterday on the Hawaiian Islands has caused severe damage to American naval and military forces. I regret to tell you that very many American lives have been lost. In addition, American ships have been reported torpedoed on the high seas between San Francisco and Honolulu.

"Yesterday the Japanese Governnment also launched an attack against Malaya. Last night Japanese forces attacked Hong Kong. Last night Japanese forces attacked Guam. Last night Japanese forces attacked the Philippine Islands. Last night the Japanese attacked Wake Island. And this morning the Japanese attacked Midway Island.

"Japan has therefore undertaken a surprise offensive extending throughout the Pacific area. The facts of yesterday and today speak for themselves. The people of the United States have already formed their opinions and well understand the implications to the very life and safety of our nation.

"As Commander-in-Chief of the Army and Navy I have directed that all measures be taken for our defense, that always will our whole nation remember the character of the onslaught against us.

"No matter how long it may take us to overcome this premeditated invasion, the American people, in their righteous might, will win through to absolute victory.

"I believe that I interpret the will of the Congress and of the people when I assert that we will not only defend ourselves to the uttermost but will make it very certain that this form of treachery shall never again endanger us.

"Hostilities exist. There is no blinking at the fact that our people, our territory and our interests are in grave danger.

"With confidence in our armed forces, with the unbounding determination of our people, we will gain the inevitable triumph. So help us God.

"I ask that the Congress declare that since the unprovoked and dastardly attack by Japan on Sunday, December 7th, 1941, a state of war has existed between the United States and the Japanese Empire."
—President Franklin D. Roosevelt, December 8, 1941

They called it the Great East Asia Co-Existence Sphere, the Japanese plan to expand their territory, initially into Manchuria and then mainland China. Their armies were on the move in the 1930s. By 1940, the United States showed what it thought of the Japanese incursions by slapping an embargo on her, covering scrap iron, steel, aviation spirit, and other potential war materials. The Americans also froze all Japanese assets in the U.S.

Japan's militant government worried about their nation's survival without their sources for strategic commodities. They especially wanted the tin, rubber, and bauxite, as well as the oil of the Dutch East Indies and Malaya, resources they believed essential for them to win victory in China. They decided they would have to go to war with the British Empire and the Dutch government in exile. And the large American military presence in the Philippines would almost certainly mean war with the U.S. too as the Americans would not tolerate this adventurism by the Japanese. Accordingly, the Japanese military planners elected to destroy the American air bases in the Philippines and the powerful U.S. Navy fleet in Pearl Harbor, Oahu, Hawaii. They saw that the total elimination of these facilites and warships was fundamental to the taking of the East Indies, Malaya and, eventually, China.

Imperial Japanese Navy Admiral Isoroku Yamamoto had been educated at Harvard and had served as a naval attaché in Washington. He had no illusions about America as an adversary and was familiar with her military strengths. As the Commander-in-Chief of the combined Imperial Japanese Fleet, he opposed war with the U.S., but accepted its inevitability. In 1940 he told a group of Japanese schoolchildren "Japan cannot beat America. Therefore, Japan should not fight America." To the limits of his influence he warned that when that war came, it would be absolutely essential to "give a fatal blow to the enemy fleet at the outset, when it was least expected. He believed that anything less than the total destruction of the U.S. fleet would "awaken a sleeping giant."

The British historian and naval authority, Hector Bywater, published a book in 1921 called Sea Power in the Pacific, which caused a stir in naval and political circles worldwide, and not least in Japan where it soon became required reading at the Imperial Naval Academy and the Japanese Naval War College.

A Bywater premise was that the Japanese home islands were largely invulnerable to assault by U.S. forces because of the distance to American supply facilities and the secondary fuel and supply consumption required in such an effort. He believed that the key to American success against Japan in a Pacific war would be an island-hopping campaign, through the Marianas to Guam and the Philippines. In 1925, in his second book, *The Great Pacific War*, Bywater speculated that Japan's military success would depend on its making a surprise attack on the U.S. Pacific Fleet and invading the Philippines and Guam, as well as thoroughly fortifying its mandate islands.

Yamamoto visited London in 1934 and there he met and had a lengthy conversation with Hector Bywater. The admiral was greatly impressed by the historian's theories and the implications for both Japanese and American strategy. Several years later Yamamoto would conceive, plan and direct the massive surprise attack on the capital ships and port facilities of the U.S. Navy at Pearl Harbor in the early morning of Sunday, 7 December 1941.

The admiral realized that some of America's warships would not be in Pearl Harbor on the day of the attack; some were stationed on the U.S. west coast, some were undergoing refit, and others were in transit between the U.S. and Hawaii or elsewhere at sea. His master plan included a vital second strike on what remained of the enemy fleet, about six months after the Pearl Harbor attack.

In the months prior to the attack, only two U.S. aircraft carriers were operating in the Pacific, the *Enterprise* and the *Lexington*. A third carrier, the *Saratoga*, was in the navy yard at Bremerton, Washington, for a major refit. The Japanese fleet numbered six carriers and all were available for the December action.

More than a year before the attack on Pearl, two waves of British Swordfish torpedo and bombing aeroplanes flying from the Royal Navy carrier HMS *Illustrious*, had attacked and inflicted heavy damage on the capital ships of the Italian fleet in the southern port of Taranto. The following May, a group of senior officers of the Imperial Japanese Navy visited their Italian counterparts on the deck of the crippled battleship *Littorio*. The Japanese were fascinated by the methods and achievement of the British who had put half the Italian fleet out of action in a single, well-planned and executed act. With the loss of only two aircraft, the British Fleet Air Arm had solved the problem of how to successfully deliver torpedoes against warship targets at anchor in a relatively shallow harbour.

Historians have disagreed over the years about the extent to which the Japanese, and Yamamoto in particular, were influenced by the techniques and results of the Taranto raid, in the planning and execution of the Pearl Harbor attack. There is little doubt though that they were inspired and motivated by the example of the British. Encouraged by the Taranto result, Admiral Yamamoto proceeded with his planning for Pearl.

As a comparison, both Taranto and Pearl Harbor were considered safe, proper anchorages by their resident warship fleet commanders. Both adjoined cities—Taranto and Honolulu—with populations of about 200,000 in 1940. Both ports were well defended and seen as powerful threats to any enemy fleet. The Japanese perceived the American facilities and presence at Pearl a prime impediment to their expansionist plans in Southeast Asia. The British, with their interests in Gibraltar, Egypt, India and Singapore, felt threatened by the Italian fleet at Taranto.

In their attack on the Italian fleet, the British carrier-based planes had to approach the harbour from the Mediterranean without being discovered by Italian reconnaissance aircraft. They had to evade the gunfire of fifty-four enemy warships and twenty-one shore batteries while avoiding the steel cables of more than fifty barrage balloons and several squadrons of Italian fighter planes. In preparing the Japanese navy to mount the raid on Pearl, Yamamoto knew he would have to assemble a thirty-two-ship task force including the six carriers *Akagi, Kaga, Soryu, Hiryu, Shokaku* and *Zuikaku* in the waters north of Japan. The force would have to sail, undetected, about 4,000 miles to a point within approximately 200 miles from the target. From there, and nearly at the limit of their range, the carrier aircraft would have to approach and face the defensive fire of the enemy shore batteries, the guns of up to sixty-eight warships, and around 100 enemy fighter planes.

The shallow harbour at Pearl adjoins the present-day Honolulu airport. The harbour is a basin surrounding Ford Island, a small airfield facility. Pearl has only a single narrow channel linking it to the open sea. On its eastern flank lay the drydocks, a submarine base, and oil storage tanks. In the morning of the attack, seven battleships of the U.S. fleet lay at anchor southeast of Ford Island. They were the *West Virginia, Tennessee, Oklahoma, Maryland, Arizona, California,* and *Nevada.* An eighth battleship, the *Pennsylvania,* was in a nearby drydock.

The greatest challenge to the Japanese planners of the attack on Pearl was how to successfully deliver torpedoes by aircraft onto target vessels in a shallow basin. Prior to Taranto, the torpedo technology of the day dictated that the missile would nearly always sink to depth of at least seventy feet before leveling and proceeding to its target. The weapon would be hopelessly mired in the mud bottom of Taranto or Pearl. But the munitions engineers of the Mitsubishi company near Nagasaki were also influenced by the achievement of Taranto, and devised a new torpedo with a special stabilizer fin. If the weapon was dropped correctly, it would sink less than the forty-foot depth of Pearl Harbor and continue unimpeded to its target. By 17 November 1941, 180 of the new torpedoes had been delivered to the aircraft carriers of Japan.

Joseph Grew was the American Ambassador to Japan in the 1930s and 1940s and like Admiral Yamamoto, Joe Grew was Harvard-educated and had known Franklin Roosevelt while there. He had a sound, thorough understanding of Japan, the Japanese and their militant government. By 1934 he was issuing clear warnings to Washington of Japan's expansionist posture towards all of East Asia: "There is a swashbuckling temper in the country, that might lead the government to any extremes and eventually to national suicide." But in the United States the people and the Congress were overwhelmingly isolationist, and President Roosevelt was limited in his ability then to respond to Japan.

By the late '30s, however, American attitudes toward Japan were subtly changing. The President requested and was granted a 20 percent increase in naval appropriations by the Congress in order to expand the nation's two-ocean navy. He used the limited powers at his command to establish an arms boycott, asking American munitions and aircraft manufacturers not to sell their products to Japan. The request was "voluntary", referred to as a "moral embargo." It was quite effective.

In October 1939, Roosevelt decided on a bit of sabre rattling in the direction of Japan by ordering the bulk of the U.S. Navy Pacific Fleet from its home base in San Diego to a new home port in Pearl Harbor. While the navy was not yet of sufficient strength for major offensive operations, and the defences at Pearl were not yet complete, he wanted to send a strong, unequivocal message to the Japanese.

Roosevelt's action seemed to provoke a different response than he had hoped for from the Japanese government. Spurred by the successes of their ally Adolf Hitler's 1940 blitzkrieg in Europe, the Japanese leaders' interest in their own plans to invade the Dutch, French and British colonies in Asia gained momentum and in early August 1940, Ambassador Grew warned Washington that the Japanese government viewed the present climate as "a golden opportunity to pursue their expansionist desires unhampered by the allegedly hamstrung democracies. The German military machine and system, and their brilliant successes have gone to the Japanese head like strong wine."

With the imposition of a new ruling cabinet in Japan, came the accession to power of two extraordinarily formidable personalities, the Minister of War Lieutenant General Hideki Tojo, and Foreign Minister Yosuke Matsuoka. The latter had been raised and educated in Portland, Oregon, and considered himself an expert on all things American. The rest of the cabinet were inclined to accept him as such and tended to allow him greater latitude in the creation and management of foreign policy than that permitted any previous foreign minister. He was seen as brilliant, arrogant, and somewhat erratic. Matsuoka was known to curry favour with his American counterpart, the Secretary of State, Cordell Hull, and concurrently tell an American newspaper correspondent that democracy was finished; that fascism would prevail in the war, and that there wasn't room enough in the world for two systems of government. Hull, for his part, had no illusions about Matsuoka and the Japanese government. He didn't trust their motives and believed they were leading to war between the U.S. and Japan.

Significantly, in another event of August 1940, Japan's most important diplomatic code was deciphered by American cryptographers who were then able to intercept and read the secret cable traffic between Tokyo and Japan's foreign embassies. Secretary Hull referred to these intercepts by the code name Magic and he had a powerful advantage. With the presentation of each seemingly sincere peace offering by ex-Admiral Kichisaburo Nomura, a Japanese special envoy sent to Washington ostensibly to resolve differences between the U.S. and Japan by diplomatic means, Hull would already have read the Magic intercepts and knew that, rather than pursuing peace, the Japanese were preparing for war. Hull despised this underhandedness and duplicity and felt a growing hatred for the Japanese government and its methods.

Beginning in September, Matsuoka made a series of moves that served only to reinforce Hull's opinion. He entered into an alliance with the fascist governments of Germany and Italy. He then began to apply pressure to acquire more Dutch East Indies oil. He also pressured the French Vichy government for permission to base Japanese troops in French Indochina (now Vietnam)—an action seen by Hull, Roosevelt and British Prime Minister Winston Churchill as preparation to invade Malaya or Burma, and possibly Singapore. With Vichy permission, Japanese soldiers and aircraft moved into Indochina in great numbers. The move came as no surprise to Roosevelt and Hull, thanks to the Magic intercepts.

As the Japanese forces entered Saigon and Da Nang in July 1941, the American president announced a total embargo of all oil shipments to Japan, having previously lowered quantities of cotton and petroleum and embargoed scrap iron and other vital materials shipments to the Japanese in an effort to warn them against continuing their war policy in China and East Asia. Finally, he froze all Japanese assets in the United States and cut off trade with Japan, as did Britain and the Netherlands. Roosevelt's actions spawned frantic activity in Tokyo. The Japanese government sent further envoys to assist Nomura in Washington, to virtually no avail. Roosevelt and Hull stood firmly in their opposition to the militant Japanese policies and told Japan that the oil embargo would remain in effect until she got out of China and Indochina, and renounced her Tri-partite agreement with Germanyand Italy. The Japanese refused to comply and countered with a demand that the U.S. stop providing arms to the Chinese Nationalist leader Chiang Kai-Shek.

Ambassador Grew worked to persuade President Roosevelt not to make the Japanese feel that they were cornered as they would then be compelled to violent reaction. By August the Japanese foreign minister had been replaced by the calmer, more reasoned Admiral Teijiro Toyoda, a man whom Grew knew and understood. The following month Grew sent a message to his boss, Secretary Hull, urging him and the president to opt for what he referred to as "constructive conciliation" rather than "economic strangulation" in their relations with Japan. He told Hull that the Japanese were wholly committed in China and would never agree to the U.S. demand, and that he believed the best route to a peace agreement between Japan and the U.S. would be for President Roosevelt to meet with Japanese Prime Minister, Prince Fumimaro Konoye, possibly in Hawaii. Lastly, he warned that the Japanese were entirely capable of readying for war while sincerely searching for peace.

Secretary Hull did not accept Grew's analysis or recommendations and would not agree to the suggested meeting of Roosevelt and Konoye. Thanks to another Magic intercept, Hull knew that Japan intended the conquest of Indochina and Thailand and had plans for elsewhere in Asia as well. While this was going on, the Roosevelt administration was under considerable pressure from the "China Lobby" and from Chiang himself, to provide more and more arms and financial assistance for their struggle against Japan. Their cry too was for an absolutely unyielding position by the administration against Japan. This hard line was strongly supported by Roosevelt's cabinet and forcefully backed by the Navy and War Secretaries, Frank Knox and Henry Stimson, respectively, both of whom believing that Japan was bluffing, probably unwilling to fight if it came down to it, and in any case, was not powerful enough militarily to be that much of a threat if war with the U.S. did result.

In England, Winston Churchill, Roosevelt's friend and ally, was urging the president to maintain a tough stand against the Japanese, even sending him notes that he hoped Roosevelt would forward to Tokyo. But Roosevelt was not about to allow Churchill or anyone else to dictate American foreign policy, and he persisted in his desire to reach some sort of acceptable accord with Japan. Also, the president had been briefed by his army and navy chiefs that U.S. armed forces were not yet ready to fight a war.

The grinding, ineffective efforts of both nations continued into the autumn, with the Japanese envoys in Washington proposing that, in exchange for a resumption of oil shipments, Japan would halt its military activity in Southeast Asia and, upon the restoration of peace in China and the Pacific region, it would withdraw its troops from all foreign soil. Hull was not impressed with the proposal. Roosevelt countered with an idea that would see the U.S. resume economic relations with Japan if Japan would stop its military moves to the north and south and renew peace negotiations with China. But the plan never went to Japan for consideration because Hull had just learned that a large Japanese task force of warships and troop transports was moving through the China Sea towards Southeast Asia and possibly the Dutch East Indies. Rather than sending the FDR idea, Cordell Hull framed a stern ten-point document demanding Japanese withdrawl from China, Indochina, and Manchuria, and the renunciation of Japan's Tripartite agreement with Germany and Italy. Hull's action served to prove the validity of Ambassador Grew's perspective. The Japanese reaction to Hull's demand showed that it had further convinced them of American intransigence and almost certainly reinforced Japanese belief in the hopelessness of any additional negotiation with the U.S. Japan's options were exhausted.

On 7 December, Kichisaburo Nomura, the Japanese envoy to Washington, requested an appointment to see Secretary of State Cordell Hull at 1 p.m. that day. Nomura later telephoned and asked that the appointment be postponed to 1:45 p.m. as he was not quite ready for the meeting. He arrived at 2:05 p.m. and was received by Hull at 2:20 p.m.

Nomura stated that he had been instructed to deliver a document at 1 p.m. which he then handed to the Secretary. He told Hull he was sorry that he had been delayed owing to the need for more time to decode the message. Hull asked why he had specified a one o'clock meeting and Nomura replied that he did not know, but that that was his instruction. Hull noted that he was receiving the message after two o'clock.

After reading the first few pages of the document, Secretary Hull asked Nomura if the document was being presented under the instructions of the Japanese Government. Nomura said that it was. As soon as he had finished reading the document, Hull turned to Nomura and said: "I must say that in all my conversations with you during the last nine months, I have never uttered one word of untruth. This is borne out absolutely by the record. In all my fifty years of public service I have never seen a document that was more crowded with infamous falsehoods and distortions—infamous falsehoods and distortions on a scale so huge that I never imagined until today that any government on this planet was capable of uttering them." Nomura then left the room without comment.

The document:
THE JAPANESE GOVERNMENT REGRETS TO HAVE TO NOTIFY HERE-

BY THE AMERICAN GOVERNMENT THAT IN VIEW OF THE ATTI-
TUDE OF THE AMERICAN GOVERNMENT IT CANNOT BUT CONSIDER
THAT IT IS IMPOSSIBLE TO REACH AN AGREEMENT THROUGH FUR-
THER NEGOTIATIONS.

One week before the document was given to Secretary Hull, the follow-ing
final warning message was issued to key American and British personnel by
the U.S. Chief of Naval Operations: "This dispatch is to be considered a war
warning. Negotiations with Japan looking toward stabilization of conditions
in the Pacific have ceased and an aggressive move by Japan is expected
within the next few days. The number and equipment of Japanese troops
and the organization of naval task forces indicates an amphibious expedi-
tion against either the Philippines, Thailand, or Korea peninsula or possibly
Borneo. Execute an appropriate defensive deployment preparatory to carrying out the tasks assigned in WPL46. Inform District and Army authorities.
A similar warning is being sent by War Department. Spenavo inform
British."

When Admiral Yamamoto made his grand plan for the Japanese attack on
the U.S. Navy in Pearl Harbor, he met with complete and absolute opposition to it by the members of the Imperial Navy General Staff. They argued
that the essential element of surprise in such an attack would be impossible
to preserve—when fielding an armada of six large carriers and more than
twenty support vessels half way across the Pacific. They pointed out that
the only route that avoided commercial shipping traffic was across the north
Pacific, making refueling inordinately difficult in the stormy seas. They
complained too that if the attack should have to be aborted, the fleet might
have to fight the American fleet in unfamiliar waters. Critically, they challenged with the point that the inherent risks outweighed the potential gains.
Yamamoto countered their arguments and, after threatening to resign his
commission and retire if his plan was not approved, he prevailed.

In late November, preparations for the strike on Pearl were well along.
Current information on U.S. Navy fleet movements, berthing positions, and
duty schedules were being cabled to Yamamoto's headquarters by the
Japanese Consul General in Honolulu. On 22 November, the Pearl Harbor
task force fleet was being assembled and would, on 25 November, sail east
from Hitokappu Bay in the Kuriles north of Japan towards Hawaii. The six
carriers, battleships, heavy cruisers, destroyers and submarines would travel in strict radio silence across the western Pacific.

In a brilliantly coordinated effort, other Japanese striking forces arrived
at their destinations around the same time as the main Pearl strike force
reached a point about 230 miles north of Oahu Island, Hawaii, where dawn
was breaking.

The Japanese task force commander, Vice Admiral Chiuchi Nagumo, had received a coded signal from Yamamoto on 2 December authorizing him to go ahead with the attack. The signal was Niitaka Yama Nabora (Climb Mount Niitaka). The task force reached the attack launch point north of the island of Oahu on 7 December and the first wave of dive bombers, horizontal bombers, fighters and torpedo bombers had launched by 6 a.m., and was assembling and climbing towards their cruising altitude. The 183 aircraft of that first wave rounded Barber's Point southwest of Pearl at 7.53 a.m. The calligraphic characters on the white hachimaki scarf tied around the leather flying helmet of their leader, Lt Commander Mitsuo Fuchida, translated as CERTAIN VICTORY. Using the code phrase Tora! Tora! Tora! (Tiger! Tiger! Tiger!), Fuchida alerted the carrier task force that the aircraft had reached the objective and were about to commence their attack.

The Japanese torpedo bombers descended first from the formation to make their low-level drops. The first warships to receive torpedoes were a light cruiser, a minelayer, and the battleship *Arizona*, which was literally blown out of the water, her bottom ripped out. Massive damage followed to the battleships *Oklahoma* and *California* when each was struck by three torpedoes. Moments later the *Oklahoma* was hit by a fourth torpedo, capsizing her. The already ruined *Arizona* was then struck by a bomb that exploded her forward magazine, blowing her apart with the loss of more than 1,000 of her crew.

While bombers and torpedo bombers worked on their capital ship targets in Pearl, other bombers and fighters from the formation dived on the Wheeler and Hickam airfields, and at Kaneohe Bay Naval Air Station, bombing and strafing the dozens of parked American aircraft. U.S. Marines who had been asleep, at breakfast, or in the showers, were machine-gunned as they ran from their barracks at Hickam. Exactly one hour after the attack began, a second wave of carrier aircraft arrived over Pearl to continue the efforts of the first.

Eight American battleships were in Pearl Harbor when the Japanese carrier-based aircraft launched the surprise attack that Sunday morning in December 1941. Two of them—*Oklahoma* and *Arizona*—were wrecked beyond repair. *California, Nevada,* and *West Virginia* were all damaged extensively and put out of action. *Pennsylvania, Maryland* and *Tennessee* suffered major damage. Three light cruisers were hit and badly damaged and three destroyers were sunk. 164 American aircraft were destroyed on the ground at the two airfields and on Ford Island, and a further 159 were damaged. 2,395 servicemen and civilians were killed in the raid with a further 1,178 wounded.

The cost to the Japanese? Nagumo's six aircraft carriers had not been detected by the Americans. Twenty-nine carrier aircraft were lost in the attack, some as the result of accidents. Two midget submarines were lost.

"I was a powder car man, running an electric hoist back and forth down to the upper handling room of the battleship USS *West Virginia*. There was nothing but powder in that room. It was directly under the projectile room where the shells were kept. We all trained so that we knew every job around the turret. I always wanted to be a gunner's mate, so I asked around to find out how I could get reassigned, and was told to see a turret captain. I went to see him and he had to check with the division officer and they took me in the turret and put me to work on the number two gun. Each man there had a part of the inside of the turret he had to take care of and wipe down and clean and shine every day.

"On December 6th 1941, a lot of us were out sunning ourselves on the upper deck, until it got so hot that you had to run down and jump in the showers. A typical Saturday in Pearl. It was good duty. On Sunday morning we had breakfast and I had the duty. My station was to handle a fire extinguisher. That day a third of the ship's company had liberty on shore. The bugle sounded 'Fire and Rescue' and I ran off to get my white hat from my locker. The Officer of the Deck at this point thought that there had been some kind of explosion over by Ten-Ten dock. A torpedo had passed under a ship there and hit a cruiser and they both sank. And then we were ordered to General Quarters. Then I realized it was the Japs. I started running aft. I went up two decks heading to the turret. On the way I saw a plane and wondered what he was doing. He turned and went toward the *California* and as he turned, I saw the red ball on the wing. Before I got to the turret there was a tremendous explosion somewhere below us. It was a torpedo. The whole ship was shaking and, by then the ladder was full. I went around to another ladder and got up to the top deck. From there I went up to the boat deck and under the overhang of the turret to my battle station in the turret.

"The explosions continued; the ship would shake and the blast covers would clang, and then we started listing slowly to port, very slowly, and I was watching that and thinking that we might have to get through that hatch door in the bottom of the turret pretty soon. Meanwhile, the damage control officer managed to counter-flood to keep the ship from capsizing. She eventually just settled to the bottom.

"The hatch cover was still open and someone stuck his head up and yelled 'Abandon ship!' 'Abandon ship!' We got out and there was no big rush. The *Tennessee* was inboard of us and we made it to the fo'c'sle, took our shoes off and jumped into the water and swam to Ford Island. When we got to shore the first thing we heard was 'Get down! Get down! Strafing!' I got down by a truck at the edge of the golf course as a plane turned toward us and began firing. The tracers seemed to be coming right at me. Only one of his guns was firing. I got under the truck and the tracers turned away from me. About then a woman came down from one of the houses there, carrying clothes. I wandered over to see what was going on and she fitted us out with dry clothes."—Richard McCutcheon, USS *West Virginia*

On Sundays the sailors of the USS *Arizona* breakfasted on beans, cornbread and coffee. The Navy allotment for food since the 1920s was forty cents per man per day.

"Properly buttoned up, the *California* could have shrugged off two or even three torpedoes, with minor listing that would have been quickly corrected by counter-flooding the starboard voids. Instead she had assumed a port list of fourteen or fifteen degrees and the list was still increasing. Suddenly I found myself sliding toward the low side of the birdbath, which brought me up sharply against the splinter shield. My earphones were jerked from my head. Before replacing them, I looked down. A hundred feet below me was nothing but dirty, oil-streaked and flotsam-filled water. Lifeless bodies from the *Oklahoma* floated face down. Motor launches were criss-crossing the channel, picking up swimming sailors.

"If the *California* capsized—and that I could see was a distinct possibility—I had at least a fighting chance to join the swimmers. My shipmates below decks had none.

"I planned to climb to the opposite side of the splinter shield as the ship went over and launch myself in a long, flat dive when the maintop touched the water. If I could avoid getting fouled in the yardarm rigging or the radio antennas, I just might get clear.

"Ahead of the *Nevada*, a large pipeline snaked out from Ford Island in a semicircle ending at the dredge *Turbine*. Since it blocked more than half the channel, the line was always disconnected and pulled clear when the battleships were scheduled to stand out. This morning, of course, it was still in place. But the sailor conning the *Nevada* squeezed her between the dredge and the drydock area without slowing down.

"The flames were now shooting up past her anti-aircraft detectors nearly to her foretop. She had been hit repeatedly, and Pearl Harbor was pouring into her hull. Her bow was low in the water. If she were to sink in the channel, she would plug up the entire harbor like a cork in a bottle. With bitter regret, we watched her run her bow into shallow water between the floating drydock and Hospital Point. The current carried her stern around, and she finished her evolution pointing back up the channel she had tried so valiantly to follow to freedom." —Ted Mason, USS *California*

At the height of his business career Kazuo Sakamaki became the head of Toyota's Brazilian operations. In December 1941, Sakamaki was a 23-year-old ensign in the Imperial Japanese Navy and one-half of the crew of a midget submarine struggling to enter Pearl Harbor. His mission was to sneak into the port unobserved, ahead of the main attack by the carrier aircraft, and be ready to sink one of the target battleships at the appropriate moment. It was a suicide mission involving five such midget subs. But the gyrocompass of Sakamaki's boat failed and the other four subs were either lost or destroyed during the attack.

Sakamaki's boat became stranded on a coral reef just down the coast and he was forced to abandon it. He was later discovered, unconscious, by an American soldier, and became the first Japanese prisoner of war of World War Two. He recalled feeling deep shame with the failure of his mission, for letting his sub fall into enemy hands, and for surviving when his comrades had died in the attempted raid. In time though, he gradually overcame the guilt he felt and went on to help his fellow Japanese prisoners in POW camps in the United States.

Where were America's aircraft carriers, the important warships that would become her new capital ships in the Second World War, on Sunday 7 December 1941? The USS *Lexington* (CV-2) had departed Pearl Harbor on 5 December in order to supplement the air defenses of Midway Island. While en route the *Lexington* commander was notified of the attack on Pearl. She launched search planes to look for the Japanese fleet and then joined with two other U.S. Navy task forces to search southwest of Hawaii, returning to Pearl on 13 December. The USS *Saratoga* (CV-3), sister ship of the *Lexington*, was entering San Diego Bay, having recently emerged from a drydock at Bremerton, Washington, where she had undergone a refit. The USS *Ranger* (CV-4), the first U.S. Navy ship to be designed and built from the keel up as an aircraft carrier, was returning to her port, Norfolk, Virginia, from a patrol in the Caribbean at the time of the attack. The USS *Yorktown* (CV-5) was at her home port, Norfolk, Virginia, on 7 December. The USS *Enterprise* (CV-6) had left Pearl Harbor on 28 November to deliver twelve Grumman F4F-3 Wildcat fighters to a Marine fighter squadron on Wake Island. She was returning to Pearl when it was attacked. Several of her aircraft were launched and eighteen of them arrived over Pearl while the attack was still under way. Six planes from *Enterprise* were lost in the action. The USS *Wasp* (CV-7) was at anchor in Grassy Bay, Bermuda, on 7 December. The USS *Hornet* (CV-8) was conducting a training cruise in the Atlantic on the day of the attack. The USS *Long Island*, a smaller escort-type carrier, was at her home port, Norfolk, Virginia, on 7 December. Five additional U. S. Navy carriers were in various stages of construction on the day Pearl Harbor was attacked. They were the USS *Essex* (CV-9), USS *Bon Homme Richard* (CV-10), USS *Intrepid* (CV-11), USS *Cabot* (CV-16), and the USS *Bunker Hill* (CV-17). No U.S. Navy carriers were in Pearl Harbor on the day of the Japanese attack, a fact that would haunt Japan's war planners and especially Admiral Yamamoto.

In the late afternoon, several hours after the last enemy raider had flown from

Pearl Harbor, two young American naval officers went over to the wreck of the USS *Arizona* in a motor launch. As the sun began to set they carefully retrieved the American flag that had furled from the stern of the battleship, but was partially submerged in oily water of the harbour. Other navy personnel visited the remains of the American warships. They brought mattress covers in which to hold the bodies and body parts they found as they explored the ruined hulks. While they worked, mass graves 150 feet long, just trenches really, were being bulldozed on Oahu to hold the hundreds of roughly-fashioned wooden boxes, some of which were leaking oil or blood.

Confusion dominated America's towns and cities that day. People across the country, including the president, his cabinet and the members of Congress, were anxious, perplexed, angry, and looking for answers. By the late afternoon in Washington, Japan had formally declared war on the United States and the British Empire. The Japanese Emperor stated: "Japan, for its existence and self-defense, has no other recourse but to appeal to arms and to crush every obstacle in its path."

THE DOOLITTLE RAID

Late in January 1942, U.S. Army Air Force Lieutenant Colonel James H. Doolittle was called into the office of his boss, General Henry 'Hap' Arnold, chief of the Air Force. Arnold asked, "Jim, what airplane do we have that can take off in 500 feet, carry a 2,000-pound bomb load, and fly 2,000 miles with a full crew?"

Doolittle considered his response for a moment. He ruled out the Boeing B-17 and Consolidated B-24 heavy bombers, knowing that neither of them would get airborne in 500 feet. That left the four medium bombers then in the USAAF inventory—the Douglas B-18 Bolo and B-23 Dragon, the North American B-25 Mitchell, and the Martin B-26 Marauder. All of them, he thought, would have difficulty getting off in 500 feet, and he was sure the B-26 would never manage it with a 2,000-pound bomb load. He asked Arnold for a little time to research the question.

The next day, having looked up the performance figures on all four aeroplanes, he told the general that both the B-23 and B-25 would meet his specifications if extra fuel tanks were installed. Arnold then said that the plane must also be able to take off in a narrow space not over 75 feet wide. Doolittle replied that the 92-foot wingspan of the B-23 would eliminate it from consideration. The B-25, with its 67 1/2 foot wingspan, was the answer. A day later, Hap Arnold ordered Doolittle off on his most important military assignment to date.

In the evening of 10 January 1942, Admiral Ernest J. King, the American Chief of Naval Operations, was working late aboard his yacht, the *Vixen*, moored in Washington Navy Yard. He had met earlier in the day with President Franklin Roosevelt who had expressed his strong wish to strike a blow at Japan as soon as possible in response to the devastating surprise attack by the Japanese at Pearl Harbor, Hawaii, the preceding month.

King was interrupted by Captain Francis S. Low, Operations Officer on his staff. Low had an idea about organising a bombing raid on Japan. He had just returned from Norfolk, Virginia, where he had inspected the Navy's newest aircraft carrier, the *Hornet* (CV 8). When taking off from the airfield at NAS Norfolk, he had noticed the outline of an aircraft carrier flight deck painted on the tarmac, where pilots were being trained in carrier take-offs and landings. He told King that the Japanese knew that the radius of action for U.S. carrier planes was roughly 300 miles, and he thought that, with a far greater range than that, some Army twin-engined medium bombers could be operated from a carrier within striking range of Japan. Low was not a pilot, and he fully expected King to be sceptical about the idea, but the admiral reacted favourably. He told Low to discuss it immediately with Captain Donald Duncan, King's Air Operations Officer—and with no one else.

When Low telephoned Duncan, he began with two questions for the Captain: Can an Army Air Force medium bomber land aboard a carrier? Can a land-based bomber loaded down with bombs, gas, and crew take off from a carrier deck? Duncan explained that a carrier deck was far too short to safely land an Army bomber, and the airframes of Army bombers are not designed to take the shock of sudden stops with arresting gear. He said he would have to look into the answer to the second question. Checking Army technical manuals for the performance capabilities of their medium bombers, as well as Navy files and historical records over the next five days, Duncan completed a thirty-page analysis. His conclusion: the North American B-25 was the only plane capable of the sort of mission Low had in mind.

Duncan began considering the demands and challenges of such a mission, starting with the fact that U.S. Army Air Force pilots were not normally required to take off in very short distances and were not trained for it. Selected pilots would need to practice take-offs with varying bomb loads on marked-out short field distances until they were able to safely get their B-25s off the deck of one of the Navy's fast carriers.

With the new USS *Hornet* scheduled to depart Norfolk for duty in the Pacific in February, Duncan felt she was the ship for the job. With her twenty-five knot steaming rate, relatively wide deck, and the support of a screening force with an additional carrier, some cruisers, destroyers and tankers, *Hornet* should be able to bring a small force of B-25s within 500 miles of Japan. The bombers could then launch, deliver their bombs and continue on to landings on airfields in China.

The planes would need substantial extra fuel capacity, adding still more weight and making the task of taking off from the short carrier deck that much more hazardous. Duncan worried about the safety of the take-offs, for the crews of the planes and that of the ship, and he added actual carrier take-off practice to his list of requirements for the mission. He knew too that strict secrecy was essential to the success of any such mission, which risked the lives of more than 10,000 men and a large task force of warships.

After nearly a week of intense discussions, research, and debate, Duncan and Low were ready to meet with Admiral King about the proposed air strike against Japan. King continued to approve their progress and told them to meet with General Arnold about it. He said that if Arnold ordered the strike to proceed, Duncan would handle the Navy end of it.

Subject: B-25 Special Project (Top Secret)
To: Commanding General, Army Air Forces

The purpose of this special project is to bomb and fire the industrial center of Japan. It is anticipated that this not only will cause confusion and impede production but will undoubtedly facilitate operation against Japan in other theaters due to their probable withdrawl of troops for the purpose of defending the home country.

An action of this kind is most desirable now due to the psychological effect on the American public, our allies, and our enemies.

The method contemplated is to bring carrier-borne bombers to within 400 to 500 miles (all distances mentioned will be in statute miles) of the coast of Japan, preferably to the south-south-east. They will then take off from the carrier deck and proceed directly to selected targets in the Tokyo-Yokohama, Nagoya, and Osaka-Kobe areas.

Simultaneous bombings of these areas is contemplated, with the bombers coming in up waterways from the southeast and, after dropping their bombs, returning in the same direction. After clearing the Japanese outside coastline a sufficient distance, a general westerly course will be set for one or more of the following airports in China: Chuchow, Chuchow (Lishui), Lushan and/or Chienou. Chuchow is about seventy miles inland and 200 miles to the south-southwest of Shanghai.

After refueling, the airplanes will proceed to the strong Chinese air base at Chungking, about 800 miles distant, and from there to such ultimate objective as may, at that time, be indicated.

The greatest nonstop distance that any airplane will have to fly is 2,000 miles.

Eighteen B-25B (North American medium bomber) airplanes will be employed in this raid. Each will carry about 1,100 gallons of gasoline, which assures a range of 2,400 miles at 5,000 feet in still air.

Each bomber will carry two 500-pound demolition bombs and as near as possible to 1,000 pounds of incendiaries. The demolition bombs will be dropped first and then the incendiaries.

The extra gasoline will be carried in a 275-gallon auxiliary leakproof tank in the top of the bomb bay and a 175-gallon flexible rubber tank in the passageway above the bomb bay. It is anticipated that the gasoline from this top tank will be used up and the tank flattened out or rolled up and removed prior to entering the combat zone. This assures that the airplane will be fully operational and minimizes the fire and explosion hazard characteristic of a nearly empty tank.

In all other respects the airplanes are conventional. The work of installing the required additional tankage is being done by Mid-Continent Airlines at Minneapolis. All production and installation work is progressing according to schedule and the twenty-four airplanes (six spares) should be converted by March 15.

Extensive range and performance tests will be conducted on airplane number one while the others are being converted. A short period will be required to assemble and give special training to the crews. The training will include teamwork in bombing, gunnery, navigation, flying, short take-off, and at least one carrier takeoff for each pilot.

If the crews are selected promptly from men familiar with their jobs and the B-25B airplane, the complete unit should be ready for loading on the carrier by April 1.

General operational instructions will be issued just before takeoff from the carrier.

Due to the greater accuracy of daylight bombing, a daylight raid is contemplated. The present concept of the project calls for a night take-off from the carrier and arrival over objectives at dawn. Rapid refueling at the landing points will permit arrival at Chungking before dark.

A night raid will be made if, due to last-minute information received from our intelligence section or other source, a daylight raid is definitely inadvisable. The night raid should be made on a clear night, moonlight if Japan is blacked out, moonless if it is not.

The Navy has already supervised takeoff tests made at Norfolk, Virginia, using B-25B bombers carrying loads of 26,000 pounds, and 29,000 pounds. These tests indicate that no difficulty need be anticipated in taking off from the carrier deck with a gross load of around 31,000 pounds.

The Navy will be charged with providing a carrier (probably the *Hornet*), with loading and storing the airplanes, and with delivering them to the takeoff position.

The Chemical Warfare Service is designing and preparing special incendiary bomb clusters in order to assure that the maximum amount that limited space permits, up to 1,000 pounds per airplane, may be carried. Forty-eight of these clusters will be ready for shipment from Edgewood Arsenal (Maryland) by March 15.

About 20,000 U.S. gallons of 100-octane aviation gasoline and 600 gallons of lubricating oil will be laid down at Chuchow and associated fields. All other supplies and necessary emergency repair equipment will be carried on the airplanes.

Colonel Claire Chennault, a former Air Corps officer and now aviation advisor to the Chinese government, should assign a responsible American or a Chinese who speaks English to physically check and assure that the supplies are in place. This man should also be available to assist the crews in servicing the airplanes. That the supplies are in place can be indicated by suitable radio code signal. Work on placing supplies must start at once.

Shortly before the airplanes arrive, the proper Chinese agencies should be advised that the airplanes are coming soon, but the inference will be that they are flying up from the south in order to stage a raid on Japan from which they plan to return to the same base.

Radio signals from the bombing planes immediately after they drop their bombs may be used to indicate arrival at gassing points some six or seven hours later.

Care must be exercised to see that the Chinese are advised just in time, as any information given to the Chinese may be expected to fall into Japanese hands and a premature notification would be fatal to the project.

An initial study of meteorological conditions indicates that the sooner the raid is made the better will be the prevailing weather conditions. The weather will become increasingly unfavorable after the end of April. Weather was considered largely from the point of view of avoiding morning fog over Tokyo and other targets, low overcast over Chuchow and Chungking, icing, and strong westerly winds.

If possible, daily weather predictions or anticipated weather conditions at Chungking and the coast should be sent, at a specified time, in suitable code, in order to assist the meteorologist on the carrier in analyzing his forecasts.

Lieutenant Colonel J. H. Doolittle, Air Corps, will be in charge of the preparations for and will be in personal command of the project. Other flight personnel will, due to the considerable hazard incident to such a mission, be volunteers.

Each airplane will carry its normal complement of five crew members: pilot, copilot, bombardier-navigator, radio operator, and gunner-mechanic.

One crew member will be a competent meteorologist and one an experienced navigator. All navigators will be trained in celestial navigation.

Two ground liaison officers will be assigned. One will remain on the mainland and the other on the carrier.

At least three crew members will speak Chinese—one on each of the target units.

Hap Arnold reacted positively when told by Francis Low and Donald Duncan of the idea for using a small force of B-25 bombers flying from a U.S. Navy aircraft carrier to make the first retaliatory air strike on Japan since the Pearl Harbor attack. He didn't bother telling them that his own staff was already working a similar plan. He called Admiral King and it was quickly arranged that Duncan would act as Navy coordinator for the project. It was then that Jimmy Doolittle was brought into it for the Air Force. Arnold told Doolittle he would have first priority on anything he needed to get the job done. "Get in touch with me directly if anybody gets in your way."

The USS *Hornet* had to sail via the Panama Canal to the U.S. west coast and be ready to leave from there on 1 April. Before leaving Norfolk, time was needed to conduct some B-25 takeoffs from the carrier. Duncan, meanwhile, was sent to Pearl Harbor to handle the Navy's task force arrangements for the project. Now the pressure on Doolittle was ratcheted up considerably. Not least among his concerns was that of maintaining secrecy around the entire effort. Without completely preserving the element of surprise, the Japanese enemy, with her numerically greater naval and air forces, would certainly be ready and waiting to punish the Americans.

By late January, arrangements had been made with the U.S. Air War Plans Division to develop five separate Air Force organisations in China under the overall command of the U.S. 10th Air Force in Burma. Jimmy Doolittle commanded the first of these organisations, the B-25s destined to raid Japan, which, after the raid, were to be used in China with the pilots and crews absorbed into the 10th. The organizations were classified 'secret' and Doolittle's outfit was given 'top-secret' classification because of the plan to bomb Japan. At that point, the only people who knew about the raid plan were Doolittle, Admiral King, General Arnold, and Captains Low and Duncan. Doolittle would keep it that way until the Navy named the man to take charge of the raid task force.

The skipper of the *Hornet*, Captain Marc A. Mitscher, was curious but not overly inquisitive about details of the project as two B-25s were hoisted aboard his ship in preparation for some experimental takeoffs. Mitscher, a naval aviator, was well aware of the dangers in such tests as the carrier steamed out of sight of land. Lieutenants John Fitzgerald and James McCarthy were at the controls of the bombers as the ship hove into a 45 mph wind over the flight deck. They would need only an additional 23 mph acceleration to take off. In the exercises, both pilots were astonished at how quickly they became airborne. The planes returned to NAS Norfolk and Donald Duncan was convinced that a fully-loaded B-25B with a five-man crew could safely get airborne from the carrier. Doolittle agreed with Duncan's assessment, provided the carrier could make at least 20 knots with a strong wind straight down the flight deck.

He was about to travel by P-40 fighter to Wright Field, Ohio, Washington, DC, Edgewood Arsenal, Maryland and elsewhere in his efforts to get the bombers ready for the their long, demanding flight. He asked General Arnold to have General Carl Spaatz, his deputy for intelligence, prepare target folders for the raid to include the most desirable industrial targets in Japan. Their locations were Tokyo, Kobe, Osaka, Nagoya and Yokohama, and specifically involved steel, magnesium, iron, and aluminium manufacturing, petroleum refineries, aircraft and shipbuilding facilities.

Next he requested information on potentially available B-25Bs and their crews. He was assigned the aircraft and personnel he needed from units commanded by Lieutenant Colonel William C. Mills and Major John 'Jack'

Hilger in Pendleton, Oregon, and by 3 February the men and planes were on their way to Columbia, South Carolina, via Minneapolis where the essential auxiliary fuel tanks were installed in the aircraft. From Columbia, Doolittle had arranged for the bombers and crews to proceed to Eglin Field, Florida, where they would undergo an intense few weeks of practice in short-field take-offs with full loads. There, Hilger served as his watchful, extremely efficient point man, in charge of the Eglin operation during Doolittle's many absences to make the necessary arrangements for the raid. The actual crew selection and make-up was handled by Col. Mills' three squadron commanders, who also provided the mechanics, armourers, radio operators and other required ground personnel.

One of Hilger's first actions was to secure the assignment of a Navy instructor to teach the Army pilots about carrier takeoffs. The man was Hank Miller and the Army pilots were nonplussed when they learned that not only had Miller never flown a B-25, but he had never even seen one. Miller studied the performance data on the aeroplane and then took three of the B-25-qualified Army pilots on some practice take-offs. On the short-field layout they were staggered to find that Miller expected them to take off in the bomber with a gross weight of 27,000 pounds at fifty miles an hour. Before their hurried carrier take-off training was concluded, they were able to take off within 350 feet (in a forty knot wind) with the airplane at a gross weight of 31,000 pounds (2,000 pounds over its maximum design load limit).

Doolittle happened to check his Form 5 Pilot's Individual Flight Record and realised that he was not yet checked out in the B-25B, a deficiency he attended to on 1 March 1942. He always believed in being proficient in every aircraft type his men were assigned to fly. To prepare himself for the raid, he took Hank Miller's course in carrier take-off procedure for B-25 pilots. He vowed that if, for whatever reason, he couldn't pass the course or wasn't as good as the younger pilots he commanded, he would go along on the raid as a copilot.

Due to the exceptionally hazardous nature of the impending mission, Doolittle insisted that all participating crew be volunteers. He told them during the training that anyone could drop out for any reason and nothing would ever be said about it. When asked by some of the men for more information about the mission, he said it was top secret and that, while they might well guess about it and their training, he ordered them to keep their guesses to themselves, not to discuss anything about the mission or the training with anyone, and if someone asked questions about it, they were to give that person's name to Doolittle and the matter would be turned over to the FBI.

From an excellent cadre, he selected the men he would rely on in their various fields of expertise. For his bombing and gunnery officer he chose

C. Ross Greening, a mid-westerner who had been a B-25 pilot with the 17th Bomb Group, before becoming part of the Doolittle Raid team. Greening would survive the attack on Japan and would later be reassigned to a B-26 group in North Africa. Shot down and captured by the Germans, he escaped after two months imprisonment, but was recaptured, having evaded for six months. He spent the remainder of the war in Stalag Luft One, Barth, Germany. A gifted illustrator, Greening produced a wealth of paintings and drawings depicting his wartime adventures including the Doolittle Raid. They were later compiled by his widow and published in the book *Not As Briefed*.

Another personnel matter arose when First Lieutenant Thomas R. White, a flight surgeon attached to the 89th Reconnaissance Squadron, learned of the need for volunteers to apply for the "special mission". He contacted Major Hilger and tried to get in on it. Hilger said that the only way he might do so was if he were a qualified gunner. So White checked out as an aerial gunner—with the second highest score of all the gunners in Doolittle's crews. He made it onto one of the crews and further served Doolittle as flight surgeon for the raiders, administering the required innoculations against typhus, yellow fever, pneumonia, small pox and bubonic plague over the three-week training period.

In the preparations for the raid, it was decided to remove the precision high-altitude Norden bombsights from the B-25 bombers used, as the bombing altitude was to be too low to require the Norden, and in fear of the highly secret bombsight falling into the possession of the enemy if any of the bombers should crash in Japanese territory. Ross Greening then designed a special two-piece aluminium bombsight for use on the raid. The sights were built in the Eglin Field metal shop at a cost of twenty cents each.

Early in the training at Eglin, Doolittle took Greening and his other three most trusted officers aside, and gave them a general briefing about the mission, the selection of the B-25, the primary objective, and the means of bringing the bombers to within range of Japan, but nothing about the specific targets. He stressed the importance of the secrecy surrounding the mission and he deliberately kept no written records of his activities relating to it.

Getting enough flight training time for the pilots and crews of the B-25s was proving a problem for Doolittle. Persistent maintenance troubles with the auxiliary gas tanks and the electrically-powered gun turrets prevented the airmen from having the level of training in day and night navigation, bombing, gunnery, and formation flying that he wanted. Problems with .50-calibre machine guns jamming and shortages of ammunition prevented the gunners from getting adequate firing practice with the weapon and, by the end of the training, none of them had been able to fire on a moving target from a B-25 in flight. The jamming problem had, however, been resolved by a representative of Delco, the gun manufacturer.

Hap Arnold was as good as his word. In the many trips Doolittle made from Eglin to Dayton, Washington, Minnesota, and Maryland seeing to the requirements for the mission, he sometimes encountered resistance to his requests. Invariably, when he invoked Arnold's name, the resistance miraculously went away. Arnold's authority in the situation soon became known amongst the suppliers involved, and the bosses in charge quickly cleared the way for Doolittle and eased his progress.

Doolittle was responsible for preparing and organising the raid and the men and planes that would fly it, but there his responsibilities ended. From his 1991 autobiography: "On one of my trips to Washington in mid-March, I dropped in to see Hap and report on the progress we were making. I said, 'General, it occurred to me that I'm the one guy on this project who knows more about it than anyone else. You asked me to get the planes modified and the crews trained and this is being done. They're the finest bunch of boys I've ever worked with. I'd like your authorization to lead this mission myself.'

"Hap stared at me and his ever-present smile disappeared. He knew I had missed combat in World War I just as he had, and understood . . . that I didn't want to miss this war. He shook his head and said, 'I'm sorry, Jim. I need you right here on my staff. I can't afford to let you go on every mission you might help to plan.'

"I thought he was going to say that and launched into a rapid-fire sales pitch I had mentally prepared beforehand. Finally, Hap gave in. He shrugged and said, 'All right, Jim. It's all right with me provided it's all right with Miff Harmon.' Miff was Brigadier General Millard F. Harmon, Jr., Hap's chief of staff.

"I smelled a rat so I saluted, about-faced, and ran down the corridor to Miff's office. I knocked and opened his door. 'Miff,' I said breathlessly, 'I've just been to see Hap about that project I've been working on and said I wanted to lead the mission. Hap said it was okay with him if it's okay with you.'

"Miff was caught flat-footed, which was what I had intended. He replied, 'Well, whatever is all right with Hap is certainly all right with me.'

"I thanked him and closed the door. Just as I did, I heard Hap's voice on Miff's squawk box. Miff said, plaintively, 'But Hap, I told him he could go.'

"I didn't wait to hear any more. I beat it back to Bolling Field, got into my B-25, and headed for Eglin."

22 March. A coded message from Donald Duncan in Pearl Harbor to Admiral King was relayed to Hap Arnold. It was the signal for Jimmy Doolittle to send the B-25s and crews to McClellan Army Air Field, Sacramento, California. At McClellan, final checks would be made on the

planes before all would proceed to NAS Alameda on San Francisco Bay, where they would be loaded aboard the *Hornet*. Before the crews left for the west coast, Doolittle called them together: "Don't tell anyone what you were doing here at Eglin—not your families, wives, anybody. The lives of your buddies and a lot of other people depend on you keeping everything you saw and did here a secret."

As the Doolittle raiders edged closer to departing the west coast of the United States, the armed forces of Imperial Japan were rapidly completing their conquest of the Philippines and pressing on toward their next major goal, the conquest of Australia. Their list of takeovers now included Hong Kong, Singapore, Rangoon, Sumatra, Java, New Britain, New Ireland, a portion of New Guinea, the Admiralty Islands and the Gilbert Islands. Nearly all the territory of the western Pacific was under Japanese control and the war situation appeared desperate to many in the Allied camp.

At McClellan Air Base Doolittle again ran into a somewhat casual, listless response to his requests, which quickly became demands, relative to the airplanes in his charge. Meeting with the depot commander there, he made it clear that the B-25s were there for final inspection only, that no one was to tamper with or remove anything from them. He pointed out that many modifications had been made to the planes and gave the commander a list of what he still needed for them—installation of new propellers, 60-gallon gas tanks fitted where the lower turrets had been removed, replacement of hydraulic valves for the gun turrets, replacement of all seat-type parachutes with back-pack type, new properly-sized covers for the leak-proof bomb bay fuel tanks, removal of the 230-pound liaison radios, new glass navigation windows to replace the Plexiglas type, and, most importantly, no one was to touch or adjust the pre-adjusted carburettors on the engines.

The ho-hum attitude to his requests and the leisurely pace at which the inspections proceeded angered Doolittle, who phoned Hap Arnold: "Things are going too slowly out here. I'd appreciate it very much if you would personally build a fire under these people. They're treating this job as 'routine' and that won't get the job done in time.

"I don't know what Hap did or said, but it seemed like only minutes before our work order became the most important mission at McClellan. We suddenly became the focus of interest for a lot of folks who wondered what was going on that was suddenly so important. Whenever the civilians would ask questions, my crews watching over them would tell them to mind their own business and get on with what they were supposed to do."

In the course of the "inspections", some of the carburettors were indeed changed and adjusted and when Doolittle heard about it, he was furious. He called Arnold and a written report was demanded of the McClellan

commander. At the end of the stay there, Doolittle was presented with a form to be filled out asking for his opinion of the work performed in the inspections on his airplanes. He scratched one word
diagonally across the form: LOUSY.

The aeroplanes were spotted on the McClellan flight line ready for the short hop to Alameda and Doolittle noticed that a number of them were sporting painted anti-Japanese slogans on their fuselages. Realising that the fate of any crewmen who might be forced down and made prisoners of the Japanese could well be made worse by these slogans, he had them removed.

When all the bombers were ready to leave for Alameda, Doolittle took off first as he wanted to be on the ramp at the naval air station to greet each crew as they arrived. He told the pilots to get in at least an hour's flying time on the hop, to thoroughly test their planes. As they arrived at the air station he met each pilot and asked if the aircraft had any malfunctions to be reported. If so, he directed that the plane be put in a nearby parking area. All the others were to be taxied to a ramp near the wharf. If any aircraft had to be left behind, the crew was ordered to board the carrier anyway. They would go on the raid as spare crew members should any other crewmen drop out. His concern for maintaining the secrecy of the raid was such that he would not allow any man who had gone through the training to be left at dockside. "The word about what we had done or speculation about what we were about to do couldn't leak out if everyone was at sea."

The B-25s were hoisted aboard the Hornet and in the afternoon of 1 April the carrier was maneuvered into San Francisco Bay where she would spend the night. Doolittle gathered his crews, cautioned them once again about secrecy and turned them loose for one last evening of liberty.

From *Not As Briefed* by C. Ross Greening: "As we rolled over the waves, our mission was carefully studied and we were constantly briefed. Targets were assigned and we had a fair idea of what to expect. We all felt ready to go and our morale was high. None of us had ever been in combat before; it would all be new to us. Doolittle planned to leave a couple of hours early, and in the dark set fire to Tokyo's Shiba ward, in order to serve as a beacon for our planes attacking later in the night. The Navy assured us that we would be taken to within 400 or possibly 500 miles from Japan. A greater distance would significantly reduce our chances of reaching airstrips near Chuchow and elsewhere in eastern China, where preparations were being made to receive us."

In consideration of Lt. Col. Doolittle's need for privacy when meeting with his air crews during the Pacific voyage, the *Hornet*'s captain, Marc Mitscher offered the use of his quarters, a conference room, bathroom and a bedroom, to Doolittle. Mitscher moved into a small bedroom just off the bridge of the carrier. As the ship left California, Doolittle received several good luck messages, from Admiral King, Generals Arnold and Marshall, and others.

Ross Greening watched spellbound as Lt. Col. Doolittle's B-25 started its take-off roll in the early morning of 18 April. A flagman immediately left of the bomber waved in a circular motion. Doolittle throttled his engines up to full power, his flaps were fully down. The B-25 leapt from the wet, pitching deck at what Greening thought a sickening angle, gained balance and headed off for Tokyo. The excitement on the flight deck of the *Hornet* was palpable.

Greening: "It was a parting of good friends. I don't think there was a man leaving who really believed he would complete the flight safely. We were 800 miles from Japan—twice the distance we had bargained for, and 200 more than was considered really feasible for the amount of fuel we carried. What we thought would be our most difficult hazard, the takeoff, turned out to be among the least of our problems. We had relatively little difficulty getting off the carrier deck.

Greening's was the eleventh B-25 to take off. "As soon as the *Hari Kari-er* was airborne with flaps and wheels up, I made a slow right turn to pass back over the carrier, checking course and drift. I then proceeded at low altitude and speed so McElroy and Bower could catch up. They fell into position for the long flight to Japan."

Greening kept the bomber as low to the surface of the sea as he dared, trying to avoid detection by the enemy. All of Doolittle's pilots had been told that if they were required to bomb Japan in daylight, they could easily lose more than half of their planes. The plan called for them all to arrive over the targets in darkness but, unfortunately, that was not to be, once the *Hornet* had been prematurely detected by Japanese patrol ships, forcing the mission to be launched much earlier than planned. The early take-offs meant that the raiders would be attacking their targets around mid-day. They all knew they were in for a rough time. Now they had to rely on their training to see them through what they were about to do. They had approximately four and a half hours flying time to think about it.

Greening's crew had selected the oil refineries at the Yokohama docks as their primary target. As a teenage seaman aboard the SS *President Cleveland* in the summer of 1933, his vessel had docked at Yokohama and he thought he would recognise various landmarks in the area. He was wrong.

The Doolittle bombers were spread over a fifty-mile front to try and make the Japanese believe they were being attacked by more aircraft than was the case. The Americans also hoped that being spread out in such a way would lessen the chances of their being detected.

As they neared the Japanese coast, Greening and his crew looked for such obvious landmarks as Mt Fujiyama and Tokyo Bay, but did not spot them. Instead, they crossed the enemy coast over unexpected hills and mountains. They later learned that most of the raider aircraft compasses were out of adjustment, causing them to arrive over Japan up to sixty miles north of their intended landfall.

Greening: "It's difficult enough to fly under 500 feet in peacetime, but even more so when you're excited, in strange terrain, and fearing for your life. It's hard to think clearly and do things rationally and deliberately. I don't think I'd ever flown so low in my life, dodging down creek beds and ducking between trees rather than going over them. I'm not sure it was necessary, but it gave a sense of security. Those minutes seemed like hours."

As his B-25 roared low across a military airfield with lines of training planes on the concrete, Greening noted that his airspeed was about 170 mph. At that moment he was startled by the noise and vibration of the top turret machine guns firing. He looked past his copilot out the right side cockpit window at a Japanese fighter on fire. The top turret gunner had scored hits on the enemy plane, which was one of a flight of four. A few moments later a second enemy fighter was seen to crash and burn. The gunner had scored again. The two remaining Japanese pilots had had enough of the engagement and backed off. In the excitement of his success the gunner kept firing, trying to add to his victories. Soon one of his guns jammed and the motors of his turret burned out from excessive use. Smoke filled the back of the plane and the turret froze in its position. The fighters seemed aware of the problem aboard the B-25 and resumed their attack. No longer able to defend themselves, Greening kept the bomber as low as he could to prevent the enemy planes from getting under him.

Greening: "We cleared the treetops by only a matter of feet or possibly inches, and passed alongside some taller ones. Ahead were high-tension power lines. In the excitement of the moment I thought if I flew under the power lines the fighters might not notice them, follow us, and hit the lines. I succeeded in getting under the power lines, but the tactic didn't work. I flew so low over an agricultural plot that I can't understand how I missed hitting a farmer plowing with his ox. I wonder what he thought when our B-25 suddenly went thrashing past his head, with two Japanese fighters shooting at us in furious pursuit. As we flew over homes and buildings, some people came out to wave at us."

Several bullet strikes appeared from the trailing edge of the right wing to the propeller. Greening knew they must drop their bomb load very soon in order to gain speed and, hopefully, outrun the enemy fighters. He alerted the bombardier to be ready to release the incendiary bomb clusters. They were just crossing over a large open field when he noticed the camouflaged pipelines and storage tanks of a refinery, not the refinery he had intended to bomb, but this would do just as well. Climbing to 700 feet, the bombardier did his work. Their incendiaries had apparently struck gasoline tanks, causing a massive explosion, forcing the B-25 into an extreme nose-down attitude. The pilot and copilot hauled back on the twin control columns to keep the bomber out of the trees. The suddenly lighter airplane immediately gained airspeed to 300 mph, enough to easily outrun the attacking fighters. The bombing seemed a success to Ross Greening as he looked back at a 1,000-foot black smoke cloud rising from the refinery site. Once free of the fighters, he reduced speed to 275 mph to conserve their precious fuel for the 1,400-mile leg to China. He could not hold that airspeed, however, as each time he achieved it the enemy fighters caught up and opened fire again. But as soon as they crossed the coast and head-ed out to sea, the fighters broke away and didn't return.

For about thirty minutes, the right engine backfired and ran roughly, worrying the Greening crew, who could not know the extent of damage sus-tained during the fighter attacks. To their great relief, the engine finally began running more smoothly as they started out across the East China Sea in deteriorating weather.

When they were about four hours from their destination, the airfield at Chuchow where they would refuel before continuing on to Chungking, it was obvious that they would not be able to make radio contact with the field. In the dark, heavy weather, they were unable to get a celestial or radio navigation fix, their fuel was rapidly running out, and they were exhausted from flying all day. The navigator had to rely on dead reckoning alone. The radio operator tried to signal other aircraft and scanned the dial to try picking up a broadcast. All he found was cello music which they lis-tened to for awhile.

Greening prepared the crew to bail out as the fuel state dropped to near-ly empty tanks. They divided the emergency rations and drinking water, the first aid kits, pistols and ammunition. He told them to bail out as close together as possible so as to meet up on the ground. Then they nearly crashed into a hillside in the rain and murk. They succeeded in climbing to 10,000 feet for the bail out. He turned on the auto-pilot and set course to try and avoid Japanese territory. He had the airplane nearly stalling at 125 mph to reduce the wind blast as they dropped from the escape hatch. Both fuel gauges read zero. Greening dropped through the open hatch after his four crewmen.

One of the last things Lt Col Doolittle told his crews in the final briefing before the raid take-offs, when asked by one of the pilots what to do if their plane was badly damaged and had to be abandoned, Doolittle said: "Each pilot must decide for himself what he will do and what he'll tell his crew to do if that happens. I know what I'm going to do. I don't intend to be taken prisoner. I'm 45 years old and have lived a full life. If my plane is crippled beyond any possibility of fighting or escape, I'm going to have my crew bail out and then I'm going to dive my B-25 into the best military target I can find. You fellows are all younger and have a long life ahead of you. I don't expect any of the rest of you to do what I intend to do." He told them to get rid of all film, identification, letters, diaries, and anything else that would link them with the Hornet, their units in the States, or the places where they had trained. The Navy would mail anything they left behind to their homes. He admonished them that, under no circumstances were they to bomb the emperor's palace. Finally, he offered them all one last opportunity to drop out. No one did. He then promised them a party they would never forget when they got to Chungking.

Up on the flight deck before the takeoffs for the raid, there were a number of last minute problems with the B-25s. Some gun turrets were not functioning properly, spark plugs were fouled, and leaks developed in gas and hydraulic lines.

Just before noon Tokyo time, Doolittle's bomber was ten miles north of the city at very low altitude when he spotted a flight of nine Japanese fighters. The fighters didn't attack the American plane, but enemy ground batteries began firing and flak struck the bomber, doing little apparent damage. He soon sighted the factory buildings of his target area, climbed the B-25 to 1,200 feet and called for the bomb bay doors to be opened. At 12:30 the bombardier toggled out the four incendiary bombs and Doolittle immediately brought the plane back down to rooftop level.

Turning west over the China Sea, the bomber ran into a powerful headwind and the navigator now estimated they would run out of fuel about 135 miles from the Chinese coast. Then their luck changed. The headwind turned into a tailwind.

Like Greening, Doolittle tried in vain to contact Chuchow airfield by radio. Without such contact he knew their chances of safely reaching the field were gone. He realised that their only real option was to continue on a dead-reckoning course towards Chuchow, abandon the bomber in midair, and trust that they would come down in Chinese-controlled territory.

They all bailed out within seconds. As he descended, Doolittle was concerned about his ankles, both of which he had broken in previous parachute jumps, but when he hit there was little shock, as he landed in a rice paddy, one well-fertilized with excrement. The none-too-fragrant pilot struggled to the door of a nearby farmhouse where he knocked while shouting the phrase "I am an American" in Chinese. The only response was the clear sliding sound of a door bolt into place. He went on walking until he happened upon the local morgue, where he spent the rest of the night shivering with cold. The next morning he made his way to a local military headquarters where the Chinese officer in charge motioned for the stinking man to hand over his pistol, which Doolittle declined to do, declaring himself to be an American who had parachuted into a nearby rice paddy during the night. The officer doubted him and Doolittle said he would gladly take the Chinese major to the spot and show him the parachute.

Surrounded by an armed escort, Doolittle was taken to the rice paddy where he had landed. The parachute was gone. When questioned by the Chinese major, the farmer, his wife, and their children at the farmhouse where Doolittle had gone for help, all denied knowledge of him, claiming they had heard no plane and seen no parachute. The major turned to Doolittle: "They say you lie!"

As one of the soldiers was about to relieve Doolittle of his sidearm, another came out of the farmhouse with the missing parachute. The Chinese major changed his tune and was all smiles and cordiality, welcoming the American flyer to China. Back at the officer's headquarters, Doolittle was offered a bath while his uniform was dried. It still smelled, however. The remainder of Doolittle's crew arrived, all of them uninjured except for the navigator, who had sprained an ankle when he landed.

Doolittle was then taken to see the wreck of his plane. "This was my first combat mission. I had planned it from the beginning and led it. I was sure it was my last. As far as I was concerned, it was a failure, and I felt that there could be no future for me in uniform now. My main concern was for my men. What had happened to my crew probably had happened to the others. If so, they had to be scattered all over a considerable area of China. How many had survived? Had any been taken prisoner by the Japanese? Did any have to ditch in the China Sea? As I sat there, Paul Leonard [Doolittle's engineer-gunner] took my picture and then, seeing how badly I felt, tried to cheer me up. He asked, 'What do you think will happen when you go home, Colonel?' I answered, 'Well, I guess they'll court-martial me and send me to prison at Fort Leavenworth.' Paul said, 'No, sir. I'll tell you what will happen. They're going to make you a general.' I smiled weakly and he tried again. 'And they're going to give you the Congressional Medal of Honor.' I smiled again and he made a final effort. 'Colonel, I know they're going to give you another airplane and when they do, I'd like to fly with you as your crew chief.' While I deeply appreciated Paul's supportive remarks, I was sure that when the outcome of this mission was known back home, either I would be court-martialed or the military powers that be would see to it that I would sit out the war flying a desk. I had never felt lower in my life."

Doolittle sent a wire to Hap Arnold in Washington: TOKYO SUCCESSFULLY BOMBED. DUE BAD WEATHER ON CHINA COAST BELIEVE ALL AIRPLANES WRECKED. FIVE CREWS FOUND SAFE IN CHINA SO FAR.

In fact, of all the raider crewmen on the mission, one had been killed bailing out, two had drowned after ditching at sea, four were seriously injured and being cared for in a Chinese hospital by Doctor Thomas White, Doolittle's flight surgeon, who had flown the raid as a member of the fifteenth B-25 to take off from Hornet. One crew had landed in Soviet territory and were interned along with their aeroplane, and eight air crew were prisoners of the Japanese. All the of the aircraft were lost and none of the motion picture cameras brought on the raid survived it. Only a few snapshots taken by Lieutenant Clayton Campbell, navigator of the thirteenth bomber from the carrier, remain of the mission itself.

Despite Doolittle's own evaluation of the mission, he and the other survivors later learned that it had had an important psychological effect on the Japanese people, who had been shocked by the attack. The Japanese leadership had been frightened and embarrassed by the appearance of the enemy in their airspace. National morale was badly rattled as an awareness of the country's vulnerability to attack spread through the population. American morale, on the other hand, rose considerably, in the aftermath of the U.S. losses at Pearl Harbor and elsewhere in the Pacific since the previous December. As for actual damage caused by the U.S. bombs and incendiaries, the raid was a pinprick producing only token destruction, especially in comparison with the devastation wrought later in the war by American B-29 fire raids all over Japan and the atomic bombs dropped on Hiroshima and Nagasaki. But President Roosevelt was particularly pleased by the Doolittle attack.

28 April. Chuchow. At the Chinese air base, Doolittle found that one of his flight engineer's predictions had been correct. He was notified that Hap Arnold had promoted him from lieutenant colonel to brigadier general (skipping the rank of colonel). In typically Doolittle style, the new general immediately set out to achieve promotions for every man who had flown the raid. On his eventual return to the States, General Doolittle was ushered into the White House where the president presented him with the Medal of Honor, confirming Paul Leonard's second prediction. Shortly after that he was indeed given the use of another B-25 bomber, fulfilling the last Leonard prediction, and Doolittle was happy to be able to offer the job of crew chief for the new plane to Leonard.

Following the raid, the Japanese propagandists ridiculed it, referring to it as the "Do-nothing Raid" and bragged about having shot down several of the enemy bombers (though none of the planes had actually been brought down by the Japanese.) In their embarrassment and fury over the American attack on their homeland, the Japanese military conducted a savage campaign of reprisals against Chinese soldiers and civilians, killing a quarter of a million of those even vaguely suspected of having aided the Americans.

Of the eighty airmen who took part in the raid, twenty-eight remained in the China-Burma-India Theater of Operations, flying further missions over the following year. Five of them were killed in action. Nineteen were reassigned to fly missions from North Africa after their return to the U.S. Four of them were killed in action and four became prisoners of war in Germany. Nine flew missions in the European Theater of Operations, with one killed in action. Twelve of the surviving aircrew were killed in plane crashes within fifteen months of the Doolittle raid. Two of the men were separated from the Army Air Force due to the severity of their injuries.

In addition to the powerful psychological impact of the Doolittle raid, it produced a strategic result, causing the Japanese to shift some Imperial Japanese Navy warships, including its main aircraft carrier task force, back to Japan, reducing the pressure the IJN had been putting on the Royal Navy and Royal Air Force.

"It was hoped that the damage done would be both material and psychological. Material damage was to be the destruction of specific targets with ensuing confusion and the retardation of production. The psychological results, it was hoped, would be the recalling of combat equipment from other theaters for home defense, thus effecting relief in those theaters, the development of a fear complex in Japan, improved relationships with our Allies, and a favorable reaction on the American people."
—General James H. Doolittle, 9 July 1942

FIGHTING LADY

From the moment in 1908 when American nickelodeon patrons first viewed "moving" images of Wilbur Wright demonstrating the flying machine that he and his brother Orville had built, the movie-going public has been hooked on aviation films. By 1910, some of aviation history's most important personalities were learning to fly from the pioneers of powered flight, the Wright brothers in the eastern United States, Glenn Curtiss on the west coast at San Diego, and others. Former U.S. President Theodore Roosevelt had just experienced his first aeroplane ride, and in Europe film fans were thronging to see documentaries about the latest aviation achievements.

In the early years of the movies the notion of flying from the decks of navy ships and the concept of the aircraft carrier were beginning their take-off run.

Flying films really took off after World War One, thanks in large part to the involvement in the fledgling motion picture industry of the former wartime aviators William Wellman and John Monk Saunders, Howard Hawks and Dick Grace, all of whom had flown in the war and landed in what was becoming Hollywood. And with their involvement, as historian Alistair Cooke wrote, "the real flavor of what was to a whole generation of Americans the most overwhelming experience of their lives" came to the cinema.

Among the first and most impressive of the early aviation war films was *Flying with the Marines*, released in June of 1918. The *New York Times* movie reviewer wrote: ". . . *Flying with the Marines* is thrilling, and that's all there is to it. The film begins with views of places and activities about the camp and then shows squadrons of airplanes rising in military formation, maneuvering in battle array and acting altogether like birds at home on the wing. Pictures of stunt flying follow, with loops, spins, dives and many eccentric, yet graceful movements pictured clearly. There are a number of views of airplanes taken from a camera itself in flight, which shows unusual close-ups of the machines above the earth. Never before, perhaps, have the camera and the airplane been brought together with such thrilling results . . ." Of another 1918 flying film, *Washington's Sky Patrol*, the *New York Times* reviewer wrote: "The intermittent applause, quick exclamation and nervous laughter . . . in the house . . . were evidence of the sensations of the spectators. They held to the arms of their chairs and dizzily watched as the (Washington) Monument revolves beneath them and the Capitol spins around like a top."

In the century-long history of naval aviation a considerable number of feature-length motion pictures have been made about navy and marine flying in war and peacetime. Many have been well-researched and imaginatively created, resulting in a relatively rewarding experience for moviegoers. Some have been less than that.

Many American and British film stars have appeared in or were involved in making movies about or including aspects of naval aviation. Many of them actually served in the Second World War as naval aviators, air crewmen, aircraft mechanics, or in other naval or marine corps aviation capacities, including Scott Brady, Fred Clark, Jeff Cory, John Ford, Bill Hayes, George Roy Hill, Rock Hudson, Brian Keith, Jock Mahoney, Ed McMahon, Kenneth More, Wayne Morris, Paul Newman, Tyrone Power, and Robert Taylor.

Here are examples of some of the notable motion pictures about naval aviation: *Devil Dogs of the Air* Filmed at United States Naval Air Station North Island in San Diego Bay, this peacetime movie about Marine Corps flying in the mid-1930s was made as a follow-on to the successful Warner Brother picture *Here Comes The Navy*, (1934) which also featured the combination of James Cagney and Pat O'Brien. Written by a high-achieving WWI flier, John Monk Saunders (*The Dawn Patrol*), there is nothing new about the story. The older and more senior Lt Bill Brannigan (O'Brien), a Marine aviator in San Diego, persuades his Brooklyn buddy Tommy O'Toole (Cagney) to come out to the west coast and enlist. Cocky and brash, O'Toole arrives and instantly earns the wrath of the entire base by buzzing the parade ground during an official ceremony, crashing his plane, which bore a large logo WORLD'S GREATEST AVIATOR, and trying to move in on Betty, Brannigan's girl (Margaret Lindsay). The rest of the story is Brannigan's effort to tame the arrogant wiseguy O'Toole and turn him into an officer, if not a gentleman.

Easily the best aspect of the film are the flying sequences and especially the final third in which Vought 02U scout planes and Boeing F4B pursuit planes take part in a dramatic war game exercise, a simulated invasion with battleships, and the air fleet in tactical formations and precision aerobatics typical of the period. Of the film, critic Leonard Maltin wrote: ". . . a tiresome potboiler with Marine Air Corps rivalry between Cagney and O'Brien. Their personalities and good stunt-flying are the only saving grace."

Of movies on a much higher plane, the 1954 film *The Bridges at Toko-Ri* was based on a novel by James Michener. U.S. Navy aviator Harry Brubaker (William Holden) had flown as a fighter pilot in the Second World War and begun his post-war career as an attorney when, as a naval reservist he was recalled to active duty for the Korean War in 1950.

Brubaker flies Grumman F9F-2 Panther jets from a carrier in the Sea of Japan and is returning from a mission when he has to ditch his battle-damaged plane in the icy water. Unless he is immediately rescued he will freeze to death. Help arrives as helicopter pilot Chief Petty Officer Mike Forney (Mickey Rooney) and AD2 Nestor Gamidge (Earl Holliman) rescue the pilot.

The carrier task force commander, Rear Admiral George Tarrant (Frederic March) had lost his son in the WW2 Battle of Midway and sees in Brubaker the qualities he had most admired in his boy. He likes Brubaker and respects the fact that the pilot is tired of war, resents having been recalled to this one and wants only to return to his family and career. He also appreciates Brubaker's acceptance of the need to fight again.

The basis of the film is the mission of the naval aviators to destroy a group of important bridges on a vital supply route used by the communist forces. But before the carrier air group begins its attacks on the bridges, Brubaker learns that his wife Nancy (Grace Kelly) and their children have arrived in Tokyo on an unexpected visit. While with them during a three-day leave, Nestor comes to their hotel and pleads with Brubaker to get Forney out of the guardhouse where he is being held after a brawl with another sailor. Nancy is frightened by the signs of combat fatigue her husband is showing and thinks he may be about to crack under the strain. She expresses her concern to Admiral Tarrant who offers his support in the situation while recalling how his own daughter-in-law nearly went insane following the loss of his son.

The pilots are briefed for the initial strike on the bridges and told of the difficult, low-level approach they must make and the intensity of the flak in the area. Brubaker foresees his death in the raid, but determines to fly the mission.

The air group is to send two waves of planes in the attack, with the first wave led by the carrier air group commander, Wayne Lee (Charles McGraw), whose pilots do not complete the task. Lee orders in the second wave, commanded by Brubaker, to come in and destroy the last remaining bridge, after which Lee orders them to attack a secondary target, an ammunition dump. Completing his run on the target, Brubaker's plane is hit by flak causing a fuel leak. Lee tries to escort Brubaker back to the carrier but the loss of fuel means that Brubaker will not make it back to the ship. He is forced to belly-land in a flat area and very soon his reliable friends, Forney and Gamidge, show up in their rescue helicopter to save him once again. But North Korean ground troops appear and machine-gun the helicopter. Nestor is killed and the helicopter is disabled. Brubaker and Forney scramble into a small ditch to defend themselves with a carbine and pistols. They are quickly overwhelmed by the enemy soldiers and both are killed.

The Bridges at Toko-Ri is easily among the best of naval aviation films. Author James Michener had served as a war correspondent aboard the aircraft carriers *Essex* and *Valley Forge* during the Korean War in the winter of 1951-52 and had based much of his novel on actual incidents in missions to destroy bridge targets in North Korea, and the rescues of two downed navy pilots. Michener believed that the men had been killed, but later learned that they had survived and been taken prisoner by the North Koreans.

Dive Bomber is an important film historically in that it is a pre-Second World War Technicolor record of some interesting historic aircraft like the Douglas TBD Devastator torpedo bomber and the Vought SB2U Vindicator dive bomber, as well as featuring colour footage of the famous aircraft carrier USS *Enterprise* (CV-6). Colour movies were still somewhat of a novelty in 1941 when *Dive Bomber* came out, and the picture was nominated for an Academy Award for Best Color Cinematography in 1942.

A U. S. Navy aircraft carrier is operating off Hawaii before the Second World War as a navy dive bomber squadron arrives over Honolulu. One of the pilots blacks out during a high speed dive and crashes. The pilot, Lt Swede Larson (Louis Jean Heydt) is in critical condition and may not survive. Navy doctor Lt Doug Lee (Errol Flynn) talks the senior surgeon into operating on Larson, but the pilot dies during the procedure. Lt Cdr Joe Blake (Fred MacMurray) blames the surgeon and Lee elects to become a flight surgeon. Lee undergoes training at NAS North Island in San Diego and one of his instructors is Blake. Rivals Blake and Lee are after love interest Linda Fisher (Alexis Smith).

After his training course, Dr Lee is made assistant to Dr Lance Rogers (Ralph Bellamy) on his project to prevent altitude sickness in dive bomber pilots. Lee flies on experimental flights with pilot Blake to observe Blake blacking out in dives. Enter Lt Tim Griffin (Regis Toomey), a naval aviator who is suffering from chronic fatigue. On a flight Griffin's condition returns and he is killed attempting an emergency landing.

Blake volunteers to be a "guinea pig" pilot in aero-medical experiments with high-altitude flying. On the first flight the cabin pressurization fails, the aircraft ices up and Blake becomes unconscious, requiring Dr Lee, a trained pilot as well, to take over the controls.

Lee and Blake jointly develop a special pressure suit and then Blake learns that he will fail his next physical exam. Blake makes an unauthorized flight to test the new pressure suit on himself. The oxygen regulator fails and he blacks out, crashes and is killed. Luckily though, his notes of the flight are retrieved from the wreckage and mass production of the pressure suit can begin. The film ends with Drs Rogers and Lee being honoured for their pioneering aero-medical science achievement.

Dive Bomber was released only a few months before the Japanese attack on Pearl Harbor and was generally well received by both the moviegoing public and the critics.

"Save for some fine, authentic Navy footage of planes in combat," wrote a *NY Times* reviewer, "*Flat Top* holds nothing new or stimulating in the way of entertainment. If this Monogram offering, featuring Sterling Hayden and Richard Carlson, becomes increasingly familiar with each reel, indeed it should. For Steve Fisher's scenario, full of hollow-sounding dialogue and clichés, focuses on a battered standby—the upper-echelon feud and its effect on a standard assortment of rookie pilots. And it adds up to a light variation of our worn old friend, 'The Dawn Patrol.'

"Dull though most of the film may be below deck (inside the studio), Monogram has had the gumption to splice to a generous compilation of official Navy photography. These awesome shots of our Pacific fleet in action include some rousing battles by our dogfighters and the Japanese Zeros and a carefully technical coverage of the galvanized carriers in action. But they hardly lend credibility to the plodding histrionics at hand.

"Nevertheless, since the entire film has been shot in an off-beat color process, the over-all effect at least is one of picturesque respectability. And while Bill Phipps, John Bromfield, Keith Larsen and William Schallert lend only fair assistance in supporting roles, Mr Hayden and Mr Carlson, as the two opposed protagonists, perform with the sensible, hard-bitten air of job-doers rather than miracle workers. Director Lesley Selander, clearly hog-tied by the story and dialogue, obviously was more interested in what the Navy, the real one, had to offer. The paying customer can expect the same reaction."

Flight of the Intruder is based on a novel by a former USN A-6 Intruder pilot, Stephen Coonts. The picture follows the experiences of Intruder pilot Lieutenant Jake Grafton and his bombardier / navigator, Lt Morgan McPhearson on their raids over North Vietnam in the 1960s war. They are operating from the carrier USS *Independence* (CV-62) and the picture was mostly made aboard the *Independence* in 1989. In the filming, the electrical equipment of the Paramount crew apparently caused a number of small electrical fires in the ship. And, a future United States Senator, Fred Thompson, played the part of a captain in

the Navy Judge Advocate General Corps. Aircraft employed in the filming include the A-6 Intruder, USAF A-1 Skyraiders, an HH-3 Jolly
Green Giant rescue helicopter, the A-7 Corsair, the C-2 Greyhound,
the F-4 Phantom II, and a North Vietnamese MiG-17.

Movie critics were generally harsh in their opinions of the picture.
Roger Ebert referred to it as "a mess. Some scenes say one thing, some
say another, while the movie develops an absurd and unbelievable
ending and a final shot so cloying you want to shout rude suggestions
at the screen."

The role of Marine Major Dan Kirby, played by John Wayne in the
film *Flying Leathernecks*, was based largely on an actual WW2 Marine
fighter ace, Major John L. Smith, who was awarded the Medal of Honor
for his performance on missions over Guadalcanal in 1942. The film,
made in 1951 by director Nicholas Ray, casts Wayne as the new commander of Marine Fighter Squadron VMF-247 on Guadalcanal. The
other pilots of 247 had expected command of the squadron to go to
Captain Carl Griffin (Robert Ryan), and soon chafed under the iron
rule and discipline of Kirby who demands a maximum effort from
them, one of them being his own brother-in-law, Vern Blithe (Don
Taylor).

The tough Kirby genuinely hates the hard decisions he is forced to
make and having to send his men to their deaths, but must put the success of their missions ahead of their potential losses. Tension between
Kirby and Griffon runs high throughout the film.

Kirby advocates low-level ground attack tactics not approved by the
higher-ups. The tactics are eventually are proven to be correct. Kirby
is shot down and injured. He must leave command of the squadron and
must appoint his own successor. He appoints Griffin despite their differences and they part amicably.

The aircraft used in the movie are the Grumman F4F Wildcat and
the Grumman F6F Hellcat.

The story goes that director Ray selected Robert Ryan for the role
of Griffin, opposite John Wayne, because Ryan had been a very good
boxer in college and was the only actor Ray knew of who could "kick
Wayne's ass."

During the Second World War writers Charles Nordhoff and James
Norman Hall produced a book called *The High Barbaree* which was
made into *High Barbaree*, a motion picture released in 1947. The plot
has Alec Brooke (Van Johnson) and Nancy Frazer (June Allyson) who
were friends as children but separated when June's family moved
away. They meet again as adults, fall in love, but are again separated,
this time by the war. Alec is a Navy aviator flying a PBY-5A Catalina
flying boat on patrols in the South Pacific when he is shot down. He

and his co-pilot are adrift in the disabled flying boat without any means of communication and are listed as missing in action—presumed dead.

Now, through flash-backs, the moviegoer learns about Alec's childhood with June and how his uncle, a Navy captain, had told him about an uncharted, mysterious, enchanted island called High Barbaree, which by the injured co-pilot's reckoning is practically right beneath their hull. Then the co-pilot dies, leaving Van to fend on his own, no food, no water, no hope. The poor guy is half-dead when he and the Catalina are finally found and his miseries are forgotten. The only problem is, there is no sign of the enchanted island.

For its time (1976) *Midway* was a long (132 minutes), big budget, all-star cast, blockbuster motion picture. It simply tells the epic story of the WW2 Battle of Midway, history's first major naval air battle. It marked the first major defeat the Imperial Japanese Navy, which outnumbered the U.S. Navy four to one, had suffered in the war. Told from both the Japanese and American viewpoints, it follows the planning of the operation by both sides and carries on through the massive air battle.

The picture begins with Col. Jimmy Doolittle's famous raid on Tokyo flown by sixteen B-25 bombers from the flight deck of the aircraft carrier USS *Hornet* (CV-8). The carrier on-board scenes were filmed aboard the *Essex*-class USS *Lexington* (CV-16) in the Gulf of Mexico. The Midway Island sequences were filmed at the U.S. Naval Air Station, Point Mugu, California, which happens to have sand dunes similar to those on Midway. In the movie, the *Lexington* was used as both the American and Japanese aircraft carriers.

The plot thickens as, unknown to the Japanese, American signals intelligence personnel crack the enemy naval codes and learn of the planned Japanese naval ambush to take place near Midway. This enables Admiral Chester Nimitz (Henry Fonda) to send his only remaining carriers to the island in order to trap the Japanese task force with his own ambush. When the Americans prevail in the great battle, Nimitz is left with the question, "were we better than the Japanese or just luckier?"

Many historical inaccuracies detract from the authenticity of *Midway*. As Robert Niemi wrote in *History in the Media: Film and Television*: "*Midway*'s clichéd dialogue and an overuse of stock footage lead the film to have a shopworn quality that signalled the end of the heroic era of American-made World War II epics . . . a final anachronistic attempt to recapture World War II glories in a radically altered geopolitical era, when the old good-versus-evil dichotomies no longer made sense."

It's not easy to be objective about the 2001 movie *Pearl Harbor*, directed by Michael Bay with a $140 million budget and a box office gross of nearly $450 million. It's another very long (183 minutes), all-star epic that featured Ben Affleck, Josh Hartnett, Alec Baldwin, Jon Voight, Kate Beckinsale, Cuba Gooding, Jr., Dan Aykroyd, and more. The movie critics were mostly lukewarm to negative about the film. Roger Ebert: "The film has been directed without grace, vision, originality, and although you may walk out quoting lines of dialog, it will not be because you admire them. There is no sense of history, strategy or context; according to this movie, Japan attacked Pearl Harbor because America cut off its oil supply, and they were down to an 18-month reserve. Would going to war restore the fuel sources? Did they perhaps also have imperialist designs? Movie doesn't say."

Rolling Stone: "Affleck, Hartnett and Beckinsale—a British accent without a single worthy line to wrap her credible American accent around—are attractive actors, but they can't animate this moldy romantic triangle."

Entertainment Weekly: "Bay's staging [of the Pearl Harbor attack] is spectacular but also honorable in its scary, hurtling exactitude . . . There are startling point-of-view shots of torpedoes dropping into the water and speeding toward their targets, and though Bay visualizes it all with a minimum of graphic carnage, he invites us to register the terror of the men standing helplessly on deck, the horrifying split-second deliverance as bodies go flying and explosions reduce entire battleships to liquid walls of collapsing metal."

New York Observer: "Here is the ironic twist in my acceptance of *Pearl Harbor*—the parts I liked most are the parts before and after the digital destruction of Pearl Harbor by the Japanese carrier planes and felt that *Pearl Harbor* is not so much about World War II as it is about movies about World War II. And what's wrong with that?"

Released in January 1942, the British production *Ships with Wings* found considerable favour with the popular press initially. Soon, however, its hype and lack of realism became apparent to much of the moviegoing public. The *New York Times* reviewer: "With all the goodwill in the world, one still cannot blink the fact that the British-made picture, *Ships with Wings*, is a large slice of mock heroics wrapped up in a technically inferior film. Especially is this disappointing, since producer Michael Balcon apparently had the cooperation of the British Navy in its making, the use of the late *Ark Royal* as a set and a story to tell of high adventure and deeds of courage in the Mediterranean fleet. Yet what he has produced is a fable which Americans will frankly recognize as 'corn' and a picture which tries such tricks with models as even a Hollywood 'quickie' producer would blush to own.

"In the routine 'stout fella' tradition, the story very clumsily tells of a flier with the Fleet Air Arm who is dismissed before the present war begins because of a fatal accident for which he is largely to blame. But later, when the war is raging and he is flying over the Mediterranean for a Greek line, he has a chance to redeem his honor by joining up with his old carrier and striking the knockout blow against the Nazis on a mythical isle.

"Except for a few undistinguished shots of battleships wallowing through the seas and a smattering of authentic glimpses of activity aboard an aircraft carrier, the entire action of this picture is played on obvious small-scale models and studio sets. Much, if not all, of the excitement of a Nazi attack upon the carrier, of a blazing flight deck and planes landing and taking off from it, is lost in the patent realization that the ship and planes are awkward miniatures. And the climactic scene, in which the hero pilots two planes (by locking his own with a Nazi's) into a dam, is preposterously artificial. They did things much better than this at the World's Fair.

"No more can be said for the performance. John Clements in the leading role and Leslie Banks, Basil Sydney and several other competent actors play extremely dubious naval men. And Jane Baxter and Ann Todd become involved in a romantic plot, to their embarrassment. Altogether, *Ships with Wings* suggests a banal adventure comic-strip. Even the name of its hero, Dick Stacey, is right in style."

Those responsible for the picture were to suffer one further indignity when Prime Minister Churchill expressed his displeasure that the film showed so many British casualties, which he thought bad for morale.

Task Force arrived in 1949, the year in which *Twelve O'Clock High*, one of the finest war films ever made was released. Next to the latter production, and following a long series of pictures made before, during, and after the Second World War, *Task Force* pales. Retiring U.S. Navy officer Jonathan Scott (Gary Cooper), who had graduated from the Naval Academy in 1917, reminisces about his twenty-seven-year campaign to promote naval aviation and the advantages of the aircraft carrier. As one would on such a career path, Scott manages to make powerful enemies in Washington. He falls for and marries the widow (Jane Wyatt) of a naval aviator who was killed in a take-off accident aboard the first American carrier, the USS *Langley* (CV-1). A part of the film is devoted to Scott fighting the Japanese from his carrier. The film is black-and-white with the last fifteen minutes colour, mainly stock footage. Cooper is ably supported in the picture by his mentor and superior, Pete Richard (Walter Brennan.)

The Eternal Sea (1955) has much to commend it, not least being the thoughtful and understated performances of Sterling Hayden as Admiral John Hoskins, Dean Jagger as Admiral Thomas Semple, Alexis Smith as Hoskins' wife, Sue, and John Maxwell as Admiral William "Bull" Halsey. Hoskins lost a leg in early war action, but carried on in command positions including commander of the aircraft carrier USS *Princeton*. He had a major role in the development of carriers for jet operations by the Korean War era. In addition to its other attractions, *The Eternal Sea* is gloriously scored with music by the excellent Elmer Bernstein who scored *The Magnificent Seven* among others.

The Fighting Lady was actually the USS *Yorktown* (CV-10), but wartime restrictions prohibited her being identified as such in 1944 when the picture was released. A kind of propaganda / documentary, it was directed by the great American photographer Edward Steichen who, at the age of 63, was asked by the U.S. Navy to run the Navy Photographic Unit in the Pacific immediately after the Japanese attack on Pearl Harbor. Captain Steichen and his staff photographed every aspect of Navy action in the Pacific theatre of operations during the Second World War. At the end of the war he edited the book *U.S. Navy War Photographs* which sold six million copies, a record for the time.

On 7 December 1941 Steichen was listening to the radio reports of the attack on Pearl. He thought, "I wish I could get into this one, but I'm too old." Of his time at sea on U.S. Navy carriers, he wrote: "Everything about an aircraft carrier is dramatic, but the most spectacular things are the takeoffs and landings of the planes. In all the takeoff pictures I had seen, the planes looked as though they were glued to the deck. They gave no impression of the terrific onrush as the planes started their run for the takeoff. Nor did they suggest the noise, which is tremendous. Each thundering plane as it takes off emphasizes the contrast between the dynamic intensity of the moment at hand and the dreamlike memories of other places, other times, another life . There was nothing I could do in the photographs to reproduce the sounds, but I was going to try to give a sense of the motion of the rushing plane. Instead of making a fast exposure to stop the motion and get a sharp picture of the plane taking off, I made a series of exposures around a tenth of a second. One shows a Hellcat fighter plane taking off, its wheels just off the deck. Even the pilot is blurred, while the skipper on the bridge, in the upper left-hand corner, looks on like a benign Zeus."

The Fighting Lady is life on board an American carrier on her way to war, and the first half of the film is devoted to the routine aspects of that experience. The balance is combat, from air strikes against Japanese bases in the Pacific, to a two-day raid at Truk in the Carolines, to the famous Marianas Turkey Shoot. Relatively short at just 61 minutes, *The Fighting Lady* is a splendid glimpse of a real aircraft carrier in action during a terrible, exhilarating time.

Among the more interesting and imaginative movies portraying carrier aviation is the sci-fi adventure *The Final Countdown*. Under the command of Captain Matt Yelland (Kirk Douglas), the nuclear-powered carrier USS *Nimitz* is preparing to depart Pearl Harbor in 1980 when a civilian observer, Warren Lasky (Martin Sheen), comes aboard. Lasky is an efficiency expert employed by Tideman Industries which had a part in designing the *Nimitz*.

At sea the carrier passes through a strange storm, after which Yelland, his executive officer, Lasky, and the rest of the crew gradually realize that the ship has gone through some sort of time warp and is now back in December 1941, on the day before the Japanese attack on Pearl. A reconnaissance aircraft from the carrier soon discovers the Japanese "attack" task force which is steaming eastward towards Hawaii. Uncertain as to what has happened, Captain Yelland launches a pair of F-14 Tomcat jets that spot a 1930s-era civilian yacht in the area. The yacht is being attacked by two Japanese Zero fighters that destroy it. The F-14 pilots down the Zeros and rescue helicopters from *Nimitz* arrive to pluck the one surviving Japanese pilot, and the yacht survivors, U.S. Senator Sam Chapman (Charles Durning) and Laurel (Katharine Ross), his assistant, from the water. The Carrier Air Group boss, Commander Richard Owens (James Farentino), an amateur historian who happens to be writing a book about the Pearl Harbor attack, recognises the Senator and knows that Chapman would have been Roosevelt's running mate in the 1944 election and eventually president.

With all possibilities exhausted, Yelland and the others are finally forced to accept that they have actually moved back through time, that the Japanese fleet is poised to attack Pearl Harbor and he, Yelland, must decide whether to use the powerful air wing and weaponry of the *Nimitz* to destroy the Japanese fleet before it can attack Pearl, and thus change the course of history—or just let history take its course as before.

The issue is debated and Captain Yelland, on the basis that the duty of his ship and men is to defend America, past, present, and future, and obey the orders of the then-Commander-in-Chief, decides to launch a massive air strike against the Japanese fleet.

Cdr Owens tells the Senator, Laurel, and the rescued Japanese pilot, that Pearl Harbor is about to come under Japanese attack. The enemy pilot grabs an automatic weapon, kills a guard and then holds Laurel hostage, threatening to kill her unless he is granted the use of a radio to warn the Japanese fleet. Marine guards kill the Japanese pilot. The Senator demands to use a radio to warn Pearl Harbor of the impending attack, but when he contacts Pearl, he is not believed. Meanwhile, Cdr Owens and Laurel are becoming interested in each other.

The Senator then demands to be flown to Pearl. Captain Yelland agrees and sends him and Laurel, accompanied by Cdr Owens, off by helicopter—but not to Pearl; to an uninhabited Hawaiian island instead. The angry Senator then tries hijacking the helicopter but ends up destroying it with him in it. Cdr Owens and Laurel are left stranded on the deserted island and Laurel discovers that Owens and the others are from the future.

The striking force is launched from the *Nimitz* to hit the attacking Japanese squadrons, but before they can engage, the carrier is again overtaken by the strange storm and is returned to the 1980s. Captain Yelland recalls the strike force, the planes return safely to the ship, and history is unchanged.

On the return of the *Nimitz* to Pearl Harbor, Warren Lasky is met on the dock by a limousine. Seated in the back are Mr and Mrs Tideman— a much older Cdr Owens and Laurel. "Mr Lasky, we have a lot to talk about."

Back now to the silent film era with *The Flying Fleet*, a romance from 1929 with Ramon Navarro and Ralph Graves as naval officers who are after the same girl, Anita Page. The graduating class of the U.S. Naval Academy includes a group of six friends who all want to be naval aviators. They go to sea with the fleet for a year and then to San Diego for flight training. Attrition has the old group down to four who move on to Pensacola. More attrition, and they are down to two, Tommy (Navarro) and Steve (Graves). Back then to San Diego where they are reunited with two of the old group, on the Navy's first carrier, the USS *Langley*.

Romance, intrigue, and a lot of silliness before Steve and three others are lost in a storm at sea on a flight to Hawaii. Aircraft from the *Langley* are ordered out on a search for the missing fliers. The search seems fruitless and is finally called off, but Tommy persuades the admiral to let him try just once more. He spots the survivors, loses his engine, sets his plane on fire as a signal to the carrier, and bails out. When they all get back to San Diego, Anita is waiting for him.

NY Times film critic: "The story is sometimes quite a bit too melodramatic, but [there were some] thrilling stunts and some splendid sequences devoted to an airplane carrier."

In April 1942 Lt Col Jimmy Doolittle led a flight of sixteen B-25 Mitchell bombers from the deck of the carrier USS *Hornet* (CV-8) in the first retaliatory strike at the Japanese home islands after the surprise attack by Japan on Pearl Harbor the previous December. The film *Thirty Seconds Over Tokyo*, was adapted from the 1943 book of the same title, by Captain Ted W. Lawson, one of the pilots who flew the raid. The picture was made during the war and released in 1944. It took the form of an eye-witness account, including the training of the crews, the preparation, the mission itself, the results and aftermath as Lawson, his crew, and the other Doolittle crews had experienced it.

In February 1942 Doolittle (Spencer Tracy) is asked to help plan a raid in retaliation for the Pearl Harbor attack. He agrees and goes to work on the problem. He asks to lead the mission and assembles his crews and trains them to take heavily-loaded B-25 bombers off in 500 feet or less from a simulated carrier deck.

Hours before the strike force is to take off, the *Hornet* is sighted by Japanese fishing boats and, with the timing of the mission now compromised, the bombers are forced to take off several hours earlier than planned and at or beyond the limit of their range. The attack succeeds, but all the bombers except one exhaust their fuel before reaching their Chinese airfields. The crews have to bail out or crash-land on or near the coast. Lawson's plane, the *Ruptured Duck*, ditches in the surf in the darkness and heavy rain. The crew survive but suffer considerable hardship as they make their way back to American lines, with the help of Chinese peasants. Lawson, who was seriously injured in the crash-landing, has to have a leg amputated while in China. At the end of the picture, he is reunited with his wife in Washington.

True, this is not a naval aviation movie in the strict sense, but it is carrier aviation.

Now considered by many critics a classic war film and the finest aviation film of the period, *Thirty Seconds Over Tokyo* was praised by the NY Times film critic Bosley Crowther: "our first sensational raid on Japan in April 1942 is told with magnificent integrity and dramatic eloquence."

As one who knew General Doolittle, I can attest that he was an extraordinarily high-achieving, extraordinarily modest man. Because the Doolittle Tokyo raid was assessed as doing little actual damage to the enemy, and because all sixteen of the bombers were lost in the effort, Doolittle felt in the aftermath of the mission that he and it had failed. But in high places others thought differently and Jimmy was awarded the Medal of Honor for his achievement.

"I feel the need . . . the need for speed." Director Tony Scott and producers Don Simpson and Jerry Bruckheimer went for all the marbles in their 1986 release *Top Gun*, a handsome, ultra-macho action vehicle for a still boyish Tom Cruise. The numbers worked pretty well too. Budgeted at only $15,000,000, the picture grossed a worldwide box office total of $353,816,701.

Wrapped around a lot of F-14 Tomcat flying in the 1980s when the U.S. Navy was still operating the aeroplane, the story has Lieutenant Pete 'Maverick' Mitchell (Cruise) and his RIO [radar intercept officer], Nick 'Goose' Bradshaw (Anthony Edwards) sent from their fleet carrier assignment to enroll in the Navy's Top Gun course at NAS Miramar near San Diego. Maverick is the son of Duke Mitchell, a Navy F-4 Phantom pilot who was killed in the Vietnam War in 1965 flying from the carrier USS *Oriskany* (CV-34). Maverick is just that, reckless, flaunts authority, does things his own way, not much of a team player. But he's a good guy and a true friend to his RIO, Goose.

Into the picture marches Charlotte 'Charlie' Blackwood (Kelly McGillis) who Maverick tries to put a move on in a bar off the base, only to find the next day that she is the instructor in the Top Gun course. The course continues through a lengthy series of combat simulations in which Maverick commits more than his share of violations, drawing the unwanted attentions of 'Jester' (Michael Ironside) and other instructors, and of the chief instructor, Cdr Mike 'Viper' Metcalf (Tom Skerritt).

The irrepressible Maverick keeps on doing things his way, in pursuit of the coveted number one pilot award in the class. In doing so he incurs the wrath of others in the class including Lt Tom 'Iceman' Kazansky (Val Kilmer) who thinks Mav is "dangerous." And while all this is going on Mav is also going after Charlie.

In the film, Viper is described as the finest fighter pilot in the world, and on one of the course hops Maverick engages him in simulated air combat. Mav's plane suffers a flameout of both engines and goes into a flat spin. He cannot recover control and he and Goose have to eject. Goose is killed and Maverick appears before a Navy board of inquiry which clears him of responsibility in the death, but Mav feels guilt and is not responsive when Charlie tries to console him. He seriously considers leaving the Navy and talks with Viper about it. Viper reveals to Mav that he had flown with Mav's father in VF-51 on the *Oriskany*, and shares the details of his father's death, which puts to rest some long-standing concerns of the pilot.

The Top Gun pilots graduate from the course and Maverick and Iceman are ordered to report to the USS *Enterprise* (CVN-65) at sea to provide air support for a stricken U.S. Navy warship that has drifted into hostile waters. Iceman is worried about Maverick's state of mind, and in the ensuing action, Maverick's aggression and confidence seem to have left him, but somehow he miraculously finds them again in time to join Iceman in downing four MiG fighters before returning triumphantly to the carrier. Later, Mav is offered the assignment of his choice. He chooses to be an instructor at Top Gun and returns to San Diego where he is reunited with Charlie.

It is rumoured that a sequel to *Top Gun* is in the works with Tom Cruise returning as Maverick in the role of a test pilot. It is believed that the aircraft appearing in the new film will be the Lockheed Martin F-35 Lightning II Joint Strike Fighter.

Yet another blockbuster effort, *Tora! Tora! Tora!* (Tiger! Tiger! Tiger!), a 1970 American-Japanese movie about the Japanese attack on Pearl Harbor, opens with the change-of-command ceremony on the Japanese battleship *Nagato*, the flagship of Commander-in-Chief of the Combined Fleet, Admiral Isoroku Yamamoto (So Yamamura) who is relieving Admiral Zengo Yoshida (Junya Usami). The American embargo of strategic materials against Japan dominates their conversation and they agree that war with the U.S. would be disastrous for Japan. But the militant Japanese government has entered an alliance with Germany and Italy and is beating the drums for a war. Threatened by the presence of the U.S. Pacific fleet in Pearl Harbor, the attack is ordered and Yamamoto plans a preemptive strike hoping to eliminate the enemy fleet in a single massive blow.

Much of the Japanese attack plan is built on an assault by torpedo planes on the U.S. battleships at anchor in the harbour. The U.S. Navy believes it is largely invulnerable to torpedo attack in the shallow depths of Pearl, but the Japanese have a new torpedo designed to beat that factor. In their favour, though, the Americans have cracked the Japanese code used for their most secret transmissions and U.S. intelligence personnel are monitoring all the enemy moves. Japanese Air Staff Officer Minoru Genda (Tatsuya Mihashi) is masterminding the air attack while Mitsuo Fuchida (Takahiro Tamura) will lead it. Lieutenant General Walter Short (Jason Robards) and Admiral Husband E. Kimmel (Martin Balsam) try somewhat ineffecually to shore up their local defences in Hawaii. Meanwhile, the Japanese envoys in Washington continue to search for peace through various initiatives with the U.S. Secretary of State and in Tokyo Army Gen Hideki Tojo (Asao Uchida) expresses his intense opposition to such efforts. A series of messages from Tokyo to the Japanese Embassy in Washington begins and it will end with a declaration of war on the United States. The Americans, however, are translating the intercepts faster than the Japanese envoys and know of the Japanese intent before they do. American intelligence people learn that the final message in the series is scheduled to reach the Japanese envoys at precisely 1 p.m. on 7 December, telling the envoys to destroy their code machines. The final message fails to reach the key American military commanders in Hawaii.

U.S. military intelligence errors, delays, inertia, miscommunication and the lack of communication continue through the morning. The Japanese envoys are slow in completing their code translations. The Japanese government intends to end diplomatic negotiations with the U.S. at 1 P.M. Washington time, thirty minutes before the start of the attack on Pearl. A final attempt at warning the Pearl Harbor command of the imminent attack fails when bad atmospherics and administrative bungling interfere. The telegram is not marked urgent and as such, is not received in Pearl until after the attack. As the Japanese squadrons round Barber's Point and approach Pearl, they are relieved at the complete lack of anti-aircraft fire ahead. Clearly, the facility has not been alerted. Unopposed, the air leader, Fuchida, radios the code 'Tora! Tora! Tora! commencing the surprise attack.'

American personnel at Pearl watch the enemy aircraft in disbelief as the Japanese pilots methodically destroy the aircraft on the ground, and the dive-bombers, horizontal bombers and torpedo bombers make run after run on their capital ship targets in the anchorage southeast of Ford Island. Two American fighter pilots at a remote airstrip manage to get airborne to go up against the enemy force.

The long raid continues and all of the U.S. Navy battleships are either sunk or badly damaged. Huge fires burn out of control around the harbour. There is chaos in Washington as word of the surprise attack slowly filters in.

Afraid that by remaining in the area and launching a third wave of attack aircraft against Pearl, he will endanger his six aircraft carriers, the Japanese fleet commander, Admiral Chuichi Nagumo (Eijiro Tono) decides against the extended attack. Admiral Yamamoto realises that his forces have not totally eliminated the American fleet and that the Americans will be enraged and furious at the Japanese action. "I fear all we have done is to awaken a sleeping giant and fill him with a terrible resolve."

The critics were mixed in their opinions of the film. Roger Ebert: ". . . one of the deadest, dullest blockbusters ever made." Vincent Canby: ". . . nothing less than a $25-million irrelevancy." Charles Champlin: ". . . the careful recreation of a historical event."

Wing and a Prayer is a curiously impressive 1944 black-and-white film about the pilots and crew of an American carrier on the defensive in the early days of the Pacific war. It is realistic and well made, if, like many of the war films of the time, a bit heavy on propaganda. It is true that, in the first weeks and months after the Pearl Harbor attack, a lot of Americans were wondering "Where is our navy? Why doesn't it fight?" With few ships remaining in the U.S. fleet, a clever secret plan is developed using one American carrier that then shows up in various locations to hopefully make the Japanese believe that several

American carriers are operating around the region. The Americans want to lure the Japanese fleet to a major confrontation near the island of Midway.

On our lone carrier, Commander Bingo Harper (Don Ameche) is hard as nails with the pilots of his air wing. A strict, by-the-book disciplinarian, Harper brooks no open-field running from his charges. When Lt Cdr Edward Moulton (Dana Andrews) and his squadron arrive for duty aboard the carrier, it is apparent to Harper that one of Moulton's pilots, Ensign Hallam Scott (William Eythe) has a rather cavalier attitude and Harper warns Moulton about him. Scott was a movie star before the war and still receives great stacks of fan mail from females in the States. Another of Moulton's pilots, Ensign Breinard (Harry Morgan) is grounded by Harper when the pilot endangers the ship by dropping a bomb too close to it during a training exercise.

In the course of the planned deception, the carrier is ordered deep into Japanese territory in the Solomon Islands chain, to "be seen" there by the enemy. The pilots and crew are under strict orders not to fight if they encounter any Japanese aircraft or warships. On a patrol Moulton's torpedo bombers do sight some enemy planes but are required to follow orders and retreat. Two of their number are lost in the encounter, and, uninformed about the grand plan of deception, Moulton's pilots are angry and disgusted with the order not to fight back. Similar incidents occur and the tension heightens as morale drops. But the plan is working and the Japanese believe that their sightings of the carrier have actually been many different U.S. carriers.

Deceived into the belief that U.S. carriers are scattered in various locations across the western Pacific, the Japanese fleet is caught and surprised near Midway by the aircraft of the Americans. In the great air and sea battle that ensues, many aircraft are lost, but the major victory goes to the U.S. Navy.

Returning to the carrier after the battle, Ensign Scott, very low on fuel, is having trouble locating the ship in the thick cloud cover. Aware of the situation, Lt Cdr Moulton pleads with Harper to shine searchlights up through the murk to guide Scott to a safe landing. Harper refuses to chance the possibility of the carrier being spotted by enemy submarines that may be in the area. Soon, Scott's engine is heard sputtering and he crashes near the carrier. Harper and Moulton quarrel but they then learn that Scott has been rescued and is safe. Harper tells the crews that he cares about them, but it is also part of his job to be willing to sacrifice some of them for the sake of the mission.

The origin of the title *Wing and a Prayer* is the 1943 song *Coming*

In *On a Wing and a Prayer*, by Harold Adamson and Jimmy McHugh.

The 1957 motion picture *The Wings of Eagles* is the story of Frank 'Spig' Wead, as well as the story of U.S. naval aviation from its beginnings through the Second World War. The movie director John Ford was a friend of Wead and made the picture in tribute to him. Wead was an early navy aviator who devoted much of his career trying to prove the value and importance of naval aviation. On the evening of his promotion to squadron commander he tumbles down the stairs in his home, suffers a broken neck and is paralyzed. His wife Min (Maureen O'Hara) consoles him but he rejects her and his children. Only his navy friends can influence and help him to get through his depression, learn to walk again and begin a new career writing screenplays in Hollywood. After achieving considerable success writing for films, Wead is finally able to return to sea duty and develops the concept of the small escort or 'jeep' carrier to supplement the aircraft carrier force. Then he is felled by a heart attack and is returned home before the end of the war.

The pre-Second World War period is represented in *Wings of the Navy*, a 1939 effort from Warner Brothers, always an important maker of aviation-related motion pictures. Another heavy piece of propaganda in which submarine officer Jerry Harrington transfers to flight cadet training at NAS Pensacola, Florida. Love finds him in the form of his brother's girlfriend, Irene (Olivia de Havilland). Cass (George Brent), Jerry's brother, also a naval aviator, is badly hurt in a crash and has to leave the navy. Jerry's flying career takes off in San Diego where he pilots flying boats while Cass is now designing new planes for the navy. One of Cass's planes is an experiemental fighter that Jerry wants to test, even if he has to quit the navy to do it. The new fighter has already claimed the life of one test pilot. Irene is left having to choose between Cass and Jerry.

The Navy gave this picture a lot of support in the making and saw it as an important recruiting asset, as it has with a number of naval aviation films from Hollywood.

CORAL SEA AND MIDWAY

Since the Japanese attack on Pearl Harbor in December 1941, almost everything seemed to be going Japan's way. Her naval and military forces had piled up a string of successes that, like those of her German ally the year before in France, seemed virtually unstoppable. Through precise planning based on excellent intelligence, her army and navy had operated throughout southeast asia and the western Pacific practically unchallenged. In the vital second phase of the Japanese plan of conquest, the goal was to secure the defences along the new frontiers of the Japanese Empire.

An internal clash of wills had the Imperial Japanese Navy wanting to take Australia to end all Allied naval presence there, but the Army preferred a plan called Operation Mo, in which a more conservative approach to taking over the area was key. It meant a two-part action around the Coral Sea, with the occupation of the island of Tulagi and its harbour the initial move before grabbing Port Moresby, the last Allied stronghold on New Guinea.

Meanwhile, the American aircraft carriers USS *Hornet* (CV-8) and USS *Enterprise* (CV-6) had steamed to a position only 650 miles from Tokyo. There, under the leadership of Lt Col Jimmy Doolittle, sixteen Army Air Force B-25 bombers were launched on 18 April in the first retaliatory raid on the Japanese home islands since the Pearl Harbor attack. Heavily modified with additional long-range fuel capacity, the planes were dispatched at the order of Vice-Admiral William 'Bull' Halsey and would deliver their bombloads on the Japanese capital, on Yokosuka, and other cities before continuing on to China. The raid shocked the Japanese as much as their strike on Pearl had shocked Americans. They now knew that their islands, and their Emperor, were vulnerable to Allied attack and it persuaded their Pearl attack planner, Admiral Yamamoto, of the necessity for a new, decisive battle with the Americans.

Yamamoto would not be able to muster the full force of the Combined Fleet for such a battle. Some of it was then being used in support of the Japanese Army's activities in the South Pacific. Still, the admiral sent the force he was able to assemble into the Coral Sea to challenge the American enemy fleet which, according to Japanese intelligence indicated the probability of aircraft carriers in that fleet. The force he sent included the heavy aircraft carriers *Shokaku* and *Zuikaku* under the command of Rear-Admiral Hara Chuichi; the cruisers *Myoko* and *Haguro*, and six destroyers. Additionally, the light carrier *Shoho* and four heavy cruisers, all under the command of Rear-Admiral Goto Aritomo, were sent along for distant cover of the Tulagi force and were then to carry on to cover the invasion force at Port Moresby. That invasion force comprised twelve troop transport ships and their escorts. Command of the force lay with Vice-Admiral Shigeyoshi Inoue.

It would be the world's first battle between aircraft carriers; a contest in the Coral Sea, southwest of the Solomon Islands group and east of New Guinea. It was also the first major sea battle that would be fought by fleets out of sight of each other.

The Japanese needed to occupy the Allied air base at Port Moresby in southeastern New Guinea, and Tulagi in the Solomons, to give them air superiority over the Coral Sea and extend the territory they controlled all the way to Australia.

On the American side, Admiral Chester W. Nimitz at Pearl Harbor had to protect U.S. convoys headed for Australia, and Australia itself, should Port Moresby fall to the Japanese. But two of his carriers, *Hornet* and *Enterprise*, were up north after the Doolittle raid and had to be rushed south towards the area where the carriers *Yorktown* and *Lexington* were assembling their task forces. The *Yorktown* force was commanded by Rear-Admiral Frank Fletcher and the *Lexington* force by Rear-Admiral Aubrey Fitch. The British Royal Navy Rear-Admiral Sir John Crace was in command of three cruisers, the Australia, Chicago, and Hobart, which were to rendezvous near the New Hebrides on 1 May. As the senior of these commanders in terms of Pacific war experience, Fletcher had been given command authority in the situation once the Allied ships arrived at the meeting point. Owing to the intercepts of Japanese war codes deciphered by U.S. intelligence personnel, Fletcher knew of the Japanese plans for Tulagi and Port Moresby.

As April ended, the Japanese Tulagi assault force departed Rabaul, New Britain, and the next day the protective Japanese carrier force sailed from Truk. Frank Fletcher's warships gathered near the New Hebrides as scheduled on 1 May for refueling. The American action plan was changed there when Australian search planes sighted elements of the Japanese Tulagi invasion force, and Fletcher took the *Yorktown* force northward at speed. At this point, the Japanese were still unaware of an American carrier presence in the area.

By 3 May, the Japanese carrier force knew the American aircraft carriers were in the region. Japanese forces were achieving a successful invasion and occupation of Tulagi and the Japanese fleet carriers then proceeded into the Coral Sea to search for and destroy the Allied warships there. As 4 May dawned over Tulagi, the *Yorktown* force arrived in the area from which Fletcher planned to launch an air attack on the enemy force. At 7 a.m. he sent eighteen TBD Devastator torpedo bombers, twenty-eight SBD

Dauntless dive-bombers, and a fighter escort of six F4F Wildcats into the cloud cover. The American attack force was made up of three waves, the first hitting its targets starting at 08:20 and continuing until 1530 when the last of the attack aircraft left the area. By then they had sunk the destroyer *Kikuzuki*, two patrol boats, and a transport, and it was now abundantly clear to the Japanese that U.S. carriers were in the vicinity. On 5 May Admiral Takeo Takagi took his carriers, *Shokaku* and *Zuikaku*, around the Solomons and into the Coral Sea where he intended to engage the American carriers. Admiral Fletcher now brought the refueled *Yorktown and Lexington* towards New Guinea where he planned to intercept the Japanese Port Moresby task group.

Though within seventy miles of each other, there was no contact by their air groups during 6 May. Only a few minor incidents occurred which served to establish the presence of both forces to each other. U.S. reconnaissance aircraft spotted the warships of the Port Moresby group, including the light carrier *Shoho*. Early in the morning of the 7th, Fletcher dispatched Crace's cruisers away from their assigned positions around the U.S. carriers, north towards the Louisiades.

The two opposing carrier forces began exchanging air strikes on each other over the course of the next two days. On the 7th ninety-two American aircraft put thirteen bombs and seven torpedoes into the light carrier *Shoho*, sinking her. Fletcher received the message from the air group, "Scratch one flattop!" The Americans suffered the loss of the destroyer USS *Sims*, and heavy damage to the fleet oiler *Neosho*, which had to be sunk a few days later by a U.S. destroyer.

Now Fletcher determined to track down the Japanese Port Moresby task group and destroy it and turned his carriers towards the Louisiades. Takagi sent his aircraft out again in an effort to locate and attack the American carriers. But the weather turned against the Takagi's pilots, with visibility closing down. In the increasing darkness, the Japanese pilots happened upon a U.S. carrier. Desperately short of fuel, the pilots were powerless to attack the enemy ship. The carrier crewmen were surprised by the sudden appearance of the enemy aircraft and the carrier gunners accounted for only one. The Japanese planes were running out of fuel and only seven of the twenty-seven made it safely back to their carrier.

The next day, 8 May, was the first day in which aircraft carriers engaged each other in battle. Early on it was only reconnaissance planes of both sides scouting the seas for signs of their enemy's task force and their hunts were successful. Within an hour of launching from the *Lexington*, the search planes located their prey and shortly after 0900 Fletcher had sent off a full-scale attack force of eighty-two aircraft.

The odds quickly changed again as intercepted Japanese radio traffic informed the American admiral that *Lexington* had been located by the enemy. Sixty-nine planes of Takagi's strike force were closing in on the American force. But the U.S. aircraft reached the enemy carriers first. Thirty-nine American planes were in position to attack the *Zuikaku* and *Shokaku* by 1015, but were foiled by a bungled timing sequence when the dive bombers were delayed by the torpedo planes who were late to strike. The delay allowed *Zuikaku* to duck into the cover of a nearby dense rain squall, temporarily obscuring her. The slip-up also enabled *Shokaku* to improve her air defences. Then the Americans hit the enemy carriers in strength as aircraft from *Yorktown* struck *Shokaku* twice with bombs, heavily damaging her bow, halting her air operations and destroying her aero engine repair facilities. *Lexington*'s aircraft, on the other hand, did little appreciable damage to the enemy ships and lost three Wildcat fighters in the process. Forty-two of *Shokaku*'s planes had to land on *Zuikaku* as repair work continued on their carrier.

The intensity of the battle grew then as the American dive-bombers dropped on the crippled *Shokaku*. As they did so, the re-organized and strengthened attack force from the Japanese carriers directed much of their attention on *Lexington*. The U.S. carrier was especially vulnerable at this point, with all of her fighter protection otherwise engaged with the enemy. She did receive the last minute assistance of twenty-three Dauntless dive bombers which managed to down four Japanese torpedo bombers, but at the cost of four of their own number to escorting Zero fighters. In the engagement, *Lexington* received two torpedo strikes as well as two serious bomb hits, causing savage interior fires, major hull flooding, the destruction of her smokestack and some of her anti-aircraft batteries, and significant loss of manouevring capability. *Yorktown* faired much better, evading all eight torpedoes that came her way and taking only one bomb hit which caused some casualties but little damage to the ship. By the end of the action, both *Yorktown* and *Lexington* appeared to be operating relatively normally with damage control working, fires extinguished, and *Lexington*'s port list corrected.

At 1247, however, a massive explosion ripped through the deep inards of *Lexington*, followed shortly by further explosions. Very soon new fires threatened the carrier's survival. In spite of valiant efforts at control, the crew was losing the battle with the fires and, at 1707, Captain Frederick Sherman ordered all hands to abandon ship. Later in the evening, the destroyer USS *Phelps* was brought in to torpedo the carrier. *Lexington* slipped beneath the waves at 2000.

Now Fletcher in *Yorktown* anticipated more battle action from the Japanese Port Moresby assault group, but both *Shokaku* and *Zuikaku* had been badly damaged, disabled in the day's activity and forced to retire to

Japan for refitting. He received orders from Admiral Nimitz to bring *Yorktown* back to Pearl immediately for rapid repair and reassignment.

The result of the battle was tactical victory for the Japanese and strategic victory for the Allies. Coral Sea marked the first time in the war that Japanese expansion was turned back. Significantly for the Allies, the damage and aircraft depletion to the two Japanese carriers meant they would not be available to take part in the Battle of Midway in June, somewhat evening the odds for the two sides. American victory in the Battle of Midway, and Japan's loss of four of her six principal aircraft carriers in the engagement, ended her designs on Port Moresby. The loss of most of her carrier capability left her far more vulnerable in the South Pacific region and open to defeat in the Guadalcanal and New Guinea campaigns, substantially contributing to her ultimate defeat in the war.

Most historians would agree that the Battle of Midway was not only the turning point after which Allied forces in the Pacific assumed a wholly offensive posture in the war, and the Japanese were forced into an entirely defensive role, but also that it was easily the most important naval battle of the Pacific campaign. Military historian John Keegan referred to the Allied victory at Midway as: ". . . the most stunning and decisive blow in the history of naval warfare."

Basically, the Japanese hoped to lure the American aircraft carriers into a trap near Midway Atoll, which they planned to occupy to solidify their expansionist position in the area. Their aim in the Midway engagement was to finally eliminate the American carriers and the U.S. Navy strategic capability in the Pacific, opening the way to total conquest in the Pacific and leading ultimately to capitulation by the United States in that theatre of operations. The outcome would be rather different, however.

Having cracked the relevant Japanese military code, the U.S. Navy was fully aware of Japan's plan for the Midway engagement, including the date, exact location and certain aspects of the enemy force disposition. The Americans then planned an ambush of their own.

The key figure in Japan's war planning strategy, Admiral Isoroku Yamamoto, had been saying all along since before the Pearl Harbor attack, that it was absolutely essential to eliminate the American capital ship and carrier force, the main threat to Japan's overall Pacific campaign. The admiral believed that hitting Pearl again, roughly six months after the surprise attack of December 1941, would draw out the entire American fleet, including her carriers this time, to fight a decisive battle. But he knew too that the U.S. now had a strong force of land-based air power in Hawaii, making such an attack too risky. He decided on the Midway atoll, 1,300 miles from Oahu, as the best place to stage the encounter, on the basis that the Americans saw Midway as a vital mid-Pacific outpost of Pearl and would certainly defend it in strength.

The U.S. Navy aircraft carrier *Hornet* (CV-8) was steaming towards a large force of Japanese warships near Midway atoll in the evening of 3 June 1942, when the pilots of Torpedo Eight entered their ready room. The torpedo squadron pilots received the plan of attack that would be employed when the two opposing naval forces clashed. Now Lt Cdr John Waldron, commanding officer of Torpedo Eight, was handing out mimeographed copies of his final message to them before what would in future be known as the Battle of Midway. "Just a word to let you know that I feel we are all ready. We have had a very short time to train and we have worked under the most severe difficulties. But we have truly done the best humanly possible. I actually believe that under these conditions we are the best in the world. My greatest hope is that we encounter a favorable tactical situation, but if we don't, and the worst comes to the worst, I want each of us to do his utmost to destroy our enemies. If there is only one plane left to make a final run-in, I want that man to go in and get a hit, May God be with us all. Good luck, happy landings, and give 'em hell."

Some of the men of the squadron then wrote letters to loved ones. It was as if they had premonitions of what lay ahead.

"Dear Mom, Dad, and Mary,
This letter will be mailed only if I do not get through battle which we expect to come off any hour. I am making a request that this be mailed as soon as possible after I fail to return.

"As you know, I am the gunner and radio man in a plane and it is up to me to shoot first and best. I would not have it any different. I want you all to know that I am not the least bit worried, and Mom, you can be sure that I have been praying every day and am sure that I will see you 'up there'.

"Perhaps I have not always done the right thing. Only hope that you do not think too badly of my action.

"The best of luck to all of you and be seeing you when life will be much different 'up there'. Be sure and remember I am only one of many and you are also one of many.
Love, Bill"

"Honey, if anything happens to me, I wish you would keep on visiting the folks, for they love you just as much as they would if you were one of their own kids. And by all means, don't become an old maid. Find someone else and make a happy home. Don't be worrying about me and I will be trying to write more often.
Love, Pete

And this, from Commander Waldron to his wife:

"Dear Adelaide,

There is not a bit of news that I can tell you now except that I am well. I have yours and the children's pictures here with me all the time, and I think of you all most of the time.

"I believe that we will be in the battle very soon. I wish we were there today. But, as we are up to the very eve of serious business, I wish to record to you that I am feeling fine. My own morale is excellent and from my continued observation of the squadron, their morale is excellent also. You may rest assured that I will go in with the expectation of coming back in good shape. If I do not come back, well, you and the little girls can know that this squadron struck for the highest objective in Naval warfare—to sink the enemy.

"I hope this letter will not scare you and, of course, if I have a chance to write another to be mailed at the same time as this, then of course I shall do so and then you will receive each at the same time.

"I love you and the children very dearly and I long to be with you. But, I could not be happy ashore at this time. My place is here with the fight. I could not be happy otherwise. I know you wish me luck and I believe I will have it.

"You know, Adelaide, in this business of the torpedo attack, I acknowledge we must have a break. I believe that I have the experience and enough Sioux in me to profit by and recognize the break when it comes, and it will come.

"I dislike having the censors read a letter from me such as this, however, at this time I felt I must record the thoughts listed in the foregoing.

"God bless you, dear. You are a wonderful wife and mother. Kiss and love the little girls for me and be of good cheer.

Love to all from Daddy and Johnny"

At 0111 officers of the USS *Hornet* were informed of an attack by four Navy PBY patrol bombers on Japanese warships southwest of Midway Island. Shortly thereafter, the pilots of Torpedo Eight were in their ready room awaiting a briefing which was delayed due to Admiral Marc Mitscher and the *Hornet* skipper, Captain Mason, being unsure of the Japanese fleet's exact position. They had to know if the Hornet was then close enough to the enemy ships for her pilots to operate within a safe fuel margin. The pilots adjourned to the ward room for breakfast and as they finished, General Quarters was sounded, followed by "All pilots report to your ready rooms." There the pilots of Torpedo Eight learned that Midway was then under Japanese attack.

Torpedo Eight TBD Devastator pilot Ensign George Gay remembered:

"There was a real commotion as we hauled our plotting boards, helmets, goggles, gloves, pistols, hunting knives and all our other gear. We took down the flight information.

"We had only six of our planes on the flight deck as there was no more room. And since we were to be alone, anyhow, we were the last to be launched. The skipper had tried in vain to get us fighter protection; he even tried to get one fighter to go with us, or even get one fighter plane and one of us would fly it even though we had never been up in one, but he could not swing it. The Group Commander and the Captain felt that the SBDs needed more assistance than we did. They had caught hell in the Coral Sea and the torpedo planes had been lucky. However, the torpedo planes had made the hits in the Coral Sea, so the Japs were going to be looking for us.

"The TBD could not climb anywhere near as high as the dive bombers needed to go, and the Group Commander and the fighter boys did not want us at two levels up there. Under these conditions Commander Waldron reasoned, our best bet was to be right on the water so the Zeros could not get under us. Since it was obvious that we would be late getting away, with nine of our planes still to be brought up from the hangar deck for launching, the problem would be overtaking to form a coordinated attack.

"As I went up to the flight deck, I suddenly ducked into a first aid station and got a tourniquet and put it in my pocket. As I got to the edge of the island, I met the skipper coming down from the bridge. 'I'm glad I caught you,' he said. 'I've been trying to convince them the Japs will not be going towards Midway—especially if they find out we are here. The Group Commander is going to take the whole bunch down there. I'm going more to the north and maybe by the time they come north and find them, we can catch up and all go in together. Don't think I'm lost. Just track me so if anything happens to me, the boys can count on you to bring them back.'

"Each of us would be tracking, and the others all knew how to do it, but it would be my job since I was navigation officer. That is also the reason why I was the last man in the formation. It gave me more room to navigate instead of flying formation so closely.

"At a little before 0900, the planes started taking off, and it was 0915 when the signal man motioned me forward to the take-off position. He only had me move forward enough so that I could unfold my wings, and so I began my take-off with the tail of my plane still sitting on the No. 3 elevator. I had more than enough room on deck in front of me to take off, and I noticed as I came back by the ship that the planes that were to follow me were being moved further up the deck with the hope of being able to bring the rest of the torpedo planes of Squadron Eight up the elevator from the hangar deck so they could get in take-off position.

"The rest of Torpedo Eight got off after what seemed to be an eternity; then we all joined up and headed away from our fleet.

"After an uneasy and uneventful hour, the skipper's voice broke radio silence: 'There's a fighter on our tail.' What he saw proved to be a Jap scout plane flying at about 1,000 feet. It flew on past us, but I knew— and I'm sure the others did—that he had seen us and reported to the Jap Navy that there were carrier planes approaching.

"We had been flying long enough now to find something and I could almost see the wheels going around in Waldron's head. He did exactly what I had expected. He put the first section into a scouting line. Each of the eight planes was to move out into a line even with the skipper's wing tips. We had never done this before, only talked about it and, in spite of the warnings and dire threats, the fellows got too much distance between the planes. I knew immediately that this was wrong, as the planes on each end were nearly out of sight. The basic idea is OK, so that you can scan more ocean, but this was ridiculous, I thought to myself.

"The skipper was upset, and he gave the join-up signal forcefully. We had just gotten together when smoke columns appeared on the horizon. The old Indian had taken us straight to the Japs.

"The first capital ship I recognized as a carrier—the *Soryu*. Then I made out the *Kaga* and the *Akagi*. There was another carrier further on, and screening ships all over the damned ocean. The smoke was from what looked like a battleship, and the carriers were landing planes. The small carrier off on the horizon had smoke coming out of her also. My first thought was, 'Oh, Christ! We're late!'

"The skipper gave the signal to spread out to bracket the biggest carrier for an attack, and that was when the Zeros swarmed all over us.

"Since we had flown straight to the enemy fleet, while everyone else was off looking for them, there was no one else for their air cover to worry about.

"Seeing immediately that the Zeros had us cold, the skipper signalled for us to join back together for mutual protection. We had not moved far apart, so we were back together almost immediately. The skipper broke radio silence again: "We will go in. We won't turn back. Former strategy cannot be used. We will attack. Good luck!'

"I have never questioned the skipper's judgement or decisions. As it turned out, it didn't make any difference anyhow. We had run into a virtual trap, but we still had to do something to disrupt their landing planes, so he took us right in. We had calculated our fuel to be very short, even insufficient to get us back to the *Hornet*, but this was not considered suicidal by any of us. We thought we had a fighting chance, and that maybe after we dropped our fish we could make it to Midway. Things started happening really fast.

"I cannot tell you the sequence in which the planes went down. Everything was happening at once, but I was consciously seeing it all. At least one plane blew up, and each would hit the water and seem to disappear.

"Zeros were coming in from all angles and from both sides at once. They would come in from abeam, pass each other just over our heads, and turn around to make another attack. It was evident that they were trying to get our lead planes first. The planes of Torpedo Eight were falling at irregular intervals. Some were on fire and some did a half-roll and crashed on their backs, completely out of control. Machine-gun bullets ripped my armor plate a number of times. As they rose above it, the bullets would go over my shoulder into the instrument panel and through the windshield.

"Waldron was shot down very early. His plane burst into flames, and I saw him stand up to get out of the fire. He put his right leg outside the cockpit, and then hit the water and disappeared. His radioman, Dobbs, didn't have a chance. When we had been leaving Pearl Harbor, Dobbs had orders back to the States to teach radio. But he had chosen to delay that assignment and stay with us.

"Much too early, it seemed, Bob Huntington [George Gay's radioman] said, 'They got me!' 'Are you hurt bad?' I asked. I looked back and Bob was slumped down almost out of sight. 'Can you move?' I asked. He said no more.

"It was while I was looking back at Bob that the plane to my left must have been shot down, because when I looked forward again it was not there. I think that was the only plane I did not actually see get hit.

"We were right on the water at full throttle and wide open which was about 180 knots. Anyone slamming into the sea had no chance of survival—at that speed the water is just like cement. That is why I was so sure that they were all dead.

"It's hard to explain, but I think Bob being put out of action so soon was one of the things that saved me. I no longer had to fly straight and level for him to shoot, so I started dodging. I even pulled up a few times, and took some shots at Zeros as they would go by. I am positive I hit one, knocking plexiglas out of his canopy. I may have scared him, but I certainly did not hurt him personally, or even damage his plane much.

"The armor-plate bucket seat was another thing that worked well for me. I could feel, as well as hear and sometimes see, those tracer bullets. They would clunk into the airplane or clank against that armored seat, and I had to exercise considerable control over when to kick the rudder.

"About this time I felt something hit my left arm and felt it to see what it was. There was a hole in my sleeve and I got blood on my hand. I felt closer, and there was a lump under the skin of my arm. I squeezed the lump, just as you would pop a pimple, and a bullet popped out. I remember thinking, 'Well, what do you know—a souvenir.' I was too busy to put it in my pocket. So I put the bullet in my mouth, blood and all, thinking, 'What the hell—it's my blood.'

"We were now in a position, those of us still left, to turn west again to intercept the ship we had chosen to attack, but the Zeros were still intent on not letting us through, and our planes kept falling all around me. We were on the ship's starboard side, or to the right and ahead of our target, and as we closed range the big carrier began to turn towards us. I knew immediately from what the skipper had said so often in his lectures that if she got into a good turn she could not straighten out right away, and I was glad that she had committed herself. At that moment there were only two planes left of our squadron besides my own. One was almost directly ahead of me, but off a bit to my left. I skidded to the left and avoided more slugs just in time to pull my nose up and fire at another Zero as he got in front of me. I only had one .30 calibre gun, and although I knew I hit this Zero also, it did little damage. When I turned back to the right, the plane that had been directly ahead of me was gone, and the other one was out of control.

"My target, which I think was the *Kaga*, was now in a hard turn to starboard and I was going towards her forward port quarter. I figured that by the time a torpedo could travel the distance it should be in the water, the ship should be broadside. I aimed about one-quarter of the ship's length ahead of her bow, and reached out with my left hand to pull back the throttle. It had been calculated that we should be at about 80 knots when we dropped these things, so I had to slow down.

"I had just got hold of the throttle, when something hit the back of my hand and it hurt like hell. My hand didn't seem to be working right, so I had to pull the throttle back mostly with my thumb. You can imagine that I was not being exactly neat about all this. I was simply trying to do what I had come out to do. When I figured that I had things about as good as I was going to get them, I punched the torpedo release button.

"Nothing happened. 'Damn those tracers', I thought. 'They've goofed up my electrical release and I'm getting inside my range.' I had been told that the ideal drop was 1,000 yards range, 80 knots speed, and 80 feet or so of altitude. But by the time I got the control stick between my knees and put my left hand on top of it to fly the plane, and reached across to pull the cable release with my good right hand, I was into about 850 yards. The cable, or mechanical release, came out of the instrument panel on the left side, designed to be pulled with the left hand. But those damn Zeros had messed up my program. My left hand did not work. It was awkward, and I almost lost control of the plane trying to pull out that cable by the roots. I can't honestly say I got rid of that torpedo. It felt like it. I had never done it before so I couldn't be sure, and with the plane pitching like a bronco, I had to be content with trying my best.

"God, but that ship looked big! I remember thinking, 'Why in the hell doesn't the *Hornet* look that big when I'm trying to land on her?'

"I remember that I did not want to fly out over the starboard side and let all those gunners have a chance at me, so I headed out over the stern.

"I thought, 'I could crash into all this and make one great big mess, maybe even get myself a whole carrier, but I'm feeling passably good, and my plane is still flying, so the hell with that—I'll keep going. Maybe I'll get another crack at them and do more damage in the long run.'

"Flying as low as I could, I went between a couple of cruisers and out past the destroyers. If you have ever seen movies of this sort of thing, you may wonder how anything could get through all that gunfire. I am alive to tell you that it can be done. I think my plane was hit a few times . . .

"The Zeros had broken off me when I got into ack-ack, but they had no trouble going around to meet me on the other side. A 20mm cannon slug hit my left rudder pedal just outside my little toe, blew the pedal apart and knocked a hole in the firewall. This set the engine on fire, and it was burning my left leg through that hole.

"When the rudder pedal went, the control wire to the ailerons and the rudder went with it. I [still] had the elevators so I could pull the nose up. Reaching over with my right hand, I cut the switch. That was also on the left side. I was able to hold the nose up and slow down to almost a decent ditching speed.

"Most airplanes will level out if you turn them loose, especially if they are properly trimmed. Mine was almost making it, but I was crosswind, so the right wing hit first. This slammed me into the water in a cartwheel fashion and banged the hood shut over me before it twisted the frame and jammed the hood tight.

"As I unbuckled, water was rising to my waist. The nose of the plane was down, so I turned around and sat on the instrument panel while trying to get that hood open. It wouldn't budge. When that water got up to my armpits and started lapping at my chin, I got scared—and I mean really scared. I knew the plane would dive as soon as it lost buoyancy and I didn't want to drown in there. I panicked, stood up and busted my way out.

"The Zeros were diving and shooting at me, but my first thought now was of Bob Huntington. I was almost positive he was dead. I think he took at least one of those slugs right in the chest, but I thought that the water might revive him and I had to try and help him. I got back to him just as the plane took that dive, and I went down with it trying to unbuckle his straps and get him out.

"The beautiful water exploded into a deep red, and I lost sight of everything. What I had seen confirmed my opinion of his condition and I had to let Bob go. The tail took a gentle swipe at me as if to say goodbye and I came up choking. I lost the bullet from my mouth and as I watched it sink in that blue, clear water, I grabbed for it but missed. Zeros were still strafing me and I ducked under a couple of times as those thwacking slugs came close. As I came up for air once, I bumped my head on my life raft out of the plane."

George Gay was the only member of Torpedo Eight to survive their attack that day. With his wits and luck, he evaded capture by the ships of the enemy fleet that drove past him as he floated near them, his head covered by a thin black seat cushion that had emerged from his sinking plane, along with a four-man life raft. That entire afternoon, in the presence of the Japanese warships, he "rode" that uninflated raft like a horse, concealing it and himself from his foes, having to wait until nightfall to inflate it. From his vantage point, he watched the destruction of three great carriers of the enemy fleet by the dive bombers of *Hornet* and other U.S. flattops. After about thirty hours in the water, Gay was saved when he was sighted by a PBY crew who landed nearby to pick him up. He was flown to Midway and later to Pearl Harbor where a doctor examined him and noted that the ensign had lost roughly a pound an hour in body weight during his time in the sea. While recovering, George Gay was visited in his hospital room by Admiral Chester W. Nimitz, Commander-in-Chief of the U.S. Pacific Fleet. The admiral had more than a casual interest in the ensign's account of what he had observed in the course of his amazing adventure. Gay later received the Navy Cross and the Purple Heart.

ACES

A military aviator credited with shooting down five or more enemy aircraft in aerial combat officially qualifies as an "ace". It is an honour among fighter pilots, as only a relative few of their number achieve it. The vast majority of enemy aircraft shot down have fallen at the hands of a small percentage of all the fighter pilots in history. Who were the best? Kill scores count for a lot, but are not the only measure. Here are some of the best of the best.

Early in the First World War, Raymond Collishaw, of Nanaimo, British Columbia, left his job on a fishing boat and enlisted in the Royal Naval Air Service. The Canadian qualified as a pilot in January 1916, flying naval patrols along the English Channel. Before moving into his stride, Collishaw, flying a Sopwith Strutter in October 1916, was bounced by six German Albatross fighters whose bullets wrecked his instrument panel and his goggles. With reduced vision he dove to low level. One of the enemy planes followed him down and crashed into a wood. When he was then overrun by another Albatross, he shot it down. Looking for a field on which to land, he put the Strutter down only to find it was a German-occupied airfield. He took off quickly and soon located a French field near Verdun. By war's end, Ray Collishaw had accounted for a confirmed 62 enemy aircraft destroyed.

Arthur Roy Brown was another Canadian ace flying with the RNAS in the First World War. He is best known for being credited with shooting down Manfred von Richthofen, Germany's "Red Baron." That credit is disputed, however. Lewis gunners of the 14th Australian Artillery Brigade claimed credit for downing von Richthofen.

After Brown viewed von Richthofen's body the day after their encounter, he wrote: ". . . there was a lump in my throat. If he had been my dearest friend, I could not have felt greater sorrow."

When the war ended, Brown returned to his native Canada and worked as an accountant. When the Second World War began, he tried to re-enlist with the Royal Canadian Air Force but was refused. He died in 1944, aged 50.

In the First World War, Stanley J. Goble, of Croydon, Victoria, Australia, became an ace and scored ten victories while commanding No. 5 Squadron, RNAS. After his flying training in 1915, he began flying anti-submarine patrols with only three hours solo flight time. A founding member of No. 8 Squadron, RNAS, Goble received the award of the Distinguished Service Order in February 1917 for "conspicuous bravery and skill" in three separate actions during the previous November. The

RNAS merged with the Royal Flying Corps in April 1918, to form the Royal Air Force, and Goble became a major in the new R.A.F. His final score in the war was ten victories.

The most high-achieving Australian ace, Robert A. Little, had a total of 47 aerial victories in World War One. Bob Little went to England in 1915 and learnt to fly at his own expense with the Royal Aero Club at Hendon before enlisting in the RNAS. He flew Sopwith Pups and Camels on the Western Front with No. 8 Squadron, racking up 38 of his kills in one year. He attained the balance of his victories with No. 3 Squadron.

In one engagement on 24 April 1917, Little forced a German pilot to land so he could claim the enemy aircraft as captured and take the pilot prisoner at gunpoint. On landing, however, Little's plane hit a ditch and flipped over. When he captured the enemy pilot, the German said: "It looks as if I have brought *you* down, not you me."

With the merger of the RNAS and the Royal Flying Corps into the R.A.F., Little became a captain, having previously joined No. 3 Squadron, RNAS, which was now No. 203 Squadron, R.A.F., commanded by Raymond Collishaw.

Flying a Sopwith Camel on 27 May. He had had reports about enemy Gotha bombers in the area and he took off on that bright, moonlit evening to hunt the raiding German aircraft. He was approaching one of the Gothas when he was hit by a bullet that passed through both of his legs. He was able to crash-land in a nearby field but suffered further injury, a fractured skull. When the wreckage of his plane was found the next morning by a policeman, Little had bled to death. He was 22. His commanding officer, Ray Collishaw, said of him: ". . . an outstanding character, bold, aggressive and courageous, yet he was gentle and kindly. A resolute and brave man."

Roderic 'Stan' Dallas was the second highest-scoring Australian WWI ace, after Robert Little. Officially credited with 39 enemy aircraft destroyed, he may well have accounted for 50 or more. In addition to his abilities as a fighter pilot, Dallas was a test pilot, an accomplished squadron leader, and a respected tactician.

He named his Sopwith Triplane *'Brown Bread'*. It was the first of several such triplanes he flew. On 23 April 1917, Stan Dallas and his wingman, Tom Culling, found and engaged a formation of fourteen enemy aircraft whom the pair had bounced from above. They attacked the Germans from opposite sides of the formation, using short bursts from their machine guns. The superior performance and handling of the Triplanes enabled Dallas and Culling to re-position themselves for twenty separate attacks on the enemy aircraft over the next 45 minutes. In that time they gradually forced the enemy pilots lower and lower and finally back across the German lines. In the fight, the pair shot down three of the German planes.

Dallas was flying the S.E.5 fighter in May 1918 when, during a lull in the fighting near Flanders, he had decided he would something to shake up the

Germans at their La Brayelle airfield. He flew down and strafed the base to get their attention before dropping a package with a note that read: "If you won't come up here and fight, herewith a pair of boots for work on the ground, pilots—for the use of." He circled, waiting for some of the Germans to come out and inspect the package, before coming down again to drop two bombs and continue to shoot up the facilities.

Stan Dallas was promoted to Lieutenant Colonel and given command of a wing on 1 June, but never received the order. He had taken off before it arrived, to go after three Fokker Triplanes in the area and was killed in the ensuing fight.

The highest-scoring fighter ace of the Royal Navy Fleet Air Arm in the Second World War is Stanley Gordon Orr. The London-born Commander is credited with destroying 17 enemy aircraft. Participating in the air actions over Dunkirk and Norway, Orr was then reassigned to HMS *Illustrious* in the Mediterranean, where he was involved in the attack on Italian warships in Taranto harbour, the Battle of Cape Matapan, the Defence of Malta, and action in Egypt. In 1944, he took part in the famous air attack on the German battle-ship *Tirpitz* in a fjord near Tromso, Norway.

Entering the Royal Navy from the RN Volunteer Reserve, Stan Orr learnt to fly and served in the First World War carrier, HMS *Argus*. As a member of 806 Squadron, he was posted to HMS *Illustrious* in June 1940. Flying a Fairey Fulmar two-seat fighter, Orr helped provide fighter cover for the Swordfish air-craft that mounted the successful torpedo attack on the capital ships of the Italian Navy at Taranto on the night of 11-12 November 1940.

Flying a Grumman Hellcat fighter, Orr was in command of the second strike group when, in March 1944, an attack was ordered on the battleship *Tirpitz* which was at anchor in Altafjord near Tromso, Norway. The battleship was a continuing threat to the great arctic convoys. The Royal Navy was maintaining a force of carriers along the Norwegian coast to give air cover for the convoys. The carriers were HMS *Furious, Victorious,* and the escort carriers *Emperor, Searcher,* and *Pursuer.* Their air strike force included Grumman Hellcats, Vought Corsairs, Grumman Wildcats, and Fairey Barracudas. Orr: "Upon arrival over *Tirpitz* it was found that the smoke screen generated by the Germans had ridden half way up the mountains on either side of the fjord. Each flight attacked their pre-briefed gun sites once it was clear that no enemy fighters were in the area. The Hellcat proved itself to be an excellent gun platform on this mission." In the raid, R.A.F. Lancaster bombers dropped 12,000-lb Tallboy bombs on the battleship, scoring two direct hits and a near miss, which caused the ship to capsize in the shallow waters. Fire spread to an ammuni-tion magazine of one of the main turrets, leading to a massive explosion. At least 900 crew members of *Tirpitz* died. Orr was awarded a second bar to his Distinguished Service Cross for his part in the raid.

Francis Dawson-Paul, a Fleet Air Arm pilot, was seconded to the R.A.F. in

1940 due to the extreme pilot shortage in the run up to the Battle of Britain. Flying with No. 64 Squadron, he was credited with shooting down 7.5 enemy aircraft before being shot down himself in the English Channel. Rescued by the crew of a German E-boat, he was taken prisoner but died of his wounds five days later. In only three weeks of combat, Dawson-Paul had become the first naval air ace of the Battle.

Shortly after being posted to R.A.F. Kenley south of London, in July 1940, he was a part the squadron's Blue Section when they were sent up to intercept an enemy aircraft. Dawson-Paul: "As Blue 2, I was ordered to scramble with Blue Section at 1830 hours to patrol base at 20,000 feet. I first reported a streak of white smoke, which I identified was condensing exhaust gases coming from what I thought was the enemy aircraft. This streak was about 14 miles ahead and to the starboard of me. I was about 2 miles behind Blue 1, as my engine was not giving full power. Crossing the coast I passed a section of Hurricanes and as I drew nearer I saw another section in line astern preparing to attack. I concluded that the enemy aircraft must have sighted the Hurricanes and Blue 1, as it started to take evasive action and lost height in a steep spiral. I followed down, drawing towards it and after the Hurricanes and Blue 1 had delivered their attacks, I overhauled it and opened fire at approximately 150 yards, closing up to about 50 yards as I gave it three bursts. I saw my bullets enter the rear portion of the enemy aircraft. I broke away to port, gained height and delivered another attack from the rear. This time the enemy aircraft turned to port and I broke to starboard and I was just positioning myself for another attack when I saw the enemy aircraft strike the water and sink almost at once. My aircraft was hit four times, twice in the starboard mainplane and twice underneath the rudder. I returned to Kenley at approximately 1955 hours."

Eugene Valencia of San Francisco joined the U.S. Navy as an aviation cadet in 1941, several months before the Japanese attack on Pearl Harbor. By war's end, Valencia had destroyed twenty-three enemy aircraft and received the Navy Cross, five Distinguished Flying Crosses and six Air Medals. He had led the most successful four-plane division of the war, Valencia's Flying Circus. A natural leader and tactician, he discovered what he believed was a flaw in Japanese fighter tactics. During additional training he recruited three fellow naval aviators to develop an imaginative and highly effective new operational unit . In February 1945, Valencia's little outfit, a part of VF-9 squadron, flew their first combat mission from the USS *Lexington*. That afternoon they returned to the carrier with six confirmed enemy aircraft downed.

Roy "Butch" Voris was a Pacific ace in the U.S. Navy in the Second World War and after the war founded the Navy's flight demonstration team, the Blue Angels.

Voris was in flight training when the Japanese struck at Pearl Harbor in December 1941. By early 1942, he was in the South Pacific flying combat missions from the carrier USS *Enterprise*. He flew the Grumman Wildcat with fighter squadron VF-10, known as the Grim Reapers. By his second cruise, with VF-2, he was flying the F6F Hellcat, initially from *Enterprise* and then from the USS *Hornet* and Guadalcanal. His squadron took part in campaigns against the Japanese at Tarawa, the Philippine Sea, in which more than 300 enemy aircraft were shot down by American Navy pilots, in a 12-to-1 kill-to-loss ratio, and at Guadalcanal island. "I shot down my first Japanese Zero at Guadalcanal. But I didn't see one coming up behind me and I got shot up and knocked out of the sky. I didn't bail out—they'll shoot you out of your parachute and if you go into the water the sharks will eat you. I was full of shrapnel wounds and had a dead stick—I'd lost the engine—but I got back to Guadalcanal. I was a lucky boy."

Richard J. "Dickie" Cork was another Royal Navy fighter ace who was seconded to the Royal Air Force to fly in the Battle of Britain. Serving with No. 242 Squadron at Duxford near Cambridge, Cork flew as wingman with Squadron Leader Douglas Bader. In his first air action with 242, the squadron shot down twelve enemy aircraft and Cork was credited with downing a Messerschmitt Bf 110 and given a share of a second 110. He became an ace on 13 September, with his fifth kill. In the Battle of Britain, 58 Fleet Air Arm pilots volunteered to fly with the R.A.F., with five becoming aces.

Returning to the Navy after the Battle, Cork flew with 880 Squadron in the Arctic, the Meditarranean and the Indian Ocean. On 12 August 1942, during Operation Pedestal, the British effort to bring desperately needed supplies to the blockaded island of Malta, he was the only Royal Navy pilot to shoot down five enemy aircraft in a single day. He received the Distinguished Service Order for the feat.

Aboard HMS *Victorious* in 1944, Cork commanded the 15th Naval Fighter Wing, three squadrons of Vought F4U Corsairs. Victorious was heading for action in the Indian Ocean when Dickie Cork was killed in a flying accident near China Bay, Ceylon, on 14 August. His final score was 9 e/a destroyed.

Arthur Van Haren Jr was a star football quarterback for his Phoenix, Arizona, high school and played for the University of Arizona. He was a member of Fighting Squadron VF-2, "The Rippers". Van Haren flew the F6F Hellcat from the carrier USS *Hornet*, participating in the famous "Marianas Turkey Shoot" during the Battle of the Philippine Sea in June 1944. In the action, he shot down three Japanese aircraft. An entry from his journal: "I took off today and almost immediately my plane started throwing oil and then started smoking to high heaven. I had a 500 lb bomb and that worried me to no end 'cause I couldn't get rid of it. The ship told me to land anyway, so I did and my old luck held right out. Just as I hit the deck, the engine burst into flames, but I wasted no time getting out of the darn thing. The boys ganged two more this morning and I wasn't on that hop. I got over the target later in the afternoon and the A.A. (anti-aircraft fire) was still pretty rough. They hit Dennis Floyd head-on. He came down in flames. He was a real fellow. They always seem to get it. It doesn't seem quite fair. He had a baby he never even got to see. What a lousy racket this is!" Van Haren finished the war with a score of twelve enemy aircraft destroyed.

The Hollywood movie actor Wayne Morris appeared in the excellent 1957 film about the First World War, *Paths of Glory*. In 1940 he joined the Naval Reserve, becoming a pilot in 1942. On the way he had pleaded with the Navy for the opportunity to be a fighter pilot, but was turned down repeatedly and told that he was simply too big to be a fighter pilot. He had an ace in the hole, however. His brother-in-law was Cdr David McCampbell, the third highest scoring American fighter ace of the Second World War. He implored McCampbell to help him and it worked. Morris was soon flying Hellcats in McCampbell's squadron, VF-15 from the carrier USS *Essex*. In his time with the squadron, Morris shot down seven Japanese planes and took part in the sinking of five enemy ships. At the age of 45, he suffered a fatal heart attack while visiting aboard the aircraft carrier USS *Bon Homme Richard* in San Francisco Bay.

David McCampbell was the U.S. Navy's all-time leading fighter ace with 34 aerial victories in the Second World War, and the highest scoring ace to survive the war. On the carrier USS *Essex*, he commanded Carrier Air Group 15 in February 1944, having previously commanded the squadron, VF-15. As CAG, McCampbell was responsible for the fighters, bombers, and torpedo bombers of the carrier air group through six months of continuous air-sea battles. His air group destroyed more enemy aircraft and sank more enemy ships than any other air group in the Pacific war theatre.

During the famous "Marianas Turkey Shoot" on the morning of 19 June 1944, McCampbell shot down five Japanese dive bombers and became an ace in a day. In a second sortie that afternoon, he brought down two more enemy aircraft. For his actions during the attacks, Commander McCampbell received the Medal of Honor, the only carrier task force pilot so honoured.

The citation for his Medal of Honor read: "For conspicuous gallantry and intrepidity at the risk of his life above and beyond the call of duty as commander, Air Group 15, during combat against enemy Japanese aerial forces in the first and second battles of the Philippine Sea. An inspiring leader, fighting boldly in the face of terrific odds, Comdr. McCampbell led his fighter planes against a force of 80 Japanese carrier-based aircraft bearing down on our fleet on June 19, 1944. Striking fiercely in valiant defense of our surface force, he personally destroyed 7 hostile planes during this single engagement in which the outnumbering attack force was utterly routed and virtually annihilated. During a major fleet engagement with the enemy on October 24, Comdr. McCampbell, assisted by but 1 plane, intercepted and daringly attacked a formation of 60 hostile land-based craft approaching our forces. Fighting desperately but with superb skill against such overwhelming airpower, he shot down

9 Japanese planes and, completely disorganizing the enemy group, forced the remainder to abandon the attack before a single aircraft could reach the fleet. His great personal valor and indomitable spirit of aggression under extremely perilous combat conditions reflect the highest credit upon Comdr. McCampbell and the U.S. Naval Service."

Hiroyoshi Nishizawa may have been the most high-achieving fighter ace of the Imperial Japanese Navy in the Second World War. His claims of eighty-seven aerial victories have attracted controversy with some believing them to be exaggerated and others that his true score is closer to 100.

Nishizawa joined the Yokaren (flight reserve enlistee training programme), completing his flying training in March 1939. On 3 February 1942, he was flying an obsolete Mitsubishi A5M fighter when he claimed his first kill, a PBY Catalina flying boat. Soon his squadron received their first A6M2 Zero fighters and were transferred to Lae, New Guinea, where he flew with other famous Japanese fighter aces, including Saburo Sakai, Toshio Ohta, and Junichi Sasai. Of Nishizawa, Sakai said: "Never have I seen a man with a fighter plane do what Nishizawa would do with his Zero. His aerobatics were all at once breathtaking, brilliant, totally unpredictable, impossible, and heart-stirring to witness."

In October 1944, Japanese pilots were ordered to fly the first kamikaze suicide missions against American warships in the Leyte Gulf. Before one such mission that he was scheduled to fly, Lt Yukio Seki was quoted as saying: "Japan's future is bleak if it is forced to kill one of its best pilots. I am not going on this mission for the Emperor or for the Empire . . . I am going because I was ordered to!" Lt Seki's A6M2 Zero fighter was carrying a 550 lb bomb when he crashed the plane into the flight deck of the escort carrier USS *St Lo*. The ship sank thirty minutes later taking the lives of 126 crewmen.

The following day, armourers loaded another 550 lb bomb onto the Zero fighter of Hiroyoshi Nishizawa. He had volunteered to take part in the morning kamikaze mission. His commander refused to permit him to go on the mission, valuing his great skill and prowess too much to spend the pilot's life in such a way. Nishizawa's Zero was flown that morning by a far less-experienced pilot, Tomisaku Katsumata, who crashed it into the escort carrier USS *Suwanee* near Surigao, causing a huge fire that engulfed eleven planes on the flight deck, killing eighty-five crewmen, and leaving 102 wounded and fifty-eight missing.

The day after this incident, Nishizawa and some of his fellow pilots of the 201st Kokutai were traveling in a transport plane from Cebu to ferry replacement Zeros from Clark Field on Luzon. The transport was attacked over Mindoro Island by two F6F Hellcats flying from the carrier USS *Wasp* and shot down, killing all aboard. Nishizawa, Japan's then highest-scoring ace was 24 years old.

Saburo Sakai was a poor student in high school. He dropped out and joined the Japanese Navy at age 16. "The petty officers would not hesitate to administer the severest beatings to recruits they felt deserving of punishment. Whenever I committed a breach of discipline or an error in training, I was dragged physically from my cot by a petty officer. 'Stand tall to the wall! Bend down, Recruit Sakai!', he would roar. 'I am not doing this because I hate you, but because I like you and want you to make a good seaman. Bend down!' And with that he would swing a large stick of wood and with every ounce of strength he possessed would slam it against my upturned bottom. The pain was terrible, the force of the blows unremitting."

Sakai was accepted into pilot training in 1937 and graduated first in his class. For that achievement he was presented a silver watch by Emperor Hirohito. He would fly the Mitsubishi A6M2 Zero in China during 1939.

Saburo Sakai is believed to have destroyed a total of sixty-four enemy aircraft in the Second World War. The majority of his aerial victories occurred while he was with the Tainan chutai (squadron) of Junichi Sasai at Lae, New Guinea. There, the high-achieving Sakai generously shared his knowledge and expertise with many of the junior pilots in the squadron.

Sakai was severely wounded on 8 August 1942 while engaged in aerial combat with some U.S. Navy Dauntless dive bombers. His close friend and fellow ace, Hiroyoshi Nishizawa, became concerned when Sakai was missing after the action, searching the area frantically for a sign of his friend. Finding nothing he returned to base at Lakunai, Rabaul. Some time later, blind in one eye and covered in blood, Sakai, who had been struck by a 7.62mm bullet that had passed through his skull leaving the left side of his body paralyzed, struggled to land his badly damaged Zero at the base, after a nearly five-hour, 640-mile flight. His fuel gauge read near empty as he desperately circled the field four times before committing to land, narrowly missing crashing into a line of parked Zeros. Nishizawa and Lts Ohta and Sasai drove Sakai to the hospital. On 12 August he was evacuated to a hospital in Japan.

Following his discharge from hospital, Sakai instructed new fighter pilots for a year until he was again permitted to fly in combat. His new unit was deployed to Iwo Jima. Sakai was one of only three pilots of his pre-war squadron to survive the war.

The Vought F4U Corsair was a handful for the average U.S. Navy pilot to land on a carrier. One of the accomplishments of John T. Blackburn during his time with VF-17 aboard the USS *Bunker Hill* was, together with his executive officer, Roger Hedrick, adapting their Corsairs to what would become the standard of the F4U-1 model, a slightly more carrier-friendly aeroplane.

The squadron was called 'The Jolly Rogers' and when they arrived in the Guadalcanal area, the Navy, which was still not satisfied with the Corsair's shipboard operating characteristics, ordered the Jolly Rogers to operate from the Ondongo airfield on the island of New Georgia in the Solomons. In their combat debut from Ondongo, the squadron ran into several Japanese Val dive bombers, downing five of them, Blackburn was credited with two.

VF-17 flew two tours of duty in the area of the Solomon Islands, accumulating 152 aerial victories and producing eleven aces. With his eleven victories, Blackburn ranked third in the squadron behind Hedrick who had twelve, and Ira Kepford with seventeen.

Lieutenant Commander Edward "Butch" O'Hare the first flying ace of the United States Navy. A recipient of the Medal of Honor and the Navy Cross, O'Hare was killed on 26 November 1943 while leading the Navy's first nighttime fighter attack from a U.S. aircraft carrier.

Butch O'Hare was a 1933 graduate of the U.S. Naval Academy at Annapolis, Maryland and in the Second World War served with great distinction aboard the carrier *Lexington* and, in September 1943, the carrier *Enterprise* where he was commander of the air group (CAG), responsible for 100 pilots and the group's F6F Hellcat fighters, SBD Dauntless dive bombers, and TBF Avenger torpedo bombers.

By 1943, daylight air superiority in the western Pacific was with the Americans and the Japanese were flying torpedo-armed Betty bombers in night missions against the U.S. Navy carriers in the area. To counter the attacks, Butch O'Hare worked with Rear Admiral Arthur Radford and Commander Tom Hamilton, Air Officer of the Enterprise, to develop what they called the "Bat Team" tactic. It involved sending an Avenger torpedo bomber and two Hellcat fighters out at night to locate, intercept and shoot down the Japanese bombers. The role of the Avenger was key to the team's success. Aviation radar then required large and bulky equipment, too big to be carried by the best fighters such as the Hellcat, so the larger Avenger became the "mother ship", to lead the Hellcats to the enemy aircraft in the darkness. From there the American fighters would close in and dispatch the Bettys.

In the first such Bat Team mission, Butch O'Hare volunteered to lead the effort on the evening of 26 November. The team was alerted just before dusk about a force of enemy bomber aircraft approaching and took off immediately. In the darkness the Hellcat pilots had difficulty from the start, first in locating the Avenger. When they found the enemy bombers, O'Hare's wingman spotted one of the Bettys behind and slightly above O'Hare's Hellcat. The rear gunner in the Avenger saw the Betty too and opened fire on it. The Japanese aircraft returned fire. It is believed that O'Hare was caught in the cross fire. The Hellcat wingman later reported seeing O'Hare's plane slide out to port and descend towards the sea.

A search of the area the next morning was unsuccessful. No trace of O'Hare or his aircraft was ever found. He was reported as missing in action. The citation to O'Hare's Navy Cross award read: "The President of the United States of America takes pride in presenting the Navy Cross (Posthumously) to Lieutenant Commander Edward Henry "Butch" O'Hare United States Navy, for extraordinary heroism in operations against the enemy while serving as

Pilot of a carrier-based Navy Fighter Plane in Fighting Squadron Two (VF-2), attached to the U.S.S. ENTERPRISE CV-6), and deployed over Tarawa in the Gilbert Islands, in action against enemy Japanese forces on 26 November 1943. When warnings were received of the approach of a large force of Japanese torpedo bombers, Lieutenant Commander O'Hare volunteered to lead a fighter section of aircraft from his carrier, the first time such a mission had been attempted at night, in order to intercept the attackers. He fearlessly led his three-plane group into combat against a large formation of hostile aircraft and assisted in shooting down two Japanese airplanes and dispersed the remainder. Lieutenant Commander O'Hare's outstanding courage, daring airmanship and devotion to duty were in keeping with the highest traditions of the United States Naval Service. He gallantly gave his life for his country." In 1949, the principal airport in Chicago was renamed O'Hare International in honour of the late naval officer.

Jefferson DeBlanc was a U.S. Marine Corps aviator with VMF-112, flying Grumman F4F Wildcats in the Solomon Islands. He was leading a flight of eight Wildcats on 31 January 1943, escorting a strike force of twelve Douglas SBD dive bombers on their way to hit Japanese shipping. During the flight DeBlanc's plane developed a serious fuel leak and he alerted rescue facilities.

Arriving at the target area, DeBlanc and his pilots spotted a pair of enemy float planes that began to attack the American dive bombers. Despite the fuel problem with his Wildcat, DeBlanc dove to attack and disrupt the enemy aircraft, destroying two. With the dive bombers successfully completing the mission, DeBlanc stayed in the area to cover their withdrawal, although his fuel status was approaching critical.

It was now late in the day and light was fading rapidly when he sighted a formation of enemy Ki-43 Oscar fighters heading for the American dive bombers. DeBlanc and his pilots roared in to attack the Oscars, and he scored his third, fourth and fifth victories of the day. Now dangerously low on fuel, he was surprised by a sudden spray of machine gun rounds hitting his Wildcat, wrecking the instrument panel and setting his engine afire.

DeBlanc was very low over Vella Lavella when he had to bail out of the stricken fighter. The seemingly lengthy, action-packed combat had actually lasted just five minutes. When he landed in the sea he finally realized that he had been wounded in the back, arms and legs. With only his life vest for partial support, he combined swimming and resting for the next six hours as he slowly made his way to shore. There he rested, his wounds unattended, surviving on coconuts for three more days. At last he was found by natives who eventually carried him to the home of a missionary, who in turn passed him on to some coast watchers who contacted Allied authorities by radio. On 12 February a Navy Catalina flying boat landed and took him back to his base where his wounds were treated. In 1946, U.S. President Harry Truman presented First Lieutenant Jefferson DeBlanc with the Medal of Honor in a White

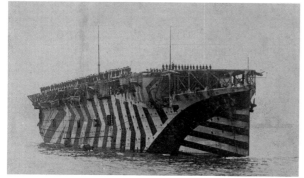

Notable among the first aircraft carriers were, from top to bottom, the British Royal Navy's HMS *Argus*, HMS *Eagle*, and HMS *Courageous*.

Pioneering aviator Eugene Ely made the first successful take-off by a fixed-wing aircraft from the deck of a ship, the USS *Birmingham*, in November 1910. below: The crew of a Royal Navy Swordfish torpedo bomber.

above: Devastation inflicted on capital ships of the U.S. Navy in Pearl Harbor, Hawaii, on 7 December 1941. right: Fleet Admiral Chester W. Nimitz, was Commander in Chief of the United States Pacific Fleet in the Second World War.

left above: A Curtiss SB2C
Helldiver dive bomber on
the USS *Bunker Hill* in
1944. left: A landing signal
officer aboard the USS
Enterprise in the Second
World War. above: The
Royal Navy light carrier
HMS *Pursuer* in WW2.

top left: The USS *Badoeng Strait*, an escort carrier in WW2. left: A Grumman TBM Avenger torpedo plane splinters the deck of the USS *Philippine Sea* in the Korean War. above: Grumman F6F Hellcat fighters about to launch on the USS *Bunker Hill*, 1944.

above: Japanese pilots
Hiroyoshi Nishizawa, left,
and Toshio Ohta, right;
U.S. Marine night-fighter
ace Bruce Porter flew
Hellcats in the Second
World War.

below: Royal Navy Sea
Harriers aboard HMS
Invincible during the 1982
Falklands War. right: Royal
Navy Commander Nigel
"Sharkey" Ward led 801
Squadron from *Invincible*
in the Falklands campaign.

below: U.S. Navy aviators in a briefing at Miramar NAS near San Diego, now a Marine Corps air station. right: An F-14 Tomcat airman suits up for a flight at Miramar.

above: An A-4C Skyhawk
is launched from the USS
John F. Kennedy, a *Kittyhawk*-class carrier .

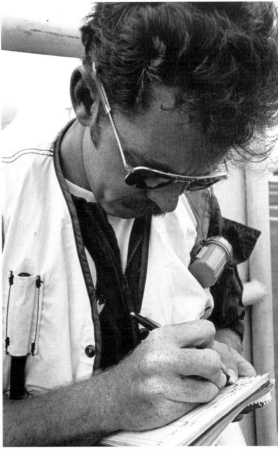

above left: The Air Boss on the U. S. Navy carrier *Coral Sea* in 1971. This officer was responsible for all operations involving aircraft, including the flight deck, hangar deck and airborne aircraft out to five nautical miles from the ship. above right: A landing signal officer of the *Coral Sea* grading landings.

above: WW2 U.S. Navy
fighter ace Stanley Vejtasa,
who would later command
the carrier *Constellation*.
above right: Naval Flight
Officer Shannon Callahan
in training at Pensacola
NAS in January 2000.

House ceremony.

Imperial Japanese Navy fighter ace Junichi Sasai was a member of the Tainan Air Group, achieving his first aerial victory in Java, Dutch East Indies on 2 February 1942 when he shot down a Brewster Buffalo fighter. As squadron leader of the 3rd Chutai, he flew with some of the best and most experienced Japanese fighter pilots, including Saburo Sakai, Toshio Ohta, and Enji Kakimoto. With help and guidance from Sakai, Junichi Sasai became a superb fighter pilot. Sasai was highly thought of by the men of his squadron, who appreciated him for his compassion. Sakai: "The Navy had a very rigid hierarchy and caste system; officers never made friends with enlisted men, it was not allowed. But Sasai was a different kind of officer."

Sasai became an ace on 4 May 1942, shooting down three P-39 Airacobra fighters in one encounter. On 11 July, he was leading twelve Zero fighters escorting twenty-one bombers from Rabaul to attack Port Moresby. On the way they met six B-17 Flying Fortress bombers and Sasai ordered an attack on the American planes. The Japanese pilots were unable to shoot down any of the American bombers, losing one Zero in the action. Sasai was reprimanded for deserting his own bombers to attack the Americans. Saburo Sakai later commented that he thought Sasai had made a poor decision in ordering the attack on the American planes, but said that all of his fellow Japanese pilots sympathized with Sasai as the B-17s had been bombing their base and they all wanted to get even. On 2 August Sasai encountered a B-17 and attacked it head-on, shooting it down.

When the Japanese command learned that American Marines had landed on Guadalcanal in the early morning of 7 August, a force of seventeen Zeros of the Tainan Group was sent up to escort twenty-seven Betty bombers in a raid on the American Navy task force supporting the invasion. Waiting for the Japanese planes were eighteen F4F-4 Wildcats and sixteen SBD Dauntless dive bombers operating from the carriers *Enterprise*, *Wasp*, and *Saratoga*. In the action, Sasai was credited with downing five Wildcats.

In his final action of the war, Junichi Sasai led eight Zeros in escort of a force of Betty bombers attacking Henderson Field on Guadalcanal. The airfield was a critical target for the Japanese as it enabled American aircraft to interupt Japan's efforts to resupply its troops in the region. In the raid, Sasai attacked a Wildcat in the Henderson traffic pattern. The Wildcat pilot, Major Marion E. Carl of Marine squadron VMF-223, retaliated, killing 24-year-old Sasai as his Zero became a fireball when it fell on the beach. Sasai's final kill score was twenty-seven.

In the morning of 26 October 1942, U.S. Navy Lieutenant Stanley "Swede" Vejtasa led three other Wildcat fighters from the deck of the carrier *Enterprise* on a combat air patrol at 09:30 to intercept a Japanese attack group that was approaching the carrier *Hornet*. Vejtasa's little group of planes was climbing at full power to 12,000 feet near the *Hornet* when they were told to watch for the enemy planes at 7,000 feet. At that moment, Vejtasa spotted at least six Japanese dive bombers above him, in a fast glide towards their diving point. As one of the enemy planes reappeared from a nearby cloud, Vejtasa positioned his fighter for a run on the Japanese pilot. He shot the enemy plane down and then downed two more.

At this point Vejtasa, who had been running his engine using his wing tanks, heard the engine quit and quickly shifted to his main fuel tank. He immediately noticed gasoline trailing from under his right wing and knew that either the tank had been holed in the combat, or a fuel line was loose.

He led the flight back up to 13,000 feet and intercepted eleven enemy torpedo bombers heading to attack the *Enterprise*. Lt Vejtasa and his wingman each got in position to attack one of the planes. Both Americans scored quickly, sending their quarries down in flames. The enemy formation now scattered and sought the shelter of a large cloud mass. Vejtasa followed a three-plane section, caught them and downed the number two aircraft. He then shot the rudder off the leader's aircraft and set that plane afire and, without pausing he went after the third torpedo bomber which tried to turn away from the action but instead fell to the American's guns.

Lt Vejtasa's next attack failed but he chased the enemy plane down to sea level and saw it crash into a U.S. destroyer. The American warships began a withering screen of anti-aircraft fire, making the situation as hazardous for the U.S. pilots as it was for the Japanese. Circling the area, Vejtasa spotted two more enemy torpedo planes attempting to escape down near the water. One of the American fighters was chasing and shooting at one of the fleeing enemy aircraft. All had flown through the flak. Lt Vejtasa went after the other torpedo plane and used the last of his ammunition on it, chasing it for nearly five miles as it jinked and twisted. Then it burst into flames and sliced into the sea.

The American fighters joined up and returned to *Enterprise* where they had to circle for over an hour until the remaining enemy aircraft ceased their attacks. Swede Vejtasa's score for the one sortie: two Val dive bombers, five Kate torpedo bombers, and one probable torpedo bomber.

One of very few Japanese fliers to experience air action over China, the Indian Ocean and the Pacific is Tetsuzo Iwamoto, whose kill score is over eighty. His diary, discovered after his death, indicates that his actual number of kills was over 200 and showing their origins as United States, United Kingdom, Australia, and New Zealand.

During the Second Sino-Japanese War in 1938, Iwamoto was the highest-scoring naval ace of that conflict, with fourteen aerial victories.

Against the wishes of his parents, Iwamoto took and passed the exam for entry into the Imperial Japanese Navy as an airman 4th Class. He completed pilot training in 1937 and, with the 13th Flying Group, flew his first combat mission on 25 February 1938 over Nanchang, China. The squadron was escorting some Type 96 land-based attack planes when they encountered several enemy aircraft. In the action, Iwamoto claimed four victories. On his return to base, he received a severe reprimand from his commander for his rash attacks.

In an illustrious career, Joseph Jacob Foss, of Sioux Falls, South Dakota, was the highest-scoring U.S. Marine Corps fighter ace of the Second World War, with twenty-six victories. In addition to rising to the rank of Brigadier General in the Air National Guard after the war, Foss served as the twentieth governor of his home state, as commissioner of the American Football League, and as president of the National Rifle Association. In May 1943, Foss received the Medal of Honor from U.S. President Franklin Roosevelt in a White House ceremony.

Joe Foss was twenty-six when he graduated and was commissioned a second lieutenant at NAS Pensacola. The Navy considered him too old to be a fighter pilot and, instead, sent him to photography school. After his repeated requests, however, he was transferred to the Fighter Qualification Program.

With Marine Fighter Squadron VMF-121, Foss and his fellow pilots were sent to Guadalcanal in October 1942. Flying from the escort carrier USS *Copahee*, they were code-named "Cactus" and became known as the "Cactus Air Force", operating from Henderson Field on the island. After a bout of malaria requiring treatment in Australia, Foss returned to Guadalcanal and continued flying combat operations there until February 1943.

The citation to his Medal of Honor awards reads: "For outstanding heroism and courage beyond the call of duty as Executive Officer of a Marine Fighting Squadron, at Guadalcanal, Solomon Islands. Engaging in almost daily combat with the enemy from October 9 to November 19, 1942, Captain Foss personally shot down 23 Japanese aircraft and damaged others so severely that their destruction was extremely probable. In addition, during this period, he successfully led a large number of escort missions, skillfully covering reconnaissance, bombing and photographic planes as well as the surface craft. On January 15, 1943, he added three more enemy aircraft to his already brilliant successes for a record of aerial combat achievement unsurpassed in this war. Boldly searching out an approaching enemy force on January 25, Captain Foss led his eight F4F Marine planes and four Army P-38s into action and, undaunted by tremendously superior numbers, intercepted and struck with such force that four Japanese fighters were shot down and the bombers were turned back without releasing a single bomb. His remarkable flying skill, inspiring leadership and indomitable fighting spirit were distinctive factors in the defense of strategic American positions on Guadalcanal."

KOREA

American and British naval aviators played a major part flying attack missions against infrastructure targets of their North Korean enemy in the "Police Action" fought between June 1950 and June 1953.

As the North Korean troops marched south across the 38th Parallel into South Korea, the Royal Navy carrier HMS *Triumph*, together with the light carrier HMS *Unicorn*, was steaming in a routine cruise from Japan to Hong Kong on 25 June. It was the initial part of *Triumph*'s return voyage to the United Kingdom where its well-worn Seafire and Firefly aircraft were to be retired. That was not to be. The ships were ordered back to Japan where they put under the command of U.S. Navy Admiral C. Turner Joy, United Nations commander in the waters around Korea. From Japan the British warships sailed to join the U.S. 7th Fleet near Okinawa. While *Triumph* was still fully operational, albeit with an air group of tired aircraft, Unicorn had been relegated to repair ship status and had also been set to return to the UK. Instead, *Unicorn* would fill an important role in the replacement of vitally needed aircraft for Royal Navy operations throughout the Korean War, steaming back and forth between Sasebo, Japan and the Royal Navy aircraft maintenance yard in Singapore.

At Okinawa *Triumph* and *Unicorn*, and the American carrier *Valley Forge* and her accompanying warships met up to form the Combined Task Force 77. The air wing aboard *Valley Forge* was a mix of Grumman F9F Panther fighters, Chance Vought F4U Corsair fighters, and Douglas A1 Skyraider attack planes. *Triumph* brought two dozen Seafire and Firefly fighters.

On the way to the Korean peninsula, 3 July, twelve Seafires and nine Fireflies of 800 Squadron flew their first air strike of the conflict, a rocket attack on the North Korean airfield at Kaishu, destroying hangars and other facilities. Aircraft from *Valley Forge* attacked an airfield at Heiju, destroying two enemy Yak-9 fighters on the ground and damaging several buildings. The Yaks were the first enemy aircraft to be destroyed by U.S. Navy jets in the war.

The air operations of the British and American carriers off the Korean coast quickly demonstrated that a serious problem existed in the execution of their joint effort against the North Koreans. Positioning the Task Force well off the peninsula posed no problem for the longer-ranging American fighters and attack planes, but the relatively short- range Seafires and Fireflies of *Triumph* were being stretched beyond the safe limits of their range, forcing the combined fleet to sail in closer to the Korean coast for launching the British aircraft. Rather than endanger the entire Task Force by doing that, it was decided to utilize the Seafires to provide defensive cover over the fleet while the Fireflies provided anti-submarine patrol against the very real threat of the North Korean submarine capability.

By August the British warships were dispatched to operate separately from the Americans near the west coast of Korea, with the Americans responsible for the east coast. Both groups were charged with effectively blockading the enemy ports and destroying enemy shipping. Freed to again operate on the offensive, the Seafires and Fireflies were flying armed reconnaissance missions, inflicting substantial punishment on the enemy port facilities and ships.

By late summer it was clear to the men of the air group aboard *Triumph* that their weary Seafires had suffered excessively through the many heavy landings often in difficult weather conditions. A plague of fuselage skin wrinkling had spread, forcing some of the aircraft to be withdrawn from service and used only as hangar queens providing spare parts for the others. The Fireflies were not fairing much better. Worse still, the supply of replacement fighters aboard HMS *Unicorn* had now dwindled to a handful and no more such types were available in the far east as they had all been previously retired, regarded as no longer being front-line aircraft.

In September the remaining aircraft of *Triumph* struggled to continue their armed reconnaissance sorties in the Wonsan area. They found and attacked supply trains both in the open and in marshalling yards, blasting them with cannon and rockets and causing great damage. But the stresses of these operations continued to take a major toll on the few Fireflies left aboard the carrier, while most of the remaining Seafires had already been grounded with wrinkles and serviceability problems. By 19 September *Triumph* was notifed that it would be relieved by the carrier HMS *Theseus* and a complement of newer Fireflies and Sea Furys. *Triumph* and her air crews had done their job and were ordered back to the UK. As the carrier left Korean waters, Admiral Joy sent a message to the Captain and crew of *Triumph*: "On the departure of HMS *Triumph* from the command of the Naval Forces Far East, I take pleasure in saying to the captain, the officers, the flying personnel and the crew of this splendid fighting ship— WELL DONE. Your enthusiastic and effective efforts have contributed immeasurably to the United Nations cause in Korea."

In the Second World War U.S. Marine Corps pilot John Bolt flew F4U Corsairs against the Japanese in the Pacific campaigns, racking up six Zero kills. In the Korean War of the early 1950s, Bolt would become the Navy Department's only jet ace of the conflict, downing six MiG-15s. "I chose an Air Force exhange tour of duty because at that point the only thing standing up to the MiGs were the F-86s. I knew that none were coming to the Marine Corps, and I was anxious to get back in the air-to-air fight. The only possibility of doing that was by getting in an F-86 squadron.

The MiGs were beating the hell out of everything else, and the F-86s were our sole air superiority plane in Korea from early on. So I managed to get a year's tour with the Air Force, and toward the end of it I managed to get into an F-86 squadron of the Oregon Air National Guard.

"I would grind out the hours in that thing, standing air defense alerts. Those were the days when the threat of nuclear war with Russia hung heavily over our heads. We really thought we were going to get into it. It was late in 1951 or early 1952 and the squadron was part of the Northwest Air Defense Command. Our guys were on standby and would be down in the ready room in flight gear, not sitting in the planes the way they did later. They would be playing bridge and so forth, but I would be up flying, getting hours in that F-86. When my Guard tour was over, I was able to get out to Korea in about May of '52 and flew ninety-four missions in F9F-4 Panthers, interdictions, air-to-ground, and close air support. We were down at K-3, an airfield near Po Hang Do, with VMF-115.

"We were using napalm to attack rice-straw thatched-roof targets. They were all supposed to contain enemy troops but I'm sure most of them were probably innocent civilians. We were attacking the villages with napalm. Then, of course, the proper military targets used thatching for waterproofing too, a supply depot for food or materiel, fuel or ammo. We used lots of napalm against all of those targets.

"My tour in Panthers came to an end and I took some R and R. I looked up an Air Force squadron commander named George Ruddell. I had met him at El Toro in 1947 when he flew an F-80 over to lecture our squadron and gave us a little demonstration of what that airplane could do. I found George at K-13 where he was commanding the 39th Fighter Interceptor Squadron. I told him about my 100 hours in the F-86F, the same type of Sabre his squadron was flying. I had the experience he needed, and he was friendly towards me and let me take a few fam flights with some of his boys.

"On a second R and R trip around Christmas of '52, it happened that Joe McConnell, who was to become the top-scoring US fighter ace of the Korean War with sixteen kills, had just been grounded from operations, and Ruddell very generously sent him over to teach me some tactics. I flew a few fam hops with McConnell and he was good. We became friends and he taught me a lot about his tactics in the F-86. He was very deserving of the fame that he had earned as the leading ace of the war. Tragically, he was killed soon after the war on a test flight at Edwards Air Force Base in California.

"After the second R and R, I put in for another Air Force exchange tour. The Group Personnel Officer said, 'Bolt, I know you've been trying to worm your way into this, going up there on R and R. I'll tell you, you've had a year with the Air Force and you ain't goin' up there. You think you are.

I'm telling you now, it ain't gonna happen.' They felt that I'd had more than my share of gravy assignments, so I got in touch with Ruddell and he got the general up there to send a wire down to the Marine Corps general. They only had two F-86 groups, the 4th and the 51st, and they had two Marines in each. One of them, a guy named Roy Reed, was leaving shortly. This was the opening I needed. The Air Force general's wire read: 'We're willing to have your pilots, but they come up here having never flown the plane, and they present a training burden on our people. But now we have a rare instance of having a pilot who's shown enough initiative to come up here and get checked out, and he's ready to go. Would you mind appointing John Bolt?'

"There was nothing else the Group could do. I was put in Ruddell's squadron and I was flying on McConnell's wing for my first half dozen flights. I was in Dog Flight. Ruddell was a very tough guy, but he was as nice as he could be. He had four or five kills, but the MiGs had stopped coming south of the Yalu River and we weren't allowed to go north of it. The Chinese were yelling about the 'pirates' that were coming over there, but that's where the action was.

"When McConnell left, I took over the command of Dog Flight, a quarter of the squadron with about twelve pilots. We lived in one big Quonset hut.

"Ruddell wasn't getting any MiGs because they weren't coming south of the river. He'd been threatening everybody that he'd kill 'em, cut their heads off if they went north of the river after MiGs. But one night he weakened. He'd had a few drinks and he called me into this little cubbyhole where he had his quarters. During the discussion tears came to his eyes— running down his cheeks—as he was saying how he wanted to be a good Air Force officer, and he loved the Air Force, and if they told him to do something, he'd do it, and if they told him not to do something, he'd not do it. But getting those MiGs meant more to him than his career and life itself. And, since he had been beating up on his own flight about not going across the river, he'd be embarrassed to ask any of them to go across it with him. He didn't know whether they would want to anyway—two or three members of Dog Flight didn't like to do it. (They would have been in big trouble if they'd been identified as going up there, I don't know if the ones they picked up later on, who were shot down north of the river, were ever disciplined when the war was over. But at the time, the threat was believed and hanging very heavily over us.) Ruddell said: 'Would you give me some of your flight? I want to go across the river. I've gotta have some action.' Ruddell's boys had been several days with no action. I said, 'Sure, I'd be delighted', so we planned one for the next day.

"I was to fly his second section. On a river crossing flight, we would take off and go full bore. We'd fly those planes at 100 percent power setting until we got out of combat. Engine life was planned for 800 hours and we were getting about 550 or so. Turbine blade cracks were developing. We were running the engines at maximum temperature. You could put these little constrictors in the tailpipe—we called them 'rats'—and you could 'rat 'em up' until they ran at maximum temperature. They were real hot rods. You'd run your drop tanks dry just about the time you got up to the river, and if you didn't have a contact, you weren't supposed to drop your tanks. We skinned 'em every time anyway. On at least four occasions, by the end of the flight I had been to over 50,000 feet. When it was empty and I still hadn't pulled the power back from 100 percent, the airplane would really get up there. The MiG-15 could get right up there too.

"On the flight with Ruddell we got up there and dropped our tanks. At least the pilots going across the river dropped them. There were big clouds up as we crossed the river. It was early morning and we heard on the radio that there was a fight going on. There were some MiGs flying this day. We came from the sunny side of the clouds to the back side of a big cumulous; there were some black puffs of flak and there were some planes down there. We were half blind from the diminished illumination on the back side of the cloud. It was a confusing situation. We dove down and there was a MiG. Ruddell got it in sight and we dropped from 43,000 feet down to about 15,000, just dropped straight down. He got into shooting position behind the MiG but didn't shoot . . . didn't shoot. I tore past him and blew up the MiG. I had experience at jumping planes and one of the things you did when you came down from extreme altitude (MiGs were frequently found down low when north of the river) was put your armor-glass defrost on full bore. It would get so hot it was almost painful, but it kept the front windscreen clear. You also tested your guns and your g-suit. Ruddell's windscreen had fogged over. He was sitting there in a kill position and couldn't see properly to shoot. So I went by him and got the MiG. Of course the squadron was abuzz that the Colonel had started crossing the river and gotten aced out of his first kill up there. I was a 'MiG killer'. I'd gotten three of four. When I got back, they had all these signs pasted up all over the Dog Flight Quonset hut. One read: MARINE WETBACK STEALS COLONEL'S MIG!

"The 'kill rules' were, if you got seven hits on an enemy aircraft, you would be given a kill. The MiGs didn't torch off at high altitude; they simply would not burn because of the air density. So, incendiary hits would be counted (we had good gun cameras) and if you got seven hits in the enemy's fuselage, the odds were it was dead, and they'd give you a kill. We knew that every third round was an incendiary so, in effect, if you got three incendiary hits showing on the gun camera film, it was considered a dead MiG.

"My first kill was at about 43,000 feet. I had missed a couple of kills before it by not being aggressive or determined enough. I was almost desperate for a MiG kill. I was leader of my flight and I'd screwed up a couple of bounces. My self-esteem and my esteem in the flight was low, and I decided that the next MiG I saw was a dead man and I didn't care where he was.

"The next MiG was part of a gaggle; MiGs as far as you could see. I made a good run on one of them and pulled into firing position, but other MiGs were shooting at me and my wingman, and they were very close.

I got some hits on my MiG and he went into a scissor, which was a good tactic. I think the F-86 may have had a better roll rate. I was trying to shoot as he passed through my firing angle. Each time I fired I delayed my turn, so he was gaining on me and drifting back. He almost got behind me and was so close that his plane blanked out the camera frame. I think he realized that I would have crashed into him and he pulled up (he was probably dead at this point). That scissor was the right thing to do; he just shouldn't have broken off. He was getting back to a position where he could have taken the advantage.

"The salvation of the F-86 was that it had good transsonic controls; the MiG's controls were subsonic. In the Sabre, you could readily cruise at about .84 Mach. The MiG had to go into its uncontrollable range to attack you, and its stick forces were unmanageable. As I recall, the kill ratio between the

F-86 and the MiG was eight to one. This was due almost entirely to the flying tail of the Sabre, although it had other superior features. The gun package of the MiG was intended for shooting down bombers like the B-29 and B-50. It carried a 37mm and two 23mm cannons, which was overkill against fighters. Although the F-86 used essentially the same machine guns as a World War II fighter, the rate of fire had been doubled, and it was a very good package against other fighters.

"Down low, where we were out of the transsonic superiority range, we wore a g-suit and they didn't. You can fight defensively when you are blacked out, but you can't fight offensively. If you had enough speed to pull a good 6g turn, you would go 'black' in 20 to 30 degrees of the turn. The MiG pilot couldn't follow you because he was blacked out too. You are still conscious, though you have three to five seconds of vision loss. When you had gone about as far in the turn as you thought you could carry it, you could pop the stick forward and your vision would immediately return. You had already started your roll, and the MiG was right there in front of you, every time, because, not having a g-suit, he had eased off in the turn. His g-tolerance was only half of yours. So he was right there and most probably would overshoot you."

YANKEE STATION

Yankee Station was a point in the Gulf of Tonkin off the coast of Vietnam, where the U.S. aircraft carriers of Task Force 77 operated to launch their air strikes during the Vietnam War. The carriers there were said to be "on the line."

For nearly two decades, from November 1, 1955 until the Fall of Saigon on April 30, 1975, the southeast Asian conflict known as the Vietnam War raged in Vietnam, Laos and Cambodia. The warring parties were North Vietnam, aided by Communist allies, against the government of South Vietnam, which had the support of the United States and other anti-Communist forces. The army of the north was known as the Vietnam People's Army, a seemingly limitless supply of troops engaged in a guerrilla war with the U.S. and South Vietnamese who relied heavily on air superiority, air strikes, and ground search and destroy operations.

The Americans were there trying to prevent a takeover of South Vietnam in a strategy to contain Communism in Asia. From the perspective of the North Vietnamese, the conflict was the extension of a colonial war they had been fighting against France. The North Vietnamese saw the government to the south as no more than a U.S. puppet state. American involvement in the war began in the early 1950s with the arrival of the first U.S. military advisors, followed by more troops whose numbers rapidly escalated through the 1960s. Actual U.S. combat units entered the fray officially in 1965. A heavy campaign of American bombing in Laos and Cambodia as well as Vietnam reached a peak in 1968 and a gradual withdrawl of U.S. ground forces followed. Peace talks were held in Paris and all the warring parties signed a peace treaty in January 1973. The American military involvement finally ended in August of that year, but fighting continued between the north and the south until April 1975, when the north captured the South Vietnamese capitol, Saigon. In 1976, the two Vietnams were reunited. 58,220 American personnel died in the war.

Rear Admiral Paul Gillcrist, U.S. Navy (Retired) was Commander Gillcrist in spring 1968. He was flying an F-8 Crusader from the carrier USS *Bon Homme Richard* (CVA-31) in VF-53. "How could I ever forget him? He did a very courageous thing . . . putting himself in great jeopardy . . . and for me . . . and he did it with such casual grace that contemplating it all these years later, still makes my throat constrict."

Gillcrist remembers it as a rather pleasant spring day, with sunny skies, a balmy breeze, a deep blue sea and a cloudless blue heaven. What more could a carrier pilot ask? "Then, of course, there were those god-damned sea snakes." As he walked forward on the flight deck towards his airplane, he looked over the starboard catwalk at the surface of the Tonkin Gulf and it nearly made him ill. As far he could see, it was alive with hundreds of thousands of sea snakes, sinuating through the water in clusters of a dozen or so. They ranged in size from about two feet to five feet and were of a yellowish-green color. They swam just below the surface with only their heads sticking out. The intelligence officer had briefed the pilots on them before they had arrived in the Gulf and told them they were the most poisonous of all reptiles on the planet. The thought of parachuting into the water filled with those hideous things made Gillcrist's stomach churn.

His flight headed inbound to a highly-defended target in the Hanoi area of North Vietnam. The mission was photographic reconnaissance to assess the damage that had been done by an air strike just thirty minutes earlier. As the target was so well defended, Gillchrist had decided to go in as photo escort, armed with four Sidewinder air-to-air missiles mounted on pylons on either side of the airplane's fuselage just aft of the cockpit. His concern was aircraft weight. The squadron's tired old F-8E Crusaders had grown in weight over the years, from structural beef-ups, to the addition of electronic counter-measures devices. The weight had become a problem, as each additional pound of gear meant one pound less of fuel which the pilots needed to get back aboard the ship.

"At first, it didn't seem to matter much . . . nothing more than a minor operational restriction with which we had to abide." But gradually, as the airplane's empty weight increased, the pilots started to realize that their number of landing opportunities was decreasing by one for every 200 pounds increase in empty weight. At night a landing used up three times as much fuel as in daytime, so, for every 600 pounds increase in the empty weight of the plane, one less night landing attempt was imposed.

In 1974, Gillcrist had done a study at the Pentagon for his own enlightenment. Using the A-4 Skyhawk, the F-8 Crusader, the F-4 Phantom, and the A-7 Corsair II as examples, he found that, on average, a Navy tactical carrier airplane grew in empty weight at the rate of one pound per day of operational life. The accuracy of that rule of thumb was startling. "So it was with careful consideration that I opted for the four-missile configuration."

Per standard operating procedure, the photo pilot, flying an RF-8, took the flight lead. Gillcrist was his escort and his protection, should the North Vietnamese elect to send out their MiGs after him. The Navy pair coasted in about twenty miles south of Haiphong at a high rate of speed. He found that, due to the drag created by the heavy load of missiles, he was using a lot more afterburner than the photo airplane.

The target was a railroad bridge between Haiphong and the capitol city of Hanoi. The amount of flak in the target area was considerable. "They were waiting for us, knowing that it was U.S. policy to get bomb-damage assessment after each major raid." Gillcrist was flying a loose wing on the photo plane, scanning the area for MiG fighters. He watched, too, for flak, as he knew that Ed, the photo plane pilot, would soon have to bury his head in his photo display shroud for the final few seconds of the filming run to be certain that the bridge span was properly framed in the camera's field of view. Both he and Gillcrist hated the possibility of messing up the photo run and having to come back another time to repeat it. During the picture-taking part of the run, when Ed was too occupied to observe flak, Gillcrist made it a habit to be in a strafing run at the most likely source of flak in the vicinity of the target. He preferred that to the always unpleasant and unnerving experience of just sitting there and being shot at.

As Ed settled in for the photo run, an eternity of about five seconds, Gillcrist heard a low SAM (surface-to-air missile) warble, the signal of a radar lock-on, followed immediately by a high warble as the SAM was launched. "My heartbeat tripled in an instant. I was on Ed's left flank and saw the SAM lift off at about the four o'clock position and only ten miles away. There was a huge dust cloud around the base of the missile as it rose. It levelled almost immediately as it accelerated towards us. There was nothing I could do but call it out, knowing that Ed would have to break off his run at the very last second. My mouth was dry as I keyed the microphone. 'One from Two. SAM lift-off at four o'clock, ten miles. Break hard right— now!' "

Both pilots broke hard right and felt the instant onset of at least nine g's squeezing the g-suit bladders on their legs and abdomens. The SAM roared by just as another high warble came through Gillcrist's headset. He couldn't see this missile and that worried him. 'No joy on the second one,' he shouted into the mike. Then he saw it, coming fast off his left wing. 'Reverse it left and down,' he yelled over the radio. As he watched, the missile tore past to the left and exploded about 200 yards out. Now both Crusaders were skimming the treetops and he called Ed, "Two. Let's get out of here." Ed responded with two clicks of his mike button. They headed toward the sea a few miles away. The two planes thundered across the beach in full afterburner at 600 knots and 100 feet.

Roughly ten miles out to sea, and well out of range of the SAMs and flak, the pilots came out of afterburner and started climbing. Ed called, apologetically, to say he had missed the photo run and they both felt exceedingly low about it. Gillcrist suggested that they report in to the carrier's strike operations center to ask what they should do, though he was sure he knew what the answer would be. They orbited at 15,000 feet over the Gulf while Ed checked with the Op center. They were told to wait while the center checked with Task Force 77 for further instructions. As Gillcrist expect-

ed, they were told to go back to the target and try again. He asked Ed
to request that an airborne tanker be made available to them for their
return to the ship.

When the pair reached the target area for the second time, the North
Vietnamese were waiting for them. The two pilots approached from a different direction this time. They got the photos, overflying the bridge in excess
of 600 knots, and turned toward the Gulf on a pre-planned heading west of
Haiphong and then nearly due east over a mostly unpopulated area. As
they had approached the target, Gillcrist was shocked when his low-fuel
warning light illuminated. They continued their egress at low level and
high speed.

Gillcrist was elated at having successfully completed the photo run and
avoiding any further missiles and flak. Ed had plenty of fuel remaining and
began his climb at full power, to get the urgently needed photos back to
the ship. Gillcrist's fuel gauge now read 400 pounds, which meant that his
engine would flame out in about fifteen minutes. He would be cutting it
very close. He headed for the rendezvous with the aerial tanker plane,
which was at 10,000 feet some twenty miles southwest of the northern
search-and-rescue destroyer on station. He was extremely happy to see the
A-4 tanker plane, but was disheartened when the tanker pilot said that he
had just given away all the fuel in his buddy tank to some other needy
pilots. Gillcrist was incredulous. How could this have happened?
Someone back at the carrier must have screwed up and failed to tell the
tanker pilot to hold back at least 1,500 pounds for him. He knew he would
not get even half way back to the ship on his 400 pounds.

The standard operating procedure for carrier pilots is to arrive back at
the ship with a reasonable fuel reserve to cope with any emergencies such
as a crash on deck, bad weather, malfunctioning recovery systems, or a
recovery delay of any sort. The low-fuel warning light in a Crusader cockpit comes on when the fuel state is down to 1,100 pounds. No carrier pilot
who wants a long, safe career should ever be caught airborne with that
light illuminated. To be 125 nautical miles from the ship with but 400
pounds of fuel is not just critical, it is way past critical.

Paul Gillcrist knew he was not going to make it back to the ship. Again,
he thought of those sea snakes. The planes levelled off at 20,000 feet, his
fuel gauge registering just 100 pounds. He began preparing himself to
eject. He was throttled back for maximum endurance, for what that was
worth.

The A-4 tanker pilot throttled back to hold position with the Crusader.
Every minute now seemed precious to Gillcrist. No more than fifty feet
away, the tanker pilot's head turned and he stared at Gillcrist for perhaps
twenty seconds. Then he looked down in the cockpit. Gillcrist saw the propeller on the nose of the tanker's buddy store begin to windmill in the

airstream. This was the driving mechanism that reeled the refuelling basket in and out.

The buddy store consisted of a fuel tank, a refuelling hose, a take-up reel and an air-driven propeller to deploy and retract the basket. The fuel tank contained 300 gallons (2,000 pounds) of fuel, when full. The tanker pilot also had the capability of transferring fuel into and out of the tank from his own internal tanks. It was the tanker pilot's responsibility to always retain enough internal fuel to get back to the ship safely. Gillcrist was amazed to see the refuelling basket reel out to its full extension. The tanker pilot looked at him and transmitted over the radio: "Firefighter Two Zero Four, I have just transferred 500 pounds of fuel into the buddy store. Go get it." "What about you?" Gillcrist asked. "You'd better take it while you can," warned the tanker pilot ominously, as though he were already having second thoughts. Gillcrist slid into position and prepared to tank.

His last glance at the gauge had shown 100 pounds. He resolved not to look at it again. The inner rim of the refuelling basket, when the Crusader's probe is centered in it, is only about a foot from the cockpit canopy. The basket seems to float around like some wayward feathery entity whenever one tries to engage it with the probe. In fact, the basket, for all its movements, is in the tight grasp of a 250 knot gale. The airstream grips it like a vice. Thus, it has all the resilience of a steel rail. If it so much as touched the canopy of the Crusader, the result would be an instant, violent implosion and fragmentation of the plexiglass into thousands of tiny shards that would end up everywhere in the cockpit. Tanking is a sensitive procedure.

"Needless to say, my tanking technique on this occasion was flawless. The tip of the probe hit the basket in its dead center with a firm clunk, a comforting sound and sensation which one can feel in his pants and right hand."

The very act of tanking, of course, uses fuel. It took Gillcrist about 100 pounds to get the 500 pounds, for a net gain of 400. But his fuel gauge now read a much more comfortable 500 pounds. He disengaged and slid out to the right side of the tanker. He looked over at the tanker pilot and asked, "Can you make it back?" After a delay the answer came, "I'm not sure. But there's another tanker up here somewhere. Maybe he's got a few pounds to give." The tanker pilot then checked with the carrier and learned that the other air tanker was indeed returning at maximum speed to rendezvous with them. Gillcrist suspected that personnel aboard the carrier knew they had really screwed up and were doing their utmost to make up for it.

Gillcrist and his tanker friend droned along at maximum endurance speed, watching their fuel gauges and the distance measuring device. Gillcrist did the math and calculated that, at their present airspeed each mile he flew was costing him about six pounds of fuel. No matter how many times he ran the numbers in his head, the result was always the same. He was going to run out of fuel before reaching the ship.

Then a target crept onto the left side of his radar scope, thirty miles out and converging. Soon the tanker pilot called "Tally ho, the tanker. Ten o'clock. Fifteen miles." The moments it took for them to complete the rendezvous seemed like forever. They were told that the newly arrived tanker had 1,400 pounds of fuel to give away. The tanker pilot told Gillcrist to go first and to take 800 pounds; he would take the other 600.

The *Bon Homme Richard* gave them priority landing clearance. They made a straight-in approach with the tanker pilot about ten miles astern of the Crusader. Gillcrist recalled that the sight of the carrier steaming into the wind with a ready deck was among the most beautiful things he had ever seen. Both planes caught the number two wire and each taxied forward for shutdown. The blast of warm air that filled the cockpit when Gillcrist opened his canopy tasted like pure oxygen. He took one last look at the fuel quantity gauge. It read 100 pounds.

Five minutes later, in the squadron ready room, Gillcrist pressed the lever on the squawkbox, "Ready room four, this is ready room two, Commander Gillcrist calling. Is the pilot of Four One Four there?" "He's listening," said a voice. "Young man," said Gillcrist, "you have cojones of brass. I owe you one." The tanker pilot replied, "No problem, Skipper, glad to be of help. It's always a pleasure to pass gas to a fighter pilot. I'll collect at the bar in Cubi."

Commander Gillcrist never got to pay off the debt. Three days later, the tanker pilot was blown out of the sky by a direct hit from an 85mm anti-aircraft shell.

FALKLANDS

Leopoldo Fortunato Galtieri Castelli was Lieutenant General and commander-in-chief of the Argentine Army as well as the de facto President of Argentina in April 1982. In a move to quell the growing anti-government demonstrations and calls for reform by his many critics, Galtieri decided to exploit the traditional patriotism and nationalism of his people. Relying, as he had throughout his military career, on the use of force where territorial disputes were concerned, on April 2nd he ordered his troops to retake the self-governing British overseas territory known as the Falkland Islands archipelago (the Malvinas Islands to the Argentines), located some 250 nautical miles east of the South American coast. The general believed that the action would spark his people to unite behind their government. It was a huge gamble, but he felt that the British were not very interested in the islands and were unlikely to respond to his move. His marines arrived first to occupy Port Stanley and its airport. Thousands of Argentine soldiers soon followed and, virtually overnight, Galtieri was seen as a new national hero in Buenos Aires.

General Galtieri came from a working-class background, a family of poor Italian imigrants. When he was seventeen he was able to enroll in the Argentine National Military Academy where he studied civil engineering. He later became an officer in the engineering branch of the army and, when he had accumulated twenty-five years as a combat engineer, he was made commander of the Army Engineering Corps. By 1976 he had attained the rank of major general and by 1980 he had risen to lieutenant general and commander-in-chief of the army.

In 1976 a military junta which Galtieri enthusiastically supported, had staged a coup, taking power in Argentina and, in December 1981, his own power and influence enabled him to oust his rival generals in the junta. His next target was the country's president, Roberto Viola, whom he removed and succeeded in office.

Galtieri vigorously pursued communists and all those he perceived as possible communists in Argentina, dealing brutally with the people he saw as left-wing subversives in the society. When he visited Washington in March 1981 he was greeted warmly by the Reagan administration whose perception of the general's regime was that of a strong barrier to the spread of communism in South America.

With the Argentine economy in deep recession and considerable unrest among the population, Galtieri tightened monetary policy, froze salaries and enacted procedures that led to a greater unpopularity of his government. To slightly alleviate the pain of recession, he brought in limited political reforms allowing a mild expression of dissent, after which anti-government demonstrations grew and with them demands for a return to democracy. And by the early spring of 1982, it was clear to the general that he had to do something to harness the ingrained patriotism of the people and defuse the demands for reform.

With the April annexation of the Falklands by Galtieri's forces, the anti-government demonstrations in Argentina were quickly overwhelmed by pro-Galtieri patriotic ones. The general expected no military response from the United Kingdom, but should it come he felt certain that the warm welcome he had received in Washington the previous year would translate into no interference by the Reagan administration, or the U.S. Central Intelligence Agency, if such a conflict with Britain were to arise.

Following the Argentine move on the Falklands, the United Kingdom, under Prime Minister Margaret Thatcher tried diplomatic pressure and negotiations, to no avail, and Mrs Thatcher then determined to retake the Falklands, ordering the deployment of a naval task force to the south Atlantic. In both numbers and geography the Argentines held the advantage, but the British were convinced that their superior technology, equipment and training would result in a relatively quick victory. In aircraft alone, the British position seemed difficult to say the least, armed as they were with a relative handful of Sea Harriers and going up against roughly 200 Mirages, Skyhawks and Etendards.

After attending Britannia Royal Naval College, Dartmouth, in the 1960s, Nigel Ward went on to fly Hawker Hunters, de Havilland Sea Vixens and McDonnell-Douglas Phantoms, in addition to his work as a qualified Air Warfare Instructor. In the Royal Navy aircraft carrier HMS *Invincible*, he was made commander of 801 Squadron in 1981 and it was then he was assigned to determine the maximum capability of the British Aerospace Sea Harrier, or SHAR, as all who were associated with the plane referred to it. It was Ward's responsibility to prove the aeroplane, its weapons and radar systems under operational conditions. In *Sea Harrier Over The Falklands*, "Sharkey" Ward described his perspective on that 1982 campaign.

"The 801 Squadron recommendations for high-level bombing against Port Stanley airfield had been accepted somewhat reluctantly by the Flag. This reluctance was not really surprising, bearing in mind that the attack relied completely on the capabilities of the [Blue Fox] radar and the Navhars [Sea Harrier Navigation Heading Attitude Reference System] for its success—bearing in mind, too, what the Flag thought of such things.

"In reply to our recommendations and after due deliberation, SAVO [Staff Aviation Officer: a member of an admiral's staff specially appointed to advise the admiral on all operational and training aviation matters] put forward several fully anticipated questions: how were the pilots going to ensure that they missed the town with their bombs? Would the line of attack take them over the town? And so on. Finally, realizing that my team had no intention whatsoever of risking the lives of the Falkland Island community, and after having been briefed in detail about the profile to be flown by attacking aircraft, the Staff agreed to the proposal. But 801, having generated and recommended the new delivery, were not the first to be tasked with trying it out. That didn't matter very much to me. The main thing was that now we could do our bit to keep the enemy awake and on the alert; the less rest the Argentines ashore got before our amphibious troops landed, the better.

"To that end—denying the enemy some sleep—we decided in *Invincible* to set up a mission that would give the opposition more than a little to think about in the middle of the night. There were two major detachments and airstrips away from Stanley. On East Falkland there was Goose Green, close to the settlement of Darwin. On West Falkland there was Fox Bay. With the Task Group well to the east, the distance to Fox Bay was about 225 nautical miles as the crow flies. The plan was very simple. I was to get airborne on my own in the small hours of the night and deliver a Lepus flare [a six-million candlepower flare, dropped or tossed from fast jets to illuminate targets for reconnaissance or night-attack purposes] attack against each defended airstrip. It was hoped that this would give the troops on the ground the false impression that a Task Force landing was under way—the flares apparently providing illumination prior to an assault.

"The mission was very straight forward. All I needed to do was enter the attack co-ordinates for each target into my navigation computer, follow the resultant HUD [Head-Up Display] directions to the target areas, check the accuracy of the navigation using my radar, and drop the flares. Outbound to the targets I would fly direct to Goose Green from the climb-out point which would take me close to Stanley. On the return leg I would approach the carrier group from 240°, that is, well clear of the islands, let down to low level and then run in to Invincible for recovery on board.

"JJ [Captain J.J. Black, skipper of *Invincible*] was pleased with the idea of the planned mission: 'Anything we have missed, Sharkey?' You know that the weather isn't too brilliant out there? The weather around the Task Group was certainly not very sharp, with high winds, towering cumulonimbus and snow showers. But over the islands the forecast was for much fairer conditions. The mission would therefore present no problems and it hurt my pride even to think that I might have a problem getting back on board. I shut my mind to snow showers and thought only of dropping the flares.

" 'No, thank you, sir. I'm very happy with all that. Can we just make sure that the Flag lets all our surface units know what's going on? One lone aircraft approaching the force at night from the south-west is just asking for a 'blue on blue'. ('Blue on blue' means own forces shooting down own aircraft.)

" 'Don't worry, we'll ensure that they let all units know.'

"There was practically no self-briefing required for the mission. It was a question of kicking the tyres, lighting the fires and getting airborne.

"I arrested my rate of climb after launch at 500 feet, settled the aircraft down to a height of 200 feet above the waves, set 420 knots and departed the ship on a north-westerly heading for 70 miles. As my eyes became fully attuned to the darkness the sea surface became visible, with the healthy wind kicking up a lot of spray and phosphorescence and clouds towering around and ahead of me like huge cliffs. Inside the cockpit I had dimmed the lighting almost to exinction, including the geometrical patterns on the HUD. Arming missiles and guns, just in case, I reached the climb-out point and headed for the stars, turning to port as I did so to get on track for the first destination.

"The aircraft climbed at a cool 30° nose up for the first 15,000 feet and very quickly I was throttling back at Mach 0.85 and 35,000 feet, enjoying the view. Under the black star-speckled sky and towards East Falkland, the cloud thinned and dissipated. Although it was the middle of the night, Stanley was well-lit and could easily be seen from the top of the climb.

"Dick Goodenough [801 Squadron Air Engineer Officer] had given me the jet with the most sought-after radar and Navhars—004. The engineers kept full records of the performance, accuracy and reliability of each radar and Navhars system. This attention to detail, which included comprehensive post- flight briefs, paid excellent dividends. But although all the aircraft performed well, 004 seemed to be the pick of the bunch. The avionics were functioning perfectly. Before passing just to the south of Stanley, I checked the navigation system accuracy with my radar and, until commencing descent for Goose Green, used the radar in its air-to-air mode to check the skies to the west for enemy fighters. There were none, nor did I expect any. I was enjoying being alone and thought of my lads back at home—they would have given anything to have been on this flight.

"I chose to run in to Goose Green up Choiseul Sound and had an excellent surface radar picture to confirm the accuracy of my desired flare-drop position. Having checked the Lepus selector switches and pylon, I monitored the Navhars readout, which was telling me time-to-go to release, and the HUD, which was guiding me unerringly to the target. Pickling the bomb button, I felt the flare body leave the aircraft, applied power and commenced the second climb of the night to high level.

"After about twenty seconds I rolled the Sea jet inverted in order to see the flare ignite. Goose Green lies on a narrow isthmus of land which separates Choiseul Sound from Grantham Sound. When the flare went off it seemed to be in the right place—right on target. Now for Fox Bay.

"The second target was well-covered in thick cloud, but that made no difference to the attack profile. My radar confirmed what the Navhars was telling me and I had no doubt at all when I pickled the bomb-release button that the Lepus was again bang on target. It was as easy as riding a bike. Having seen the glow from the flare through the cloud, I turned to the east in the climb and set off on the long dog-leg home.

"At 140 miles to go to the deck, I was suddenly illuminated with fire-control radar from a ship below. The relative silence of the cockpit was shattered by the radar warning receiver alarm. I had detected a vessel on radar earlier and had presumed it was on detachment from the Task Group.

Thoughts of the Argentine Navy firing Sea Dart at me flashed through my mind. I broke hard to starboard and descended to the south-west away from the contact which was only 20 miles to the north. But I was still locked-up by the fire-control radar, and having taken initial avoiding action I started to analyze the threat. It certainly wasn't Sea Dart—the noise in my earphones didn't have the right characteristics—and so I was pretty safe now, 30 miles south. I turned port onto east, arresting my descent as I did so, and climbed back up to 30,000 feet. I would circum-navigate the ship that had shown such an unhealthy interest in me. At the same time I would interrogate it on radio. I found the culprit on the pre-briefed Task Group surface/air frequency. 'Warship illuminating lone Sea Harrier, come in.'

"The warship had obviously not been briefed on the SHAR mission and was unwilling to believe I was who I said I was. Being now a little short of fuel after three and a half climbs to high level, I left my personal signature encoded in terms of four-letter words and bid them goodnight. If
I had been on a slightly different track and hadn't had my radar informa-tion to tell me where to evade to, I could have been engaged by my own forces. So much for the promise to pass information to all ships.

"By the time I began my final descent towards the carrier group I was back amongst the clouds. They were massive and very turbulent. After I had descended to low level and was running in to the expected position of the ship via the safety lane, I called, '004 on the way in. Estimating 280° 25 miles. Over.'

"Tony [Direction Officer in *Invincible*] was immediately on the air.

" 'Roger, 004. Read you loud and clear. I have no contact on you, repeat no contact. Clutter from snow clouds too intense.' He was concerned. Good old Tony; there's a man you can really trust. He'd do anything to get his pilots down safely.

" 'Roger. I'll conduct my own approach and call out my ranges to go.' I was feeling confident thanks to two important facts. Firstly, when Invincible gave a ship's estimated position for the recovery of aircraft, you could bet your pension on her being in that position when you returned from your flight; especially in bad weather. So I was very sure in my mind that I could find the deck using my Navhars information. The second fact was that I had practised self-homing to the deck on many occasions, and we had also carried out the trials on the software for self-homing when ashore in the Trials Unit. It was no higher workload for the pilot than following instructions from the ship's precision approach controller.

"On my radar screen, the *Invincible* 'position destinations marker' that I had selected on my nav computer sat less than 2 miles from one of the ship contacts in view. I had already programmed the 'marker' with the ship's pre-briefed recovery course and speed and was happy to see it was holding good information on the contact nearest to it. That had got to be *Invincible*—I hadn't enough fuel left to make mistakes. There was enough for one approach only.

"It was a simple matter to update the radar 'marker's' position by fixing the radar onto the contact. The 'Self-Controlled Approach' programme in the Navhars computer software was provided so that the pilots could safely carry out their own precision approach to a chosen destination. My chosen destination was the ship, and as I lined up 5 miles astern of what I thought was Invincible, I selected the precision approach mode on the HUD. I also locked the radar onto the ship to keep the 'destination' information as accurate as possible. Now I was all prepared for recovery to the ship.

" 'Five miles on the approach', I called.

" 'Roger. Still no contact.' Tony must be sweating buckets down there.

"I was at 800 feet and the world outside was black. Approaching 3 miles I prepared to commence descent. The radar was firmly locked on to the contact ahead.

" 'Three miles.'

" 'Still no contact.'

"Was I on the right ship? I began to wonder as I started down the slope. My jet was being tossed around a bit by turbulence from heavy clouds, which would certainly account for the clutter Tony had mentioned. There was no other course but to wait and see. I cleared the doubts from my mind.

" 'Have you now at 1 ? miles. On the glide slope.' Tony sounded relieved. I was relieved.

"Tony continued with his calls all the way to half-a-mile. He had passed the wind over the deck as 40 knots gusting to 50. It felt like it in the cockpit, too. The buffeting increased as I got lower.

" 'Half-a-mile.' My head-up information said the same. I delayed selecting hover stop for a few seconds because of the strong head-wind, then nozzles down, power going on. At a quarter of a mile I called 'Lights'. And there, behind the radar cross in the HUD, appeared the ship's island. As usual the cross was just about on Flyco. Radar off and concentrate on controlling the jet. As I was moving sideways over the deck from alongside, the wind backed through 30°. I ruddered the nose into it before setting onto the deck with an uncharacteristic thud.

" 'That's my excitement over for the night', I thought. It was 0400 hours, and a long day lay ahead . . .

"By the time June arrived we had grown well-used to operating in the unpredictable South Atlantic weather, and to our routine air transits to and from the islands for CAP [Combat Air Patrol]. Combat opportunities against the Argentine Air Force and Navy pilots were becoming less and less frequent. But there was never a moment to relax vigilance on CAP because the enemy had not given up. On the contrary, they still held all the strategic points on the islands, and although Jeremy Moore's [Land Forces Deputy] men had landed they were not yet in a position to displace the occupation forces.

"Intelligence gleaned from various sources indicated that Port Stanley was still being supplied by air on a nightly basis by AAF Hercules aircraft, and the same aircraft were making regular use of the landing strip at Fox Bay to support their logistic re-supply efforts. Without a radar look-down-over-land capability, there was little we could do to intercept these night re-supply flights, especially with the Task Group positioned between 200 and 230 nautical miles to the east of San Carlos Water. The majority of the Sea Harrier effort by day continued to be spent on maintaining CAP stations around the beach-head and, at that range from the carriers, our on-task time had come down to about 25 minutes over the Sound (and that was pushing it). It was, nevertheless, effort well spent, and the SHAR's continuous presence to the west of the Amphibious Operating Area continued to deter and disrupt enemy air attacks.

"On 1 June my section had launched after daybreak and we had carried out our CAP duty over Falkland Sound without any sign of trade. Everything appeared quiet in the skies to the east as our two jets commenced the climb-out to the north of San Carlos en route to the ship. Our home transit would be at 35,000 feet and, on the climb, Steve [Thomas] kept his Sea Jet in neat battle formation on my starboard beam.

"HMS *Minerva* was the Local Area Control Ship and we had not yet switched from her control frequency. The craggy north coast of East Falkland Island was well below us when my headphones crackled as *Minerva* called us up.

" 'I just had a 'pop-up' contact to the north-west of you at 40 miles. Only had three sweeps on the contact and it has now disappeared. Do you wish to investigate? Over.' I could tell from the controller's voice that he really felt he had something but didn't want us to waste our time if he was wrong. After all, 40 nautical miles was a long way in the wrong direction when our aircraft could be running low on fuel.

"He needn't have worried; neither I nor Steve would dream of turning down the slimmest chance of engaging the enemy. Before he had finished his call I had already started a hard turn to port with Steve following in my wake. I was flying aircraft side number 006 and its radar was on top line.

"In the turn and using the radar hand-controller thumb-wheel, I wound the radar antenna down to just below the horizon, and as we steadied on a north-westerly heading, there was the target. The green radar blip stood out as bold as brass in the centre of my screen at just less than 40 miles.

"Judy! Contact at 38 miles. Investigating.' This was a chance we couldn't miss.

"I decided to try to lock the radar to the target to get some accurate height information on it. The radar locked easily, telling me as it did so that the target had to be a large one at that range, and gave me what I wanted to know, a height difference of 4,000 feet. I was at 12,000; that made the target at 8,000. I broke the lock so as not to alert the target (he would be listening out on his radar warning receiver) and wound our speed up to 500 knots in a shallow descent. Target range decreased rapidly to 34 miles, 30 miles—then it seemed to hold. There was only one possible reason for that.

"Steve, I think he's turning away. He's now at right 10° at 28 miles. 4,000 below.'

" 'Roger. Contact.' Good! Steve also had contact.

"I locked the radar again. Still about 4,000 feet below, but we had already come down to 10,000 feet in descent.

" 'He's definitely turned away and he's descending. Must have seen us.' The short control radars of the Argentine forces must have monitored the start of our intercept and then passed the information to the target.

"It was now a race against time and fuel. Invincible was over 200 miles away and we should have been heading home. But there was an easy alternative. I called *Minerva* on the radio.

" 'We may be too short of fuel to get back to Mother after this. Can you ask the assault ships to prepare to take us on board in San Carlos?'

"A short pause before *Minerva* came back. 'We have decks ready to take you if you need it.'

" 'Roger. Please check that weapons will be 'tight' in the missile zone if we pay you a visit.' I knew it wasn't necessary to remind *Minerva* of that, but it was better to be safe than sorry.

" 'Roger. No problem.' The ship-borne controller then settled down to monitor the chase—if we destroyed the target it would all be as a result of his sharp radar pick-up and concentration.

"Having sorted the fuel problem out in my mind, I could give my full attention to tracking the target, which was now heading west and had descended to low level below the cloud. We were still cracking along above the cloud in brilliant sunshine. I checked my missile and gun switches; safety flaps were up and everything was live and ready to go.

"The sea state was markedly rough and as we continued to close the fleeting target from above, I wished that the Flag and his Staff could have been in the cockpit with me to witness the radar's performance in these look-down conditions. The radar was holding contact with the target on every sweep.

"We were now approaching the cloud-tops at 6,000 feet and catching the fleeing aircraft fast. To stand any chance at all of survival, the slower target ahead would need to stay in the cloud layer and try to evade us with hard manoeuvring. But there was little chance of that being successful either, since I had had a lot of practice against large evading targets in cloud by day and night.

" 'Steve, you'd better stay above the cloud until I am visual with the target below.' If he popped up through the cloud layer, Steve would get him.

" 'Roger. Still good contact at 9 miles.'

"I descended steeply into the cloud layer, breaking through the bottoms at 1,800 feet. I still had the enemy on my radar screen; a fat blip at 6 miles and closing fast. I looked up from the radar and flight instruments and there it was at 20° left, a Hercules heading for the mainland as fast as it could go. It was at a height of about 300 feet above the waves.

" 'Tally ho, one Herky-bird! Come and join me down here, Steve.'

"I closed the four-engined transport fairly quickly and when I felt I was just within missile range and had a good growl from the seeker-head I fired my first Sidewinder. As usual, it seemed an eternity before it came off the rails and sped towards its target. I had locked the missile to the left-hand pair of engines. The thick white smoke trail terminated after motor burn-out and the missile continued to track towards the Hercules' left wing. I was sure it was going to get there, but at the last minute it hung tantalisingly short and low on its target and fell away, proximity-fusing on the sea surface below.

"There was no mistake with the second missile. I locked up the Sidewinder on the target's starboard engines, listened to its growling acquisition tone, and fired from well under 1 ? miles. It left the rails with its characteristic muffled roar and tracked inevitably towards the right wing of the Hercules, impacting between the engines. Immediately, both engines and the wing surface between them burst into flames.

"Our fuel state was now getting marginal, to say the least. The job had to be finished, and quickly. Otherwise the Argentine aircraft might still limp home and escape. I knew the Hercules had an excellent fire suppression system in the wings and we couldn't let it escape now.

"I still had more than 100 knot's overtake as I closed to guns range and pulled the trigger. My hot-line aiming point was the rear door and tailplane and all of the 240 rounds of 30mm high-explosive ammunition hit their mark. There were no splashes in the sea below.

"As I finished firing, and with its elevator and rudder controls shot away, the large transport aircraft banked gracefully to the right and nose-dived into the sea. There could have been no survivors.

"Pulling off the target hard to port, I called *Minerva*.

" 'Splash one Hercules! Well done on spotting it!'

"As the controller's excited voice came back on the air, I could hear the cheers of the Ops Room staff in the background. They also knew that the Hercules force had been running supplies into Stanley on a daily basis, usually at night and always at very low level. To our ground forces they were a high-priority target. This Hercules had shown some complacency by popping up to 8,000 feet, and had paid the price.

" 'Nice one.' It was the *Minerva* controller. 'Do you wish to land in San Carlos? We'd all like to see you both.'

" 'Roger. Wait. Steve, check fuel.'

" '2100,' came the reply.

"I had a couple of hundred less and the ship was 230 miles away. We couldn't rearm my aircraft on board the assault ships and as I thought we could just squeeze home to Invincible, I decided to turn down *Minerva*'s kind invitation.

" 'Sorry, we can just make it back to Mother, so we'd better do that. Thanks anyway for standing by.'

"We were already in the climb and in less than half an hour were touching down on deck. There had been a tail-wind so we ended up with about 400 pounds of gas in the tanks—more than I had expected.

"During the preceding weeks there had been much talk in our crew room about knocking down a Hercules or similar large transport. Given the chance, everyone favoured flying up alongside the cockpit and signalling to the crew to jump out. We felt no animosity towards the Argentine pilots; they were just doing what they had to do, and if their lives could be spared then they would be. Sadly there had been no time for such chivalry on this occasion. The choice was chivalry, thus possibly giving the enemy aircraft the opportunity to survive and maybe running our Sea Jets out of fuel, or a quick kill. Circumstances and, in particular, fuel states dictated that it had to be the latter choice. I didn't lose any sleep over it, but wished that we had had more time to play with.

"The Hercules intercept turned out to be the last kill of the air war in which the Sea Harrier weapon system was able to play its full part."

The British victory in the Falklands campaign was achieved in little more than two months. The Falklands capital Stanley was retaken by British forces in June 1982. Days later General Galtieri was removed from power and placed under house arrest for the next eighteen months, during which a form of democracy was returned to Argentina. In 1983, the general, and several other members of his military junta, were charged in a military court with various human rights violations and mismanagement of the Falklands war. Galtieri was stripped of his rank and sentenced to twelve years in prison. In 1989, he and thirty-nine other convicted officers were pardoned by President Carlos Menem. In 2002 he was again charged with further crimes from the era of the military junta and again placed under house arrest. He died in Buenos Aires in January 2003.

THE PLANES

In the first hundred years of naval aviation one concept has become gospel among airmen the world over: If it looks right it will probably fly right. There have, of course, been exceptions, but for the most part that idea has proven correct. This selection from some of the more significant naval aircraft largely, though not entirely, supports that notion. It is essentially chronological in organization and, while the majority of the aircraft featured are American in origin, many of these have also been operated by squadrons of the British Royal Navy and Fleet Air Arm, as well as by the naval and air forces of other nations. In terms of roles, these aircraft represent nearly all the basic assignments in naval aviation history, excepting helicopters, which are covered in a separate chapter. Apologies to all whose favourite naval aircraft types have been omitted due to limitations of space.

The prototype of the 'Torpedo-Spotter-Reconnaissance' bomber of the Fairey Aviation Company, known as the Swordfish, and to its crews affectionately as 'the Stringbag', maid its first flight in April 1934. The Swordfish was actually obsolete by 1939, but it continued to serve both effectively and impressively through much of the Second World War. Most notably, the biplane torpedo bomber distinguished itself in the Royal Navy's attack on warships of the Italian Navy in the harbour of Taranto in November 1940. Flying from the British carrier HMS *Illustrious*, the little aircraft sank an Italian battleship and severely damaged two others as well as disabling a cruiser in the battle. On visiting Taranto after the raid, officials of the Imperial Japanese Navy were greatly impressed by the achievement of the Swordfish crews. They took the information they gathered there back to Japan, incorporating the lessons of the British torpedo attack on the warships in the shallow Italian harbour, into the planning of the Japanese attack on Pearl Harbor, Hawaii, in December 1941, which drew the United States into World War II.

An equally impressive achievement by Swordfish crews took place in May 1941 when aircraft from the carrier HMS *Ark Royal* flew in an attack against the German battleship *Bismarck*. The *Bismarck*, and her sister ship, the *Tirpitz*, were the largest and most powerful battleships ever built by Germany. Completed in the summer of 1940, the big warship, together with the heavy cruiser *Prinz Eugen*, was under way in her first (and only) offensive operation in May 1941. She was assigned to break out into the Atlantic and attack Allied shipping from North America to Britain. British naval units had detected the two German vessels off Scandinavia and sailed to block them.

The British battlecruiser HMS *Hood* and the battleship HMS *Prince of Wales* were dispatched to intercept Bismarck on her way to attack the convoys. On 24 May *Hood* was hit by several shells from *Bismarck* in the Battle of the

Denmark Strait and exploded. The shocking loss of the *Hood*, pride of the Royal Navy, caused British Prime Minister Winston Churchill to order the Navy to "sink the Bismarck".

Warships of the Royal Navy pursued the German battleship for the next two days as she raced for the relative safety of occupied France. It was during this dash that Swordfish torpedo bombers from HMS *Ark Royal* caught up with *Bismarck*. One of the Swordfish crews managed a hit on the battleship's rudder, jamming her steering gear and leaving her unsteerable. The next morning, the German battleship was destroyed, but the cause of her demise is still debated, with German survivors of *Bismarck* claiming that, in fact, they scuttled her, while the official position of the Royal Navy is that the battleship was destroyed by torpedoes fired from the cruiser HMS *Dorsetshire*. There can be no disputing, however, the effect of the Swordfish attack that disabled the German battleship, leaving her helpless in the Denmark Strait.

The Fairey Swordfish is a torpedo bomber that began service with the Royal Navy in 1936. It has also served with the Royal Air Force, the Royal Canadian Air Force and Navy, the Royal Netherlands Navy, and the Royal Australian Air Force. A total of 2,391 Swordfish aircraft were built. Crew: pilot, observer, and radio operator/rear gunner. Powerplant: one Bristol Pegasus IIIM.3 radial engine of 690 hp. Maximum speed: 139 mph at 4,750 feet. Range: 546 miles loaded. Service ceiling: 19,250 feet. Armament: one forward-firing .303 Vickers machine gun, one .303 Lewis or Vickers machine gun in rear cockpit; eight RP-3 rockets; one 1,670 lb torpedo or one 1,500 lb mine or 1,500 lbs of bombs. Origin: United Kingdom.

The Grumman F4F Wildcat is a carrier-based fighter that first flew in September 1937 and entered service with both the U.S. and Royal Navys in 1940. Its first combat role was with the Royal Navy where it was then called the Martlet. The Wildcat was the early-war workhorse of the United States Navy and Marine Corps in the Pacific Theater of World War Two. In most respects the Wildcat was inferior to its principal opponent, the Japanese Mitsubishi A6M Zero fighter. However, the sturdy construction of the Grumman plane, together with the superior training and tactics of the American pilots who flew it, resulted in the Wildcat ending the war with a final kill-to-loss ratio 6.9 to 1.

The renowned British test pilot Eric Brown on the F4F: "I would still assess the Wildcat as the outstanding naval fighter of the early years of World War II. I can vouch as a matter of personal experience, this Grumman fighter was one of the finest shipboard aeroplanes ever created."

In the mid-1930s, the American Navy planners were considering the purchase of an advanced monoplane fighter and they were comparing the relative merits of an early version of the Wildcat against those of the Brewster

Buffalo. They favoured the Brewster plane and ordered it into production in 1936, causing Grumman to redesign the Wildcat. The Navy still preferred the Buffalo, believing its overall performance to be superior to that of the Grumman plane and Grumman then substantially improved the Wildcat, gaining a production order for it in early 1940. The French also ordered the plane but, before their first aircraft could be delivered France had fallen to the Germans and the aircraft of her order went to the British instead.

The combat career of the Grumman plane began on Christmas Day 1940 when a land-based British Martlet downed a German Junkers Ju 88 bomber over the Scapa Flow naval base in the Orkney Islands off the north-east coast of Scotland. It was the first combat score achieved by an American-built fighter operated by the British in the Second World War. In another significant action, six Martlets flying from HMS *Audacity* during September 1941 on a convoy escort mission, shot down several Focke-Wulf Fw 200 Condor bombers.

It was in the Pacific, though, that the Wildcat achieved its greatest fame. It was outperformed by the Japanese Zero, but its U.S. Navy and Marine pilots managed to prevail in most combat engagements thanks to the superior armour and self-sealing fuel tanks of the Wildcat, as well as its more substantial airframe, and the quality of their training and tactics. And as the Allied pilots gained experience in the Grumman, they became even more formidable to their opponents. One of the Japanese pilots who encountered the Wildcat on several occasions was top ace Saburo Sakai who later wrote of one such experience: "I had full confidence in my ability to destroy the Grumman and decided to finish off the enemy fighter with only my 7.7mm machine guns. I turned the 20mm cannon switch to the 'off' position, and closed in. For some strange reason, even after I had poured about five or six-hundred rounds of ammunition directly into the Grumman, the airplane did not fall, but kept on flying. I thought this very odd—it had never happened before—and closed the distance between the two airplanes until I could almost reach out and touch the Grumman. To my surprise, the Grumman's rudder and tail were torn to shreds, looking like an old torn piece of rag. With his plane in such condition, no wonder the pilot was unable to continue fighting! A Zero which had taken that many bullets would have been a ball of fire by now."

Grumman had learned many lessons from the combat career of the Wildcat, and applied the knowledge in the design, development and construction of their successor to the F4F, the new F6F Hellcat, a vastly superior machine to both the Wildcat and the Zero. The Grumman production line stopped building Wildcats early in 1943 to make way for the Hellcat, and the carmaker General Motors took over the continuing production of Wildcats for both the U.S. Navy and the Royal Navy. Now the Wildcats, with their slower landing speeds, were shifted to operate from the shorter decks of the small escort carriers where they continued to perform with distinction against the aircraft, submarines, and shore threats of the Japanese enemy. The shift made room for the big new fighters like the Hellcat and the Chance Vought F4U Corsair aboard the larger fleet carriers.

Perhaps the most impressive accomplishment of the Wildcat occurred on 20 February 1942 when U.S. Navy Lieutenant Edward "Butch" O'Hare, flying an F4F-3 from the carrier USS *Lexington* near Bougainville, Papua New Guinea, shot down five Mitsubishi twin-engine bombers in only a few minutes.

The Grumman Wildcat is a carrier-based fighter that began service with the U.S. Navy in December 1940. It has also served with the Belgian Air Force, the French Aeronavale, the Royal Canadian Navy, the Royal Navy Fleet Air Arm, and the U.S. Marine Corps. A total of 7,785 Wildcat and Martlet aircraft were built. Crew: one pilot. Powerplant: one Pratt & Whitney R-1830-86 double-row radial engine of 1,200 hp. Maximum speed: 320 mph. Range: 830 miles. Service ceiling: 34,000 feet. Armament: six .50 Browning machine guns. Origin: United States.

The reliable and rugged Douglas SBD Dauntless dive bombers of the U.S. Navy were responsible for sinking more Japanese warships and cargo vessels than any other aircraft in the Second World War. Produced between 1940 and 1944, the Dauntless was designed by a team led by Ed Heinemann who was also responsible for the superb Douglas A1 Skyraider attack aircraft. The most produced variant of the six SBD types, the SBD-5, was built at the Tulsa, Oklahoma Douglas plant, which produced more than 2,400 of the model which was equipped with a 1,200 hp radial engine.

Initial combat operations for the SBD began during the Japanese attack of 7 December on Pearl Harbor when eighteen of the Douglas dive bombers, flying from the carrier USS *Enterprise*, arrived over Pearl in the midst of the attack. A mix of U.S. Navy and Marine Corps aircraft, seven of the Dauntlesses were lost to enemy fire. In the raid itself, most of the ground-based Marine squadron VMSB-232 were destroyed at their Ewa Mooring Mast Field by the marauding Japanese fighters and dive bombers.

Shortly after the Pearl Harbor attack, SBDs began to prove themselves when, flying from the carriers *Lexington, Enterprise,* and *Yorktown,* they participated in heavy air strikes against enemy installations in the Marshall Islands, Gilbert Islands, Rabaul, New Guinea, Wake and Marcus Islands, as well as in the Battle of the Coral Sea.

While flying an SBD with U.S. Navy Scouting Squadron Five in January 1942, Stanley "Swede" Vejtasa took part in the first American strikes on Japanese targets in the Gilbert and Marshall Islands. In March, he flew in raids on enemy shipping near New Guinea, sharing in the destruction of three Japanese vessels, earning him the Navy Cross. In April, flying from the carrier USS *Yorktown,* which was then delivering air strikes on Tulagi in the

Solomon Islands, Vejtasa shared in the downing of an enemy floatplane. On 7 May, during the Battle of the Coral Sea, he scored a direct hit on the Japanese carrier *Shoho*, sharing credit for its sinking. The following day his combat air patrol was ambushed by several A6M Zero fighters. In the encounter Vejtasa shot down three of the enemy aircraft, earning him a second Navy Cross. Swede Vejtasa survived the war and completed thirty years in the U.S. Navy as an aviator and, ultimately, as commanding officer of the carrier USS *Constellation*.

The Battle of Midway in June 1942 was the high point for the Dauntless. In that epic clash the SBDs managed to sink or cause the demise of four Japanese carriers, three of them, *Soryu*, *Akagi* and *Kaga*, in only six minutes, in addition to heavily damaging two enemy cruisers. The achievement of the Dauntless pilots was attributable to the fact that the Japanese carriers were exceptionally vulnerable at the time of the attack by the SBDs—busy preparing their bombers for launching, with live ordnance and fueling hoses all over the hangar decks. Additionally, the protective fighter cover for the Japanese carriers had been drawn away from the enemy ships by TBDs from the U.S. Navy carriers, leaving the Dauntlesses carte blanche to hit the enemy carriers without interference.

Test pilot Eric Brown: "Mundane by contemporary performance standards, the Dauntless was underpowered, painfully slow, short on range, woefully vulnerable to fighters, and uncomfortable and fatiguing to fly for any length of time, being inherently noisy and draughty. But it did possess certain invaluable assets that mitigated these shortcomings. Its handling characteristics were, for the most part,, innocuous and it was responsive; it was dependable and extremely sturdy, capable of absorbing considerable battle damage and remaining airborne and, most important, it was an accurate dive bomber.

"Throughout the Pacific war, it remained the principal shipboard dive bomber available to the U.S. Navy; it was the only U.S. aircraft to participate in all five naval engagements fought exclusively between carriers, and, deficiencies notwithstanding, it emerged with an almost legendary reputation as the most successful shipboard dive bomber of all time—albeit success that perhaps owed more to the crews that flew it in truly dauntless fashion than to the intrinsic qualities of the aeroplane itself."

By 1944 it was clear that the SBD was long since obsolete and most of them had been replaced by the newer Curtiss SB2C Helldiver, an action not appreciated by many of the pilots reassigned to fly the Curtiss, who gave it the nickname Son of a Bitch 2nd Class, and much preferred the slower, reliable and deadly Dauntless. The last production SBD Dauntless emerged from the Douglas El Segundo, California, plant in July 1944. The type had flown more than a million operational hours; more than 25 percent of all the operational hours flown by U.S. Navy carrier aircraft in the Second World War.

In its operational career the Dauntless had been responsible for the destruction of six principal Japanese aircraft carriers, fourteen enemy cruisers, six destroyers, fifteen transports and cargo ships and many other enemy vessels.

The Douglas SBD Dauntless is a carrier-based dive bomber that began service with the U.S Navy in 1940. It has also served with the Chilean Air Force, the French Air Force and the French Aeronavale, the Mexican Air Force, the Moraccan Desert Police, the Royal New Zealand Air Force, the Royal Air Force, the Royal Navy Fleet Air Arm, the U. S. Army Air Force, and the U. S. Marine Corps. A total of 5,936 Dauntless aircraft were built. Crew: two. Powerplant: one Wright R01820-60 radial engine of 1,200 hp. Maximum speed: 255 mph at 14,000 feet. Range: 1,115 miles. Service ceiling: 25,500 feet. Armament: two .50 forward-firing Browning machine guns; two .30 Browning machine guns in rear; 2,250 lbs of bombs. Origin: United States.

It was called Zero or Zeke by the Allies—the Mitsubishi A6M long-range Reisen long-range and Navy carrier fighter. The naval version was referred to as: Navy Type 0 Carrier Fighter, thus the nickname Zero. From the first days of deployment aboard the fleet carriers of the Imperial Japanese Navy, the A6M developed a powerful reputation as the best carrier-based fighter in the world. Its long range and excellent manoevrability added to its legendary status as a dogfighter with an established combat kill ratio of 12 to 1.

To the American and British pilots encountering the Zero in the first year of World War Two, it must have seemed insurmountable, a fighter plane so efficient, effective, manoeuvrable, so fast and long-ranging, indeed so superior in every respect to anything else in the air at the time, that it was simply incomparable—and unbeatable. The best fighters the Allies could present in those dark days, the Grumman F4F and the Curtiss P-40, the Supermarine Spitfire and the Hawker Hurricane, were utterly out-classed by the swift, ultra-lightweight, extraordinarily agile Zero, though, of the lot, in the hands of several above-average U.S. Navy and Marine Corps aviators, the F4F often proved formidable in those early contacts with the Japanese fighter. When Japan's top aces were at the controls of the A6M, however, men like Hiroyoshi Nishizawa with 104 confirmed victories, Tadashi Nakajima with 75, Saburo Sakai with 64, Naoishi Kanno with 53, it was a different story. For most of that first year, the Zero and its pilots were virtually invincible.

As good as it was, the performance characteristics of the Zero deteriorated dramatically as the aeroplane neared its practical combat ceiling altitude. What frequently saved it and its pilot in that situation was the fact that most of the Allied fighters it engaged up there suffered an even greater fall-off in performance. And at lower and medium altitudes, everything seemed to favour the Japanese fighter.

One factor that is often overlooked about the Zero is that in some ways it was the highly impressive forerunner of the most successful long-range escort fighter of the war, the North American P-51 Mustang. With far greater range than any other fighter of the period, the A6M was shepherding Japanese bombers enormous distances to their Chinese targets even before the start of the main Pacific war. The phenomenal range of the Zero allowed the Japanese carrier air groups to easily out-range the American carrier air groups. In the Pearl Harbor attack of December 1941, the amazing 1,600-mile range of the naval variant Zero fighter enabled it to operate much
further from its carrier than its enemy could possibly anticipate.

The performance and firepower of the Zero in 1941 made nearly all the Allied aircraft it faced pale in comparison and it readily disposed of them, including the fine British Spitfire. The Zero could easily out-turn and out-climb the British fighter, and could remain airborne three times as long.

Six months after the Pearl Harbor attack, however, the balance of power began to shift as the availability of better Allied aircraft and improved Allied training and tactics began to even the aerial odds. Those odds moved ever-more towards the side of the Allies over the next year as the basic weakness-es in the A6M construction and the absence of a more powerful aero engine for the type made it less of a threat to the newer, more advanced and sophis-ticated fighters of the Allies, aircraft with increased armament, speed and performance capabilities which first approached and then surpassed those of the Japanese fighter. Japanese Zero pilots struggled on through the remain-ing war years, mismatched against the excellent qualities of the newer Grumman Hellcat, the Lockheed Lightning, and the Chance Vought Corsair, known to the Japanese as "whistling death" for the eerie howl it produced when it passed low overhead at high speed. Near the end of the war, desper-ate Japanese air unit commanders utilized their remaining Zero fighters in kamikaze suicide strikes against the Allied warships, their primary targets being the American fleet carriers.

Two Allied tactics were developed that began to turn the tide against the Zero even before the advent of vastly improved American fighters like the Corsair and the Hellcat. Allied pilots quickly realized the folly of engaging in a conventional dogfight with the extremely agile A6M. They discovered that it was far safer and more effective to gain altitude over the Zero, dive on it in an accurate high-speed firing pass, and then zoom back to altitude. More often than not, this practice resulted in flaming the relatively delicate Japanese plane. The practice was employed and honed by the famous Flying Tigers, the American Volunteer Group operating against the Japanese in the China-Burma-India theater of operations in 1941-42. Secondly, the develop-ment of the "Thach Weave" by U.S. Navy Lieutenant Commander John S. Thach further contributed to reducing the odds for the Zero. Thach reasoned that when two Allied fighters flew about 200 feet apart, if a Zero pilot positioned himself behind one of them for a kill, and the two Allied planes turned towards each other, the Zero pilot would follow his original intended target through their turn into position to be fired on by the target's wingman. The effectiveness of this tactic was proven in the great Battle of Midway.

Japanese military planners had been dissatisfied with the new A5M fighter as soon as it entered service in 1937 and immediately issued a specification to aircraft manufacturers Mitsubishi and Nakajima for a new carrier-based fighter to replace the A5M, whose performance in China had been less than impressive. The plane the planners wanted had to have a top speed of 370 mph. It had to climb to 10,000 feet in less than 3.5 minutes. With a normal power setting, and drop tanks, it had to have a two-hour endurance, and six to eight hours at an economical cruising speed. It had to be armed with two 20mm cannon, two .303 machine guns, and two 130 lb bombs. It had to carry a complete radio set and a radio direction finder for long-range navigation. Manoeuvrability was to be at least the equal of the A5M, and the wingspan could not exceed 39 feet for practical storage aboard a carrier (evidently they had no involvement at the time with the concept of folding wings for carrier-based aircraft.) In the context of these demanding requirements, the challenge for the designers would have been enormous, considering the power limitations of the aero engines available to them at the time. In fact, Nakajima believed that the requirements were unachievable and withdrew from the design competition.

Jiro Horikoshi, Mitsubishi's chief designer, thought the specifications challenging but achievable, providing the weight of the plane could be kept to an absolute minimum. To that end he insisted on incorporating every conceivable weight-saving consideration into the company's design. He even specified the use of a new and secret aluminium alloy known as Extra Super Duralumin (ESD) for the airframe and all appropriate applications in the construction. The ESD was both stronger and lighter than the other aluminium alloys then in use, but was also more brittle and more subject to corrosion.

For simplicity, and to save weight, no armour was provided for the pilot, the engine, or any other vital areas of the aircraft. Even the use of the relatively new technology of self-sealing fuel tanks was excluded. All of these measures, and very low wing-loading, served to make the Zero lighter and more agile than virtually all other fighter aircraft in the early part of the war. The downside included a higher probability of fire and explosion when the plane was hit in combat.

In June 1942, American military officials had the opportunity to carefully examine and flight test an A6M Zero when, during a Japanese air raid over Dutch Harbor in the Aleutian Islands, one of the fighters was brought down by ground fire. The pilot was killed, but the largely undamaged aircraft was shipped to the North Island Naval Air Station at San Diego where it was repaired and flight-tested to determine its strengths, weaknesses, and secrets. They learned that a fully loaded A6M weighed just 5,200 pounds, roughly half the weight of a typical American naval fighter. They were particularly interested in the unusual "one-piece" construction method used by Mitsubishi with the wings and fuselage; a far slower, more labour-intensive method, but one that produced great strength and significantly improved manoeuvrability. Test pilot Eric Brown: "I don't think I have ever flown a fighter that could match the rate of turn of the Zero. The Zero had ruled the roost totally and was the finest fighter in the world until mid-1943."

The Mitsubishi A6M Zero is a carrier fighter that began service with the Imperial Japanese Navy in July 1940. It has also served with the Royal Thai Air Force, the Indonesian Air Force, and the Republic of China Air Force. A total of 10,939 A6M aircraft were built. Crew: one. Powerplant: one Nakajima Sakae 12 radial engine of 950 hp. Maximum speed: 331 mph. Range: 1,929 miles. Service ceiling: 33,000 feet. Armament: two .303 machine guns in engine cowling; two 20mm cannon in the wings; two 132 lb bombs or one 551 lb bomb for use in kamikaze attacks. Origin: Japan.

In an inauspicious combat debut, five of six Grumman TBF Avengers of Torpedo Squadron 8 participating in the Battle of Midway were shot down, but the type itself went on to earn a record as probably the best torpedo bomber of the Second World War. Even with the losses suffered by the American torpedo bombers, they were ultimately credited with diverting the enemy combat air patrols, enabling American dive bombers to successfully attack the Japanese carriers. As the war progressed and the Allies gradually gained air superiority in the Pacific theater, improved American tactics, together with better trained and more experienced American pilots allowed the Avengers to show their full range of capability.

Avenger pilots remembered it as the heaviest single-engine aircraft of the war years, with only the Republic P-47 Thunderbolt approaching it in maximum loaded weight. Among the innovations introduced by the TBF was Grumman's efficient, space-saving wing-folding system, a mechanism also installed on later models of the company's F4F Wildcat and its superb F6F Hellcat fighters.

The Avenger was operated by a crew of three—a pilot, a turret gunner, and a radioman/bombardier/ventral gunner. The plane was fitted with a large bomb bay to carry one Mk 13 torpedo or one 2,000 lb bomb or up to four 500 lb bombs. Like Grumman's other fine products, the Avenger was appreciated by its crews for its sturdy construction and ability to absorb punishment in combat situations and still return to its carrier. It was appreciated too, for its handling and stability, its excellent radio system, and its impressive range. In range and overall performance it easily equalled or exceeded those of the other U.S. Navy torpedo bombers as well as its Japanese counterpart, the

Nakajima Kate.

At about the time the attacking force of the Imperial Japanese Navy was delivering their surprise raid on Pearl Harbor that early Sunday morning in December 1941, officials of the Grumman Aircraft Engineering Corporation were cutting the ribbon to celebrate the opening of their new manufacturing plant at Farmingdale, New York. The star of the show was their new TBF torpedo bomber being shown to the public for the first time. By the end of the ceremony word of the Japanese attack on Pearl had spread through the crowd and the Grumman people acted to seal off the facility against the possibility of sabotage by enemy sympathizers.

Combat successes began accumulating for the Avenger in August 1942 when 24 TBFs, flying from the carriers Enterprise and Saratoga, took part in a naval action in the eastern Solomon Islands, sinking the enemy carrier *Ryujo*. The achievement was followed in October by Navy and Marine Corps Avengers attacking and sinking the Japanese battleship *Hiei*.

As Grumman geared up to mass-produce the highly capable new Hellcat fighter, it began phasing out Avenger production, turning the work over to the Eastern Aircraft Division of the car maker General Motors which took over manufacture and assembly of the TBF at its Tarrytown, New York, plant in mid-1944. There GM built the new TBM-3, an improved Avenger with a better and more powerful engine, and hard points under the wings for rockets and fuel drop tanks. More TBM-3 Avengers were built than any other variant of the plane.

Two famous personalities were associated with the Avenger in wartime. The future President George H. W. Bush flew a TBM from the carrier *San Jacinto* on 2 September 1944 over the island of Chichi Jima, was shot down, releasing his bombload on target before he bailed out. He was awarded the Distinguished Flying Cross for the action. Actor Paul Newman tried to qualify for U.S. Navy pilot training, but his colour blindness prevented it. He flew instead as a rear gunner in an Avenger operating from the escort carrier *Hollandia*.

In addition to its achievements in torpedo attacks on enemy surface ships, the Avenger is credited with the sinking of at least thirty Japanese submarines in both the Pacific and Atlantic theaters of operations. In the Atlantic, the plane excelled in providing vital air cover for the Allied convoys between North America and Britain. Among the greatest achievements of the Grumman Avenger was its participation in the sinking of the two Japanese super battleships, *Yamato* and *Musashi*.

The Grumman TBF/TBM Avenger torpedo bomber began service with the U.S. Navy in 1942. It has also served with the Brazilian Navy, the French Aeronavale, the Royal Canadian Navy, the Japanese Maritime Self-Defense Force, the Royal Netherlands Navy, the Royal New Zealand Air Force, the Royal Navy Fleet Air Arm, the United States Marine Corps, as well as the

Uruguayan Navy. A total of 9,839 Avenger aircraft were built. Crew: pilot, turret gunner, radioman/bombardier/ventral gunner. Powerplant: one Wright R-2600-20 radial engine of 1,900 hp. Maximum speed: 275 mph. Range: 1,000 miles. Service ceiling: 30,100 feet. Armament: one .30 nose-mounted Browning machine gun; two .50 wing-mounted Browning machine guns; one .50 dorsal-mounted Browning machine gun; one .30 ventral-mounted Browning machine gun; up to eight 3.5 inch rockets or 5 inch rockets of high velocity rockets; up to 2,000 lbs of bombs or one 2,000 lb Mk 13 torpedo. Origin: United States.

The Grumman F6F Hellcat carrier-based fighter and the Chance Vought F4U Corsair were the principal U.S. Navy fighters in the last half of the Second World War. The Hellcat was the high-achieving successor to the Grumman Wildcat, the main U.S. Navy fighter in the early years of the war. The Hellcats of the U.S. Navy, U.S. Marine Corps, and the Royal Navy's Fleet Air Arm, were credited with the destruction of more enemy aircraft than any other Allied aircraft type, a total of 5,271.

In its design work on the Hellcat, Grumman was determined to surpass the overall performance capability of the Japanese A6M Zero fighter, an aeroplane clearly superior in manoeuvrability and rate of climb to the Hellcat's predecessor, the Wildcat. The Wildcat did have some advantages over the Zero—it was better armed and better able to withstand battle damage. It was also faster in a dive and thus able to evade enemy attackers when necessary. The Grumman designers intended the Hellcat to be both faster than the Zero and to have appreciably greater range.

Test pilot Eric Brown: "No more outstanding example of skill and luck joining forces to produce just the right aeroplane is to be found than that provided by the Grumman Hellcat, unquestionably the most important shipboard fighter of World War II. U.S. Navy observers . . . had learnt that speed, climb rate, adequate firepower and armour protection, pilot visibility and manoeuvrability were primary requirements in that order. In the case of the shipboard fighter, these desirable qualities had to be augmented by ample fuel and ammunition capacity, and the structural sturdiness that was a prerequisite in any aeroplane intended for the naval environment. The Grumman team had . . . formulated its own ideas on the primary requirements in a Wildcat successor, these having been arrived at by consensus: the opinions of U.S. Navy pilots had been canvassed and the results equated with analyses of European combat reports.

". . . so spacious was the cockpit that when I first lowered myself into the seat, I thought I would have to stand up if I was to see through the windscreen for take-off! There was a great deal of engine ahead, but in spite of the bulk of the Double Wasp, the view was not unreasonable, thanks to the Hellcat's slightly hump-backed profile. The take-off was straight forward, with a tendency to swing to port requiring gentle application of rudder, and acceleration was very satisfying, although the noise with the canopy open was quite something. In a dive it was necessary to decrease r.p.m. to 2100 or less in order to reduce vibration to acceptable levels. The Hellcat had to be trimmed into the dive and became tail-heavy as speed built up, some left rudder being necessary to counter yaw. With bombs under the wings, speed built up very rapidly indeed and there was considerable snatching of the elevator and rudder. Final approach to the deck was at 80 knots and the Hellcat was as steady as a rock, with precise attitude and speed control. I always used a curved approach to get a better view of the deck and left the throttle cut as late as possible to prevent the heavy nose dropping and allowing the main wheels to contact the deck first, thus risking a bounce, although the Hellcat's immensely sturdy undercarriage possessed very good shock absorbing characteristics.

"The Hellcat had twice the power of the Japanese Zero-Sen, but it also carried twice the weight. The Japanese fighter was supremely agile and its turning radius was fabled. At airspeeds below 200 knots the Zero-Sen's lightly loaded wing enabled it to outmanoeuvre the Hellcat with comparative ease, even though the airframe of the latter allowed more g to be pulled. At higher speeds the controls of the Japanese fighter stiffened up and the turn rate disparity was dramatically reduced.

"The Hellcat could not follow the Zero-Sen in a tight loop and U.S. Navy Hellcat pilots soon learned to avoid any attempt to dogfight with the Japanese fighter, and turn the superior speed, dive and altitude characteristics of the American fighter to advantage. These characteristics usually enabled the Hellcat to acquire an advantageous position permitting the use of tactics whereby the Zero-Sen could be destroyed without tight-manoeuvring combat.

"The Hellcat had not been the fastest shipboard fighter of World War II, nor the most manoeuvrable, but it was certainly the most efficacious, and one of its virtues was its versatility. Conceived primarily as an air superiority weapon with the range to seek out the enemy so that he could be brought to battle, as emphasis switched to offensive capability, the Hellcat competently offered the strike potential that the U.S. Navy needed to offset the reduced number of bombers aboard the service's fleet carriers. The Hellcat was certainly the most important Allied shipboard aircraft in the Pacific in 1943-44, for it turned the tide of the conflict, and although Japanese fighters of superior performance made their appearance, they were too late to wrest the aerial ascendancy that had been established largely by this one aircraft type."

The Second World War ended in August 1945 with the Japanese surrender aboard the battleship USS *Missouri* in Tokyo Bay. In November the last production Hellcat rolled from the Grumman assembly line for a total run of 12,275 aircraft. In its operational history, the Hellcat began with a bang, in November 1943 when Hellcats encountered a large formation of Japanese

Zeros over the island of Tarawa and shot down thirty of the enemy fighters with the loss of just one Hellcat. Hellcats were the main U.S. fighter type taking part in the Battle of the Philippine Sea, also referred to by air crews as the Great Marianas Turkey Shoot. In all, the Grumman fighter was credited with 75 percent of all aerial victories in the Pacific war. It had an overall kill ratio of 19 to 1.

The Grumman F6F Hellcat fighter began service with the U.S. Navy in 1943. It also served with the French Aeronavale, the Royal Navy Fleet Air Arm, the U.S. Marine Corps, and the Uruguayan Navy. A total of 12,275 Hellcat aircraft were built. Crew: one pilot. Powerplant: one Pratt & Whitney R-2800-10W radial engine of 2,000 hp. Maximum speed: 380 mph. Range: 1,530 miles. Service ceiling: 37,300 feet. Armament: six .50 Browning machine guns or two 20mm cannon and four .50 Browning machine guns; six 5 inch rockets or two 11.75 inch rockets. Origin: United States.

The Chance Vought F4U Corsair is a carrier and land-based fighter that served in the Second World War and the Korean War. Its superior performance and considerable capability put it in great demand, so much so that its manufacturer was unable to supply it in the numbers requested and additional production facilities were required with both the Goodyear and Brewster companies joining the Corsair building programme. A total of 12,571 Corsairs in sixteen variants were produced between the initial deliveries in 1940 and the final delivery in 1953.

Readying the Corsair for carrier operations proved a major issue for the U.S. Navy. The advanced technology of the aeroplane, the configuration of its landing gear, its stall characterisitics in landing, the aft-positioned cockpit and the long nose, oil from the hydraulic cowl flaps spattering on the windscreen and reducing visibility during the landing approach, along with several other factors contributed to the concerns about flying the Corsair from carriers. Test pilot Eric Brown: "The incipient bounce during landing resulting from overly stiff oleo action . . . was found to be most disconcerting by pilots fresh to the F4U-1, but not so disconcerting as the virtually unheralded torque stall that occurred all too frequently in landing condition. Compounded by a serious directional instability immediately after touchdown, and coupled with the frightful visibility from the cockpit during the landing approach—it was small wonder that the U.S. Navy concluded that the average carrier pilot was unlikely to possess the necessary skill to master these unpleasant ideosyncrasies, and that committing the Corsair to shipboard operations until these quirks had been at least alleviated would be the height of foolhardiness.

"Oddly enough, the Royal Navy was not quite so fastidious as the U.S. Navy regarding deck-landing characteristics, and cleared the Corsair for shipboard operation some nine months before its American counterpart. The obstacles to the Corsair's shipboard use were admittedly not insurmountable, but I can only surmise that the apparently ready acceptance by their Lordships of the Admiralty of the Chance Vought fighter for carrier operation must have been solely due to the exigencies of the times, for the landing behaviour of the Corsair really was bad, a fact to which I was able to attest after the briefest acquaintance with the aircraft.

"I was well aware that the U.S. Navy had found the Corsair's deck-landing characteristics so disappointing in trials that it had been assigned for shore duties while an attempt was being made to iron out the problems, and although the Fleet Air Arm was deck-landing the aircraft, I knew that, by consensus, it had been pronounced a brute and assumed that shipbord operations with the Corsair were something of a case of needs must when the devil drives. The fact that experienced U.S. Navy pilots could deck-land the Corsair had been demonstrated a couple of months earlier. I was most anxious to discover for myself if the Corsair was the deck-landing dog that it was reputed to be. It was!

"In the deck-landing configuration with approach power, the Corsair could demonstrate a very nasty incipient torque stall with dangerously little warning, the starboard wing usually dropping sharply. With the large flaps fully extended the descent rate was rapid, and a simulated deck-landing at 80 knots gave very poor view and sluggish aileron and elevator control. A curved approach was very necessary if the pilot was to have any chance of seeing the carrier, let alone the batsman! When the throttle was cut the nose dropped so that the aircraft bounced on its mainwheels, and once the tailwheel made contact the aircraft proved very unstable directionally, despite the tailwheel lock, swinging either to port or starboard, and this swing had to be checked immediately with the brakes. Oh yes, the Corsair could be landed on a deck without undue difficulty by an experienced pilot in ideal conditions, but with pilots of average capability, really pitching decks and marginal weather conditions, attrition simply had to be of serious proportions."

In time the majority of the Corsair's negative characteristics were overcome and her pilots came to appreciate the plane and its excellent performance. In the Second World War Corsair pilots destroyed 2,140 enemy aircraft in combat against a loss of 935 Corsairs.

The Chance Vought F4U Corsair carrier and land-based fighter began service with the U.S. Navy in December 1942. It also served with the Argentine Navy, the El Salvador Air Force, the French Aeronavale, the Honduran Air Force, the Royal New Zealand Air Force, the Royal Navy Fleet Air Arm, and the U.S. Marine Corps. F4U-4 Corsair. Crew: one pilot. Powerplant: one Pratt & Whitney R-2800-8 radial engine of 2,000 hp. Maximum speed: 446 mph. Range: 897 miles. Service ceiling: 41,500 feet. Armament: six .50 Browning machine guns or four 20mm cannon; eight 5-

inch rockets or 4,000 lbs of bombs. Origin: United States.

In 1944 the U.S. Navy requested design proposals from various American aircraft manufacturers for a new attack aircraft: a carrier-based, single-seat, high performance dive/torpedo bomber to succeed the Curtiss Helldiver and the Grumman Avenger. Curiously, the Navy had not invited a proposal from Douglas Aircraft. However, Ed Heinemann, chief designer for Douglas, and a few members of his team, decided to enter the competition anyway and, in a Washington DC hotel room they worked overnight to make preliminary drawings of their proposed aircraft. The following day Navy officials saw the drawings and ultimately Douglas prevailed in the contest. On 18 March 1945 the Douglas prototype flew for the first time and was impressive. The Navy sent Douglas a letter of intent to purchase 543 of the new planes (reduced after the Japanese surrender to 277) and the company continued development and testing the plane that would in 1946 be called the AD-1 Skyraider. 3,180 Skyraiders were built in seven versions including night attack, photo reconnaissance, electronic countermeasures, and early warning variants.

The Skyraider was a truly amazing performer, able to lift more than its own weight in ordnance, carrying that load over a substantial combat radius. It was big and heavy, and well armoured against the threat of ground fire to protect it in its primary ground attack role. The aeroplane is probably best known for flying close air support missions with the U.S. Navy over Korea and Vietnam in the 1950s and 1960s and by the U.S. Air Force over Vietnam. The first generation of supercarriers began to enter service in the 1960s and with it the Skyraiders remaining in fleet service were mostly transferred to the smaller *Essex*-class carriers then still serving; the Skyraiders having been replaced on the supercarriers by the Grumman A-6 Intruder as the primary medium attack aircraft for the carrier-based air wings.

Arriving with the fleet too late for service in the Second World War, the Skyraider became the backbone and workhorse of the U.S. Navy and Marine Corps air wings through the era of the Korean War in the early 1950s where it served with great distinction and achievement. Among its most famous roles in the Vietnam conflict was that of the "Sandy" helicopter escort on combat rescues. Two United States Medal of Honor awards were presented to Skyraider pilots for their participation in those missions.

The Douglas A-1 Skyraider began service with the U.S. Navy in 1946. A total of 3,180 Skyraiders were built. The Skyraider was also operated by the navies or air forces of Cambodia, the Central African Republic, Chad, France, Gabon, South Vietnam, Thailand, Sweden, the United Kingdom, the United States, and Vietnam. Crew: one pilot. Powerplant: one Wright R-3350-26WA radial engine of 2,700 hp. Maximum speed: 322 mph. Range: 1,316 miles. Service ceiling: 28,500 feet. Armament: four 20mm cannon; up to 8,000 lbs of ordnance including bombs, torpedoes, mine dispensers, unguided rockets, or gun pods. Origin: United States.

The Hawker Sea Fury naval fighter-bomber flew for the first time on 21 February 1945. It was designed by Sydney Camm, who had designed the Hawker Hurricane and the Hawker Tempest fighters. The Sea Fury was the among the fastest single-engine propeller-driven fighters ever built and was the last propeller-driven fighter to serve with the Royal Navy. A de-militarised Sea Fury holds the current unofficial speed record for a piston-engined aircraft in level flight—547 mph.

With the Japanese surrender in August 1945, all work on the land-based Fury version was suspended but work on the navalized Sea Fury continued. By August 1947 the aircraft had been approved for carrier landings. From then it remained the primary fighter-bomber of the Fleet Air Arm until 1953.

Sea Furies flying from the carriers HMS *Glory, Ocean, Theseus,* and the Australian carrier HMAS *Sydney*, operated as ground-attack aircraft. One of only a few incidents in which a propeller-driven aircraft engaged and downed a jet fighter occurred on 8 August 1952 when Lieutenant Peter Carmichael of 802 Squadron flying from HMS *Ocean* encountered and shot down a MiG-15 during the Korean War.

The Hawker Sea Fury began service with the Royal Navy Fleet Air Arm in October 1945. A total of 860 Sea Fury aircraft were built. The Sea Fury was also operated by the navies or air forces of Australia, Burma, Canada, Cuba, Egypt, Germany, Iraq, Morocco, the Netherlands, and Pakistan. Crew: one pilot. Powerplant: one Bristol Centaurus XVIIC radial engine of 2,480 hp. Maximum speed: 460 mph at 18,000 feet. Range: 700 miles. Service ceiling: 35,800 feet. Armament: four 20mm Hispano cannon; twelve 3 inch rockets or 2,000 lbs of bombs. Origin: United Kingdom.

The British Aerospace Sea Harrier is a vertical / short take-off and landing strike fighter developed for the Royal Navy from the Hawker Siddeley Harrier. The Sea Harrier, also known as the SHAR, entered naval service in April 1980 and took on the air defence role for the carriers of the Royal Navy. Operating mainly from aircraft carriers, the plane flew with distinction in the 1982 Falklands War (see The Falklands chapter), downing twenty enemy aircraft for the loss of one Sea Harrier to ground fire. The aircraft was withdrawn from RN service in 2006 and will ultimately be replaced by the V/STOL version of the Lockheed Martin F-35 Lightning II joint strike fighter.

In the 1960s the British Navy was shrinking. Its last battleship, HMS *Vanguard*, had been retired from service in 1960 and, in a continuing economic climate of austerity, the government cancelled the planned next class of large aircraft carriers, the CVA-01. Navy planners, mindful of the political sensitivity surrounding any discussion of future naval aviation funding, now referred to development of another new class of ships as "through-deck cruisers", tip-toeing around the term "aircraft carrier", to somehow evade the hostility of the existing political atmosphere regarding costly new capital ships. A new class of vessels known as *Invincible* emerged from the dens of British naval planners in 1973. The new ships were rather small; HMS *Invincible*, the namesake of the ship class, displacing just 22,000 tons with a flight deck only 689 feet in length. Her air group consisted of eight Sea Harriers and twelve Sea King helicopters. The other carriers of the class were HMS *Illustrious* and HMS *Ark Royal*. In the construction of the new ships, a ski-jump was added to the flight deck to enhance the carrier capability of the Sea Harriers. In 1981 the Sea Harrier was finally declared operational on board *Invincible*.

Largely based on the Harrier GR3, the Sea Harrier is a subsonic strike, reconnaissance and fighter aircraft powered by a Rolls-Royce Pegasus turbofan engine of 21,500 lbs thrust. It has four vectorable nozzles in addition to its conventional controls and, using the ski-jump on the above-mentioned carriers, the Sea Harrier can take-off with a heavy load from the relatively short flight deck. It has a raised cockpit canopy for better visibility in carrier operation and an extended forward fuselage to accommodate the Blue Fox radar system. The FA2 Sea Harrier was equipped with an improved radar, the Blue Vixen, among the most advanced pulse doppler radar systems in the world when this version was built.

The Hawker Siddeley/British Aerospace Sea Harrier strike fighter began service with the Royal Navy in August 1978. A total of 75 Sea Harrier aircraft were built. The Sea Harrier was also operated by the Indian Navy and a version of the Harrier, the AV-8B Harrier II, built by McDonnell Douglas, is operated by the U.S. Marine Corps. Crew: one pilot. Powerplant: one Rolls-Royce Pegasus turbofan engine of 21,500 lbs thrust. Maximum speed: 735 mph. Range: 620 mile combat radius. Service ceiling: 51,000 feet. Armament: two 30mm Aden cannon; total payload of 8,000 lbs rockets, missiles, bombs and nuclear bomb. Origin: United Kingdom.

The Grumman C-2A Greyhound is a COD (carrier onboard delivery) aircraft used by the U.S. Navy since the 1960s to bring cargo and passengers to and from aircraft carriers at sea. The newer version of the C-2A is considerably improved over the original COD aircraft, with engines of one-third more horsepower, improved navigation and communications equipment, better insulation for a quieter interior in flight, a public address system for communicating with the passengers and updating them on catapult launch, and arrested landing procedures on carriers, improved weather radar, an automatic carrier landing system, and a 25 percent payload capacity increase.

The Grumman C-2A Greyhound began service with the U.S. Navy in the 1960s. A total of 58 Greyhound aircraft were built. Crew: two pilots and two aircrew. Powerplant: two Allison T-56-A-8B turboprop engines of 4,600 shp each. Maximum speed: 352 mph. Range: 1.496 miles. Service ceiling: 33,500 feet. Origin: United States.

The Northrop Grumman E-2C Hawkeye is an all-weather airborne early warning and control aircraft. It entered service with the U.S. Navy in 1964. The Hawkeye and its sister ship, the Greyhound, are the only propeller-driven aeroplanes currently operating from U.S. Navy aircraft carriers. The primary mission of the Hawkeye is patrolling the approaches to the fleet to detect impending attack by hostile aircraft, missiles, or sea forces. Additionally, the plane provides strike and traffic control, area surveillance, search and rescue guidance, navigational assistance, and communications relay services.

Hawkeye is capable of all-weather operations and its sophisticated electronics equipment gives it enormous flexibility in its various assignments. Hawkeyes were first embarked aboard the carrier USS *Kittyhawk* in 1966. The five-person crew (two pilots and three equipment operators) can monitor many aircraft at a given time and direct strike aircraft to assigned targets in all weather conditions; this while watching for hostile forces anywhere within the long range of the plane's radar. A team of Hawkeyes operate by surrounding the fleet with an early-warning ring for directing air defences against any enemy threat.

Over the years major improvements have been made to the radar and computer systems of the Hawkeye, along with expansion of its surveillance and command control capability. So extensive is the overall capability of the plane that its equipment operators are able to detect targets anywhere within a three-million-cubic-mile surveillance envelope while simultaneously monitoring maritime traffic. Each Hawkeye can also maintain all-weather patrols, track automatically and simultaneously more than 600 targets, and control more than forty airborne intercepts.

The Northrop Grumman E-2C Hawkeye airborne early warning and control aircraft began service with the U.S. Navy in January 1964. A total of 210 Hawkeye aircraft have been built. The Hawkeye was also operated by the Egyptian Air Force, the French Aeronavale, the Israeli Air Force, the Japan Air Self-Defense Force, the Mexican Navy, the Republic of Singapore Air Force, and the Republic of China Air Force (Taiwan). Crew: five—two pilots, a combat information center officer, an air control officer, a radar operator. Powerplant: two Allison/Rolls-Royce T56-A-427A turboprop engines of 5,100 shp. Maximum speed: 350 knots. Ferry range: 1,462 nautical miles. Service ceiling: 34,700 feet. Origin: United States.

The aeroplane to replace the F-4 Phantom in the interceptor/air superiority and multirole combat task for the U.S. Navy was the Grumman F-14 Tomcat, a supersonic, twin-engine, two-seat, variable-sweep wing fighter that first flew in 1970. The Tomcat was finally retired from service with the fleet in September 2006, being replaced by the Boeing F/A-18E/F Super Hornet. The original aim of the Navy in the late 1950s was to acquire a new long-range, high-performance, high-endurance interceptor to defend and protect its aircraft carrier battle groups from long-range anti-ship missiles launched from Soviet submarines and jet aircraft. The new fleet air defence plane would require a more powerful and capable radar system and longer range missiles than those carried in the F-4 Phantom II. In developing the Tomcat it was determined that the aircraft must have the close-in dogfighting capability as well as the standoff missile fighting ability.

The Tomcat's two-seat cockpit has a high-bubble canopy for exceptional pilot visibility. Its variable geometry wings swing automatically during flight for optimum performance. For high-speed intercept the wings are swept back. They swing forward for lower speed flight. The F-14 design takes advantage of many lessons learned in the air combat operations of F-4 Phantoms during the Vietnam War. The fuselage and wing design of the F-14 allow it to climb faster than the F-4 and its twin-tail configuration provides greater stability. The large flat area in the fuselage between the engine nacelles stores fuel and the avionics systems.

The variable geometry wing can sweep between 20° and 68° in flight and is automatically controlled by the aircraft's central air data computer, maintaining optimum lift-to-drag ratio through the changes in aircraft speed. Light, strong, rigid titanium is used extensively in the construction of the Tomcat, including in the upper and lower wing skins, the wing box and pivots. As the Tomcat is an air superiority fighter in addition to being a medium and long-range interceptor, the aeroplane is fitted with an internal 20mm M61 Vulcan cannon for dogfighting.

In the 1970s proposals to upgrade the Tomcat to a more advanced version were rejected by the Navy, which chose to ultimately retire it in favour of the F/A-18E/F Super Hornet in the fleet defence and strike roles.

The Grumman F-14 Tomcat interceptor/air superiority and multirole combat aircraft began service with the U.S. Navy in September 1974. A total of 712 Tomcat aircraft were built. The Tomcat has also been operated by the Islamic Republic of Iran Air Force. Crew: a pilot and a radar intercept officer. Powerplant: two General Electric F110-GE-400 turbofan engines of 13,810 lbs thrust each. Maximum speed: 1,544 mph. Combat radius: 575 miles. Service ceiling: 50,000 feet. Armament: one 20mm M61 Vulcan cannon; 14,500 lbs of ordnance and external fuel including AIM-54 Phoenix, AIM-7 Sparrow, and AIM-9 Sidewinder missiles. Origin: United States.

The Northrop Grumman EA-6B Prowler electronic warfare/attack aircraft entered fleet service with the U.S. Navy in July 1971. It has also been used by the U.S. Marine Corps. The Prowler is a twin-engine aircraft modified from the basic A-6 Intruder aircraft design. Since 2009 the Prowler is gradually being replaced in the fleet by the Boeing EA-18G Growler, a development from the F/A-18F Super Hornet. In the course of its naval career, the Prowler has flown many radar jamming and radio intelligence gathering missions against enemy air defence systems.

The Prowler is capable of high subsonic speeds. It is a complex and aging aircraft, making it high-maintenance. While it is principally tasked with electronic warfare and command-and-control work for air strike missions, it is also able to fly attack missions against surface targets on its own, especially surface-to-air missile launchers and enemy radar sites.

The EA-6B Prowler electronic warfare/attack aircraft began service with the U.S. Navy in 1971. A total of 170 Prowler aircraft were built. The Prowler has also been operated by the U.S. Marine Corps. Crew: a pilot and three electronic countermeasures officers. Powerplant: two Pratt & Whitney J52-P408A turbojet engines of 10,400 lbs thrust each. Maximum speed: 651 mph. Range: 2,022 miles. Service ceiling: 37,600 feet. Armament: up to 18,000 lbs of missiles and external fuel. Origin: United States.

Probably no naval aircraft exemplifies the U.S. Navy today better than the McDonnell Douglas F/A-18 Hornet multirole fighter. Easily the most versatile plane in the current Navy inventory, the Hornet is a twin-engine supersonic, all-weather, carrier-capable jet fighter designed for both dogfighting and ground attack. The design was derived from the YF-17, a 1970s joint project between Northrop and McDonnell Douglas for the Navy and the U.S. Marine Corps. In its fighter role, the Hornet flies as a fighter escort, in suppression of air defences, fleet air defence, air interdiction, close air support, and aerial reconnaissance. In the plus column is the plane's versatility and reliability. Not without its critics, however, it has been faulted for its limited range and payload capabilities. The follow-on to the Hornet answers these criticisms though. The Boeing F/A-18E/F Super Hornet is bigger and heavier, with improved range and payload. It offers an even wider range of mission capabilities than the Hornet, including operating as an aerial refueling tanker and, in the EA-18G version, as an electronic jamming platform.

One of the most remarkable characteristics of the Hornet is that it requires much less down time for mainentance than its counterpart aircraft, the F-14 Tomcat and the A-6 Intruder. The Hornet was designed specifically to achieve that aim; those counterpart aircraft experienced part or system failure three times more frequently than the Hornet, which requires half the maintenance time. With engines that were designed for maximum reliability, operability, and maintainability, but are not of particularly exceptional performance rating, they are definitely exceptional in their robustness in all conditions and their resistence to stall and flameout. Without the use of special equipment, a four-person maintenance team can easily remove a Hornet engine in less than twenty minutes.

F/A-18 Hornets have flown combat missions since 1986, including the 1991 Gulf War, Operation Desert Storm, Operation Southern Watch, Operation Enduring Freedom, and Operation Iraqi Freedom.

The McDonnell Douglas F/A-18 Hornet began service with the U.S. Navy in 1983. A total of 1,480 Hornet A,B,C, and D aircraft have been built. The Hornet has also been operated by the air forces of Australia, Canada, Finland, Kuwait, Malasia, Spain, Switzerland, and by the U.S. Marine Corps. F/A-18C/D: Crew: a pilot and a weapon system officer. Powerplant: two General Electric F404-GE-402 turbofan engines of 11,000 lbs thrust each. Maximum speed: 1,190 mph at 40,000 feet. Range: 1,250 miles. Service ceiling: 50,000 feet. Armament: one 20mm M61 Vulcan cannon; 13,700 lb capacity for rockets, missiles, bombs, decoys, countermeasures, and external fuel tanks. Origin: United States.

The newest multirole strike fighter, expected to join the U.S. and Royal Navy fleets after 2016, is the Lockheed Martin F-35 Lightning II joint strike fighter. This fifth generation multirole fighter aircraft with stealth features was designed to handle air defence missions, reconnaissance, and ground attack assignments.

The F-35 first flew in 2006. Among the most complex and sophisticated aircraft ever developed, it is the result of the Joint Strike Fighter programme initiated in 2001 to replace the American F-16, A-10, F/A-18A/B/C and D, and the AV-8B aircraft. Three versions of the new plane were planned. The F-35A is intended to be a conventional take-off and landing aircraft. The F-35B is a short-take-off and vertical-landing variant, and the F-35C is a carrier-based variant. The F-35 is intended to be the premier strike aircraft through at least 2040 and a Lockheed Martin spokesman has stated that the plane will be four times as effective as the best previous fighters in air-to-air combat, eight times more effective in air-to-ground combat, and three times as effective in suppression of air defences and reconnaissance—with greater range and a lesser requirement for logistical support.

The United States has planned to purchase 2,443 F-35s. The United Kingdom planned to purchase an unspecified number of the planes for the Royal Navy.

In July 2007 then-British Defence Secretary Des Browne announced the government contract for two new *Queen Elizabeth* Class aircraft carriers to be constructed for the Royal Navy and expected to enter service in 2016. The ships would be the *Queen Elizabeth* and the *Prince of Wales* and would have a 65,000-ton displacement, a 920-foot flight deck, a ship's complement of 679 and an air group complement of 1,600. They would be the largest warships ever built for the Royal Navy, far larger than the previous *Invincible* class carriers it had been operating, and much closer in size to the American *Nimitz* class supercarriers.

The Royal Navy intended that the two carriers would be built in the Short Take-off and Vertical Landing configuration to operate the F-35B (STOVL) version of the joint strike fighter. However, with the 2010 Strategic Defence and Security Review, the British government elected to purchase the F-35C carrier version of the plane and ordered that the two carriers be reconfigured to a Catapult Assisted Take-Off Barrier Arrested Recovery configuration. The F-35C carrier-based plane will have greater range (very important in carrier operations), a greater weapons capacity and the latest in stealth technology; in short, a significantly more capable aircraft than the F-35B (STOVL) model. In May 2012, with the information that implementation of the change to the carriers was going to cost around twice that of the original reconstruction estimate, and with austerity seeming to take precedence over all other considerations, the current government announced it was going to revert to the originally approved carrier design.

Conventional military logic dictates that the greatly reduced Royal Navy, which currently operates just nineteen warships is, to say the least, highly unlikely ever to use one of the new large carriers against one of the emerging powers like India or China, both of whom are in the large carrier race. Conventional wisdom sees any such future nation v. nation conflicts more likely being fought in cyberspace. Far more likely is the use of the new carriers against Islamist insurgents in Somalia or Yemen, or in an effort to keep the Strait of Hormuz open to giant oil tanker traffic.

In March 2012, the U.S. Navy intervened in the UK position on the design and construction of the two new British carriers. The Assistant Secretary of the American Navy wrote to the British defence procurement minister that the required equipment involved would cost £458 million before installation and expert estimates put installation at about £400 million. The American stated too that the cost of the new, sophisticated and untested catapult and arrestor wire systems then intended for the British carriers would be underwritten by the United States, which was installing the new systems on one of its own carriers. He stated too, that "The Department of the Navy is committed to supporting the success of the UK CVF (conventional carrier)."

On 9 May 2012, the current British government made its U-turn, abandoning plans to purchase the conventional take-off version of the joint strike fighter, reversing one of the principal decisions of the defence review. The 2010 decision to install the new catapult and arresting gear systems on the British carriers was expected to delay completion of the ships until at least 2020, with potential delays in completion of the conventional version of the F-35 aircraft possibly pushing that date back further to 2023. Such delays would leave Britain without an operational carrier for at least another decade. Further considerations relating to the May decision to revert to the STOVL carrier configuration include the fact that development work on the jump-jet version of the F-35 is going more smoothly than anticipated, with the plane now expected to be available for carrier operation as early as 2018. And, with adoption of the jump-jet and that version of the carriers, the Royal Navy would now have two operational new carriers. Under the conventional carrier plan, one of the new ships would have to be mothballed, rather than made operational, to save money.

The joint strike fighter is by no means an all-American project. The United States is the main financial sponsor of the plane, and the principal customer, but the United Kingdom, Italy, the Netherlands, Canada, Turkey, Norway, Denmark, and Australia have contributed a total of $4.375 billion to the development costs of the programme. It is estimated that the development costs will be more than $40 billion, to be underwritten mainly by the United States.

The Lockheed Martin F-35 Lightning II is expected to begin service with the U.S. Navy after 2014. A total of 5,500 F-35 aircraft constructed is anticipated. The F-35 will also be operated by the U.S. Air Force, the Royal Navy, and the air forces of Italy, the Netherlands, Canada, Australia, Turkey, Norway, and Denmark. F-35A: crew—one pilot. Powerplant: one Pratt & Whitney F135 turbofan engine of 28,000 lbs thrust. Maximum speed: 1,200 mph. Range: 1,200 nautical miles. Service ceiling: 60,000 feet. Armament: one General Dynamics 25mm cannon; a 15,000 lb weapons capacity including missiles and bombs. Origin: United States.

CARRIER STRIKE GROUP

Ernie Pyle, a great American war correspondent in WWII wrote: "An aircraft carrier is a noble thing. It lacks almost everything that seems to denote nobility, yet deep nobility is there. A carrier has no poise. It has no grace. It is top-heavy and lop-sided. It has the lines of a well-fed cow. It doesn't cut through the water like a cruiser, knifing romantically along. It doesn't dance and cavort like a destroyer. It just plows. You feel it should be carrying a hod, rather than wearing a red sash. Yet a carrier is a ferocious thing, and out of its heritage of action has grown nobility. I believe that today every navy in the world has as its number one priority the destruction of enemy carriers. That's a precarious honor, but it's a proud one."

The main job of the aircraft carrier is to function as a sea-going air base, deploying and recovering aircraft, allowing a naval force to project air power over great distances without the need to depend on local bases and land-based aircraft. The supercarrier is the current primary capital ship, the role formerly occupied by the battleship prior to the Second World War. But unescorted aircraft carriers are considered vulnerable to attack by other surface ships, aircraft, submarines, and missiles, and they operate in the company of a carrier battle group, now known as the Carrier Strike Group.

For as long as there have been aircraft carriers, and inter-service rivalry, an argument has raged about the vulnerability and viability of the carrier and its strike group: proponents of the unmatched firepower and force it projects, versus opponents pointing to the ship being increasingly vulnerable to cruise missiles and arsenal ships. The debate continues.

The United States operates eleven supercarriers and their strike groups. Other nations operate and maintain aircraft carriers, including the United Kingdom which currently has no active carriers but is building two new *Queen Elizabeth*-class carriers that are expected to enter service with the Royal Navy in 2016 and 2018 respectively. The French navy operates the nuclear-powered carrier *Charles de Gaulle* and a second carrier is in the design stage though, as of this writing a decision to build the ship has not yet been taken. Currently the Russian navy operates the carrier *Admiral Kuznetsov* and it is believed that Russia plans to construct at least one more carrier whose design is under way. A new carrier for the Indian navy is under construction and is expected to enter service in 2016. India has also purchased the Soviet-built carrier *Admiral Gorshkov* carrier from Russia. It is being refurbished and is to be renamed the *INS Vikramaditya*. China has purchased an uncompleted *Admiral Kuznetsov*-class carrier called *Varyag* from Ukraine, which is in the sea trials phase. Two new Chinese aircraft carriers are under construction. Brazil currently operates a small carrier called the *Sao Paulo*, formerly the French aircraft carrier *Foch*. The United States, United Kingdom, France,

Republic of Korea, Japan, and Thailand all operate small helicopter carriers.

While the supercarrier represents its country as a fearsome and impressive projection of power, capable of bringing massive force to virtually anywhere on the planet, it is not invulnerable and relies heavily on the Carrier Strike Group for support and protection. The Carrier Strike Group has replaced the Carrier Battle Group and, in company with the aircraft carrier it supports, provides the ability to strike rapidly at any trouble spot in the world.

The first such carrier battle groups were developed and deployed in the Second World War when the United States was engaging the Japanese in the Pacific. Then there were many more warships taking part in the support role with their carriers, both American and Japanese. The Battle of Midway is the only occasion when such battle groups have fought each other.

When the Japanese attacked Pearl Harbor in December 1941, they employed six aircraft carriers, the *Kaga, Akagi, Shokaku, Zuikaku, Hiryu,* and *Soryu*, their 300 strike aircraft, two fast battleships and a small group of additional warship escort vessels. The power of this battle group was sufficient to destroy two American battleships and take five more out of action for a long while.

Without a functional battleship force, the United States was largely compelled after Pearl Harbor to adopt the battle group strike force around its own carrier fleet strike force which was comprised of the *Enterprise, Saratoga, Lexington, Yorktown, Hornet,* and *Wasp* in the early part of the war. Experience gained through hardfought air and sea actions with these carrier battle groups led directly to the development and construction of the twenty-four *Essex*-class carriers that served the U.S. into the Cold War period. The concept of the U.S. carrier battle group embraced protecting the carrier via layers of defence capability; utilizing cruisers and battleships to provide anti-aircraft support and destroyers to prevent submarine attacks. Into the Cold War, however, the Soviets emphasised their strong submarine fleet armed with cruise missiles, requiring the American carrier battle group composition and goals to change accordingly.

Following the Second World War, with the introduction of atomic weapons, a new vulnerability stalked the American carriers, whose use had often been designed within the framework of large task force fleets which sometimes included up to eight fast carriers. In the nuclear age, such a grouping was no longer realistic, thus leading to the individual carrier battle group concept.

Throughout the Cold War years, the primary role of the carrier battle group was to protect the Atlantic supply routes between the United States and Europe. The main concern then for the Americans was the potential use by the Soviets of a substantial number of anti-ship cruise missiles, a tactic that the Argentinians tried to employ in the 1982 Falklands War.

Operationally, in the U.S. Navy, Carrier Strike Groups are normally deployed at sea for six months, depending on the current requirements of the command to which the CSG is assigned. The CSG is fundamentally a small fleet of specialized warships and their crews of about 7,500 personnel, that accompany their carrier in its role of projecting power at sea and in the air. Being vulnerable to attack from submarines, aircraft, missiles, and other surface ships, the carrier must be protected from these threats so it and its air wing can continue to provide their offensive firepower. The aircraft of the carrier's air wing also contribute to the group's defence through combat air patrols as well as airborne anti-submarine efforts.

Carrier Strike Groups are charged with accomplishing a variety of wartime missions. In peacetime, their role is in forward presence operations in helping to form the strategic environment, deter conflict, work with Allies, and respond to crises. The U.S. Navy regularly rotates its strike groups on six-month cruises to meet the demanding requirements of the United Combatant Commands. The carrier strike group missions are: Gaining and maintaining sea control in coastal regions, the open ocean, bounded seas, and choke points; power projection ashore against a wide range of operational, strategic, and tactical targets defended by sophisticated air defense systems by day and night, in all weather; the protection of commercial and military shipping; humanitarian assistance and disaster relief; the protection of a U.S. Marine Corps Amphibious Ready Group prior to or during an amphibious operation; surveillance and intelligence to achieve and maintain a comprehensive operational picture of the littoral environment including surface, air, undersea, and relevant land areas; command and control of assigned U.S. and multi-national forces; establishment of air superiority or air supremacy by seizing and maintaining control of a designated airspace; theater ballistic missile defence of littoral areas, and selected theater-wide areas, against attack; and operations in support of the peacetime presence mission, including supporting United States diplomacy through cooperative engagement with designated Allied forces, normal peacetime operations, and shows of force.

In the nineteenth and the early twentieth centuries, gunboat diplomacy, in which one nation pursues its foreign policy objectives with the aid of conspicuous displays of military power, implying or constituting a direct warfare threat should terms not be agreeable to that superior military force, was practiced. Today, that term has been replaced by power projection, but, it is still essentially implementing policy by means of force, or the threat of force. Parking a supercarrier near the coast of a crisis area is often sufficiently persuasive to soften the intentions of the country or countries involved.

The captain of the supercarrier in a Carrier Strike Group is directly responsible to the commander of the CSG, who is usually a rear admiral. As commanding officer of the CSG, the carrier is his flagship and he operates from it, utilizing its advanced combat direction centre and communications suite. The Commander, Air Group (CAG) reports directly to the commander of the CSG. The CAG has overall responsibility for up to nine squadrons and has the same seniority as the captain of the carrier.

Ultimately, the CSG is responsible to the U.S. government, for which it can provide a range of options, from simply showing the flag, to attacking targets at sea, ashore, and in the air. The supercarrier CSG can also participate in sustained operations with other forces. Currently, five carrier strike groups are based on the U.S. west coast, five are based on the east coast, and one is forward-deployed at Yokosuka, Japan.

The actual composition of the Carrier Strike Group may be modified to meet the specific requirements of certain roles, missions, or expected threats. Typically though, the CSG is made up of one to two Aegis guided missile cruisers—a multi-mission surface combatant equipped with Tomahawk missiles for long-range striking capability; two to three guided missile destroyers—multi-mission surface combatants mainly for anti-submarine and anti-aircraft warfare and also equipped with Tomahawk missiles; and one to two Los Angeles-class attack submarines to operate with the group or independently—to seek out and destroy hostile surface ships and submarines; and a combined oiler-ammunition-supply ship, to provide logistical support for the group on station.

The supercarriers and their strike groups require no permissions to sail anywhere in recognized international waters. With critical national interests around the world, and a shortage of forward U.S. bases in many areas, the United States must rely on a combination of the cooperation of friendly Allied host nations, and carrier strike groups positioned offshore of crisis situations, if it expects to have a continuing role in international events.

In 2012 there were ten *Nimitz*-class supercarriers and one *Enterprise*-class supercarrier, each with an embarked Carrier Strike Group assigned in the U.S. Navy. These nuclear-powered carriers are *Enterprise* (CVN-65), *Nimitz* (CVN-68), *Dwight D. Eisenhower* (CVN-69), *Carl Vinson* (CVN-70), *Theodore Roosevelt* (CVN-71), *Abraham Lincoln* (CVN-72), *George Washington* (CVN-73), *John C. Stennis* (CVN-74), *Harry S. Truman* (CVN-75), *Ronald Reagan* (CVN-76), and *George H. W. Bush* (CVN-77). Currently operating eleven such carriers and their carrier strike groups, the United States is also building a new class of aircraft carrier, the *Ford*-class of which the USS *Gerald R. Ford* (CVN-78) and the USS *John F. Kennedy* (CVN-79) will be the first examples.

Balancing the maintenance and deployment schedules of the carrier strike groups, while providing appreciable consideration for the needs and interests of the embarked sailors, marines, and aviation personnel, is vitally important to the Navy. Typically, of the eleven operational carrier strike groups, two to three are scheduled for what the Navy calls Deep Overhaul, including nuclear refueling in the three principle shipyards at Newport News and Norfolk, Virginia, and Bremerton, Washington. Two to three of the strike groups are involved in Yearly/Periodic Maintenance, normally carried out dockside at the ship's home ports. The other six to seven are functioning in an eighteen-month activity cycle of three phases: a) Leave/ Unit Training Period—six months of rest and training for crew personnel coming off deployment; b) Work-up Period—six months combined training to refresh combat skills and sharpen the crew's ability in joint operations before the next deployment; c) six months when the assembled carrier strike group is forward-deployed on actual operations.

In the U.S. Navy, the current fleet of *Nimitz*-class carriers are the largest warships in the world. Their flight decks are 1,092 feet long and 252 feet wide. The length at the waterline is 1,040 feet. Their displacement is 103,300 tons. Their maximum navigational draft is 37 feet. They are powered by two A4W nuclear reactors, four steam turbines and four shafts. Their maximum speed is 30+ knots or 35+ mph. Their range: unlimited distance over 20-25 years. Their crew: With embarked air wing is 6,500 officers and personnel. Ship's company is 3,200; Air wing is 2,480. Their armament: two Mk 57 Mod 3 Sea Sparrow; two RIM-116 Rolling Airframe missiles; three Phalanx CIWS guns. Their aircraft carrried: ninety fixed-wing and helicopters. Their launch catapults: four. Their aircraft elevators: four.

On a *Nimitz*-class carrier, the four catapults and four arresting-gear engines enable the ship to launch and recover aircraft rapidly and simultaneously. The 4.5 acre flight deck is extremely active during flight operations, with crew members, aircraft, and equipment functioning at a high level of efficiency and intensity. The four large aircraft elevators bring aircraft to and from the hangar deck below the flight deck. Many of the ship's aircraft are stored and maintained on the hangar deck. Low-built tractors spot the planes on the flight deck. The aviation fuel is pumped up from below the flight deck and ordnance, bombs, and rockets are brought up from the magazines below. The steam catapults can accelerate a 37-ton jet aircraft from zero to a safe flying speed of up to 180 mph in 300 feet and less than three seconds. The exact weight of each aircraft ready for launching is determined and the launch catapult is then set to the required amount of thrust.

When the carrier is recovering landing aircraft, the pilots use a system of lenses to guide their aircraft along and down a "glide slope", the correct glide path to the deck landing. Four arresting wire cables, each two-inches thick, are connected to hydraulic rams below decks. As the tail-hook of a landing aircraft engages one of the arresting cables, the aircraft, landing at 150+ mph, is dragged to a stop in less than 400 feet.

High up in the "island", a seven-storey control structure above the starboard edge of the flight deck, the "air boss" and his staff coordinate the flight deck operations which are also monitored by the captain on the bridge.

The functions of the many flight deck and hangar deck personnel are identified by the shirt colours they wear: officers and aircraft directors wear yellow, fuel handlers wear purple, catapult and arresting gear crews wear green, tractor drivers wear blue, chock and chain runners wear brown, and ordnance handlers and crash and salvage teams wear red.

These nuclear-powered carriers have virtually unlimited range. They carry enough food and supplies to operate unreplenished for up to ninety days. They are equipped with four distilling units and can make more than 400,000 gallons of fresh water from seawater a day for the use of the propulsion plants, the catapults, and the crew. The *Nimitz*-class carrier stores about three million gallons of fuel for her aircraft and her escorts, as well as sufficient weapons and stores for extended operations. The carriers have extensive, sophisticated repair facilites for aircraft, electronics, and ship repair requirements. Like small, highly efficient communities, these carriers provide the services and facilities of a post office, radio and tv station, a newspaper, library, hospital, general store, two barber shops, and a fire department.

For ship defence, the *Nimitz*-class carrier is equipped with the NATO Sea Sparrow missile system comprised of two launchers with eight missiles each. Sea Sparrow is a short to medium range, radar-guided missile capable of engaging aircraft and cruise missiles. For close-in defence, the ship has mounts with search and track radar and six-barrel 20mm cannon.

By the end of the Second World War, the British and American navies were attempting to introduce the use of jet aircraft aboard carriers and were facing serious problems. The jets of those days were relatively low-performance aircraft with sluggish power and handling and the fear was that their higher landing speeds would be too high for carrier operation. The Royal Navy decided to try a new design concept on one of their carriers, which were smaller than the American vessels. Their idea incorporated an angled deck configuration, with arresting cables and had aircraft landing at ten degrees off the centreline of the flightdeck. With an angled deck, when a landing pilot fails to catch an arresting wire with his tail hook he simply accelerates and goes around for a second landing attempt. Before, with the straight deck layout, a missed landing attempt endangered aircraft parked or spotted on the forward end of the ship. The angled deck also frees up space in the flight deck layout for more catapults, thus more aircraft movements, for greater operational efficiency. Over 4,000 test landings were carried out on both HMS *Triumph* in 1952 and subsequently on USS *Antietam*, which demonstrated greater safety and efficiency than the previous conventional flight deck layout. The angled deck configuration was adopted and has been the standard for U.S. carriers since. While initially used by the Royal Navy as well, a different deck configuration, one utilizing a ski-jump ramp for Harrier jump jets, became the standard for British carriers until planning got under way for the next generation of RN carriers.

Another brilliant innovation came about after the adoption of the angled flight deck—the mirror landing sight. Prior to its development (also by the British initially), pilots approaching to land on a carrier relied on what the British called a "batsman" and the Americans referred to as a "landing signal officer", who used a pair of paddles to signal the pilot if his plane was too high, too low, etc. If the pilot's final approach to land was unsafe, he would be given a "wave-off" signal and would have to abort his landing and go around for another try. The original mirror landing system was somewhat crude by today's standard, but it worked. The current versions, a Fresnel array, which must cope with high-speed, high-performance jets, is more sophisticated and safer for all concerned. The fast jet must land under considerable power and in "dirty" configuration with all flaps and lift devices deployed, so it can safely accelerate away from the flight deck if the landing attempt fails.

When a pilot has flown his plane to a point roughly three-quarters of a mile from the carrier in his final approach to the deck, the ship's air traffic control centre delegates control of the aircraft to the landing signal officer (LSO) who, with his half dozen assistants, many with binoculars trained on the incoming plane, checks first to be sure that its landing gear and flaps are in the proper down position, that the plane is lined up on the centreline of the flight deck, that its wings are level, and that it appears to be descending at the correct rate to catch one of the four arresting wires when it slams onto the deck.

Bringing a hot and heavy jet like an F/A-18 Hornet aboard a carrier is a precise, demanding task, with little margin for error. The pilot must establish his plane's position and attitude on the glide slope and then fly it down the slope at an exact three-and-a-half degree angle. If, when he arrives over the ramp, he has flown the slope perfectly, his tail hook will cross the ramp fourteen feet above it. If he is more than a few feet too high, his hook will miss the arresting wires, or bounce over them, for what is known as a "bolter". Procedure requires U.S. Navy pilots to put the throttle (or throttles in multi-engine aircraft) to full-power the instant the aeroplane contacts the flight deck. When the plane's tail hook catches an arresting wire, bringing it to an abrupt halt, the pilot immediately retards the throttle(s), and the plane is allowed to roll back a few feet so the tail hook is disengaged from the wire. The hook is raised and the aircraft is guided away from the active landing area. The arresting gear is then reset for the next approaching plane. Should a pilot experience a bolter and his tail hook fail to catch an arresting wire, his engine is at full-power so he can get airborne and go around for another landing attempt. With every approach, the LSO and his back-up each hold an up-raised "pickle" switch that either of them can use to activate flashing red lights on the Fresnal array, signalling a wave-off to the pilot. The wave-off is not optional.

LSOs grade every landing approach to a carrier. They use a Trend Analysis form to chart the on-going record of every pilot's performance. When all the landings in a flight operation have been completed, members of the LSO team visit the pilots who have just landed, to discuss their grades for the task. Few things in the life of a carrier aviator are more important than these grades. If he cannot consistently and safely bring his aeroplane aboard the ship, the pilot is all but worthless to the Navy and will be sent to the beach. The grade given by an LSO for a landing approach is nearly always final and not subject to appeal. The grades given range from OK—a good approach with no problems, to NO GRADE—unacceptable deviation from the correct approach, to WAVE-OFF—the approach was too far from correct, was unsafe and had to be aborted, to BOLTER—try again. Competition among pilots for good grades is naturally high. When a pilot has done everything well and made a good approach, his tail hook should catch either the number two or number three wire. If the approach was a little high or fast, he may catch the number four wire; if a bit low or slow he may get the number one. Both numbers one and four are less safe than two and three—three being the most desirable.

One of the most dangerous things a human being can do is a "night trap"; landing on a carrier at night. Nothing a pilot must do requires greater skill, is more demanding and genuinely frightening. Poor performance in carrier night landings is the biggest cause of naval aviators losing their wings, and some pilots say that even after hundreds of night carrier landings, they never get easier. Some feel that the more night landings they do, the more nervous and uneasy they are about them. "Doing a night trap concentrates the mind wonderfully", commented one F/A-18 pilot. It is the lack of visual cues that creates the problem for pilots on night traps. Landing at night on an airfield offers a whole range of vital cues with which a pilot can judge how he is doing in his approach. Nighttime at sea is black-on-black. Often there is no horizon, making the experience even more disorienting. Setting up a proper approach can be a genuine waking nightmare. However, many people believe that a little fear, in combination with intelligence and a high degree of capability, in such a demanding situation, can be a good thing. It keeps you sharp, focused.

Former U.S. Navy fighter pilot, Frank Furbish: "During work-ups and refresher quals, I was on the flight deck when a good friend's career came to an end. Bhudda and his RIO (radar intercept officer) Boog, were out for a refresher night qual during work-ups for a cruise, when he pulled off a little too much power for a little too long. The F-14 has a slow 'spool-up' time for the engines, and it was too little too late. He hit the round-down with the tail and the hook of the airplane. He continued down the deck and once again became airborne as I saw a large piece of the nettings steel support rattle by. The back of the plane was engulfed in flame and he was instructed to eject. Luckily, they both got out and were uninjured. They were picked up by the helo within minutes. Bhudda never made it back. He was given all the help he needed, but could never get past the fear of night traps and, eventually, quit the Navy. He had excelled for two years of arduous training, was one of the best in all phases of flight, and yet, due to one mistake, he never made it to the fleet."

When carrier-based planes have to come to the boat in foul weather, there is a wide spectrum of electronic aids ready to assist them on modern U.S. carriers, from the instrument landing system (ILS), to the tactical air navigation system (TACAN), to the carrier controlled approach (CCA),to the automatic carrier landing system (ACLS). The latter is capable of bringing a plane to touchdown when the pilot has no visual contact with the ship, much less the flight deck. In ACLS, a precise guidance radar on the ship locks on to the automatic pilot in the plane when the plane is eight miles out from the carrier. Computers on the carrier and in the plane feed position updates to each other and the ACLS sends signals to the plane's autopilot which establish the approach. With this method, the autopilot can fly the plane to a safe landing on the carrier without the pilot having to touch the stick.

Among the most formidable threats to the current American aircraft carriers is the anti-ship missile, and in particular, the Soviet SS-N-22 Sunburn (NATO designation) anti-ship missile, two versions of which have been designed. One, the Raduga Moskit, is ram-jet propelled and launched by a small solid-fuel rocket. It is intended for use by certain destroyers, corvettes, and other small warships. This Mach 3 weapon is considered to be among the most lethal anti-ship missiles in existence, allowing a target just 25-30 seconds reaction time.

During the Second World War, the German Air Force experimented with the use of a radio-controlled "glide bomb" against various Allied targets. But it was not until 1967 that the effective use of an anti-ship missile began when, in the Israeli-Egyptian conflict of that time, an Egyptian missile boat sank the Israeli destroyer *Eilat* near Port Said. That action influenced anti-ship missile development by other nations including the United States, France, Italy, Norway, Sweden, China, and Israel, as well as air-launched versions; the French Exocet or flying fish prominent among them. Exocet was used by Argentina to sink the Royal Navy Type 42 guided-missile destroyer HMS *Sheffield* in the 1982 Falklands War.

When a strike aircraft like the Argentine Navy Super Etendard found and briefly illuminated a target like the *Sheffield* on the aircraft's radar, it input the range and bearing information to the computer in the Exocet missile.

When launched, the missile automatically descended to a pre-determined altitude until it had flown approximately two-thirds the distance to its target, when it dropped to wave-top height, making it very difficult for enemy radar to detect it. The radar of the missile was not turned on until the missile was about five miles from the target. Once the missile's radar had locked on to the target, the only defence for the target vessel was to destroy the missile with guns or a defensive missile system such as SeaRam. The typical gun used against such a missile was the multiple-
barreled 20mm Vulcan Phalanx with a firing rate of 3,000 rounds a minute. There was no time for such a reaction in *Sheffield*.

An earlier version of Sunburn, known as the Zubr, was developed for the submarine-launch capability. The nations known to possess and operate the Sunburn launchers and missiles are Russia, the People's Republic of China, India, Vietnam, and Iran.

Several years ago, when the Soviets were puzzling over how to overwhelm the force and firepower of the American Navy's carrier strike groups, they concluded that it was simply not feasible to outspend the U.S. in that category. In looking for vulnerabilities in the U.S. carrier strike forces, they set out to design and develop a number of supersonic anti-ship missiles, which led to their success with the Sunburn, a weapon specifically created to defeat the U.S. Aegis radar defence system. One credible defence source is quoted about the missile: "The Sunburn's combined supersonic speed and payload size produce tremendous kinetic energy on impact, with devastating conse-quences for ship and crew. A single one of these missiles can sink a large warship, yet costs considerably less than a fighter jet . . . the U.S. Navy's only plausible defence against a robust weapon like the Sunburn missile is to detect the enemy's approach well ahead of time, whether destroyers, subs, or fighter-bombers, and defeat them before then can get in range and launch their deadly cargo. For this purpose U.S. AWACS radar planes assigned to each are kept aloft on a rotating schedule. The planes 'see' everything with-in 200 miles of the fleet, and are complemented with intelligence from orbit-ing satellites. But U.S. naval commanders operating in the Persian Gulf face serious challenges that are unique to the littoral, i.e. coastal environment. A glance at a map shows why: The Gulf is nothing but a large lake, with one narrow outlet, and most of its northern shore, i.e. Iran, consists of mountain-ous terrain that affords a commanding tactical advantage over ships operat-ing in Gulf waters. The rugged northern shore makes for easy concealment of coastal defences, such as mobile missile launchers, and also makes their detection problematic." The mission for the supercarriers is nothing if not challenging.

WOMEN ON BOARD

Twenty-year-old Baillie Campbell is making her way from the United States Naval Academy at Annapolis, Maryland, to primary flight training at Pensacola, Florida, where she expects to ultimately emerge as Ensign Alison Baillie Campbell, navy aviator. She is fictitious, her journey is real.

Baillie earned a bachelor's degree in engineering at the academy, was ranked sixth in her class, and, as a midshipman, was part of the Naval Reserve Officers' Training Corps (NROTC) program. Of the approximately 13,000 applicants for admission to the Naval Academy each year, fewer than ten per cent are accepted. Of these, most bring exemplary academic records, a history of leadership, and an impressive sports background. An applicant must be at least eighteen years of age and a U.S. citizen, by birth or naturalization. He or she must pass the Aviation Selection Test Battery, a standard examination that originated in the Second World War. It consists of five timed subsets—mathematics and verbal, mechanical comprehension, aviation and nautical, spatial perception, and a survey gauging interest in aviation. Successful applicants must also take and pass a battery of physical, psychological and background tests, as well as a flight physical. His/her vision must be no worse than 20/40, correctable to 20/20, to become a naval aviator and he/she cannot have depth perception problems or be colorblind.

At NAS Pensacola, the would-be pilot undergoes primary flight training before going on to specialization in a particular type of aircraft. If you want to fly helicopters, you remain at Pensacola's Whiting Field for six months to train in the Bell Sea Ranger. If you are selected to fly tactical jet aircraft, your training will be at either Kingsville, Texas, or Meridian, Mississippi. All naval aviator training begins with ground school, including aerodynamics and meteorology. Most students then move on to fly the British Aerospace-McDonnell Douglas T-45 Goshawk, a fully carrier-capable jet, for intermediate and advanced training. Multi-engine maritime patrol aircraft training takes place at NAS Corpus Christi, Texas, and those who will fly the E-2C Hawkeye or the C-2A Greyhound turboprop planes learn about them at Kingsville. All of the aircraft types operated by the U.S. Navy require a minimum of 100 flight hours of training.

As a candidate to become a navy aviator, one must either hold a private pilot certificate (or higher), have completed a solo cross-country flight in a civilian aircraft, or undergo introductory flight screening in which you are required to take twenty-five hours of instruction at a certified flight school, and complete at least three solo flights, one being a cross-country.

At Pensacola, Baillie will study aviation physiology, aerodynamics, engines, and navigation, before continuing on to specialized training in the use of devices to cope and survive if she should be cast into the sea in an aircraft mishap. Her primary training begins at Whiting Field with instruction in the Navy's main basic trainer, the Beechcraft T-34C Mentor. After more than 100 hours in the Mentor and in a T-34 simulator, she will have learned basic flight skills, aerobatics, night and formation flying in preparation for her next training phase.

Baillie has long wanted to be a naval aviator and especially, a fighter pilot. If she qualifies, and there is an opening at that time, she will be trained to fly the McDonnell Douglas (now Boeing) F/A-18 Hornet, the backbone of U.S. Navy fleet aviation. The Hornet is supersonic and a highly capable all-weather, multirole jet fighter designed for air defence, fighter escort, suppression of enemy air defences, air interdiction, close air support, and aerial reconnaissance. Or, she may be assigned to fly the F/A-18E or F, the Super Hornet; larger and more powerful, these single-seat and tandem derivatives of the Hornet have advanced weaponry and extended range.

In 1974, six women earned their Navy wings of gold and became the first female pilots in the U.S. military. Later that year, the Army followed suit and trained its first female helicopter pilots and, in 1976, the U.S. Air Force began admitting women to its pilot training program. Initially, there were gender quotas, combat exclusionary rules, and limitations on the types of aircraft women were allowed to fly—until 1993, when the rules were changed.

Air Force Lt Col. Martha McSally was among the first American women to fly in combat as a fighter pilot. She became the first female in American military history to fly a combat sortie in a fighter during her 1995-96 tour of duty in Kuwait. She also flew more than 100 combat hours in an A-10 attack plane over Iraq in the mid-1990s and was a flight commander and trainer of combat pilots. By 2004, there were more than 500 female pilots in the U.S. military services.

This then is the eventful introduction of women into air combat roles by the United States Navy, their training and initial carrier assignments, the pressures and the wide-spread institutional resistance to their presence in America's greatest warships, their dignity and perseverance through the experience, the adjustments they, their male counterparts, and the Navy have made, and the issues they faced in their first thirty-five years in naval aviation.

"There is a world-old controversy that crops up whenever women attempt to enter a new field. Is a woman fit for that work? It would seem that a woman's success in any particular field would prove her fitness for that work, without regard to theories to the contrary." —Ruth Law, 1920

Shannon Callahan is the granddaughter of a U.S. Navy enlisted man who served on the aircraft carrier, *Gambier Bay*, a small carrier that was sunk in the Battle of Leyte Gulf during the Second World War. In March 2000, she completed the Naval Flight Officer course at NAS Pensacola and was selected for the EA-6B Prowler "community", as the Navy refers to those who fly a particular type of aircraft. "When I was in high school, I took a trip to the Air Force Academy and fell in love with the place. I definitely wanted to go there. But the Air Force officers I talked to convinced me that, to be in the Air Force one should really be a pilot, and I didn't think I could be a pilot because I didn't have 20/20 vision. I looked at the other service academies and decided on the Naval Academy, where I learned that even without 20/20, (I have 20/40) I could qualify to be a Naval Flight Officer. It is ironic that I actually could have been a pilot in the Air Force, because their eyesight requirements are lower than those of the Navy, but I didn't know that at the time. Fortunately, I found my calling because I really love carrier aviation. I went out on a carrier on a midshipman cruise one summer while at the Academy, and was enamoured with the whole thing. I got five cat-shots in a Prowler and after that there was no going back. I graduated from the Academy in '98, got my Masters degree in National Security, and showed up at flight school in Pensacola in '99.

"My first choice was RIO [Radar Intercept Officer] on an F-14 Tomcat [no longer in the Navy inventory]; second choice was Electronic Countermeasures Officer on an EA-6B Prowler. The Prowlers are being replaced by the E/A-18G; they call it the Growler. So it seems like I will end up in the Super Hornet if I stay in, which I really want to do. Every aviator loves their platform [assigned aircraft type]. Nobody ever regrets the direction they went or their choice. Everyone is positive and always trying to sell you on their platform.

"Every event, every training flight, is graded. They keep track of how each student is doing with what they call Navy Standard Scores (NSS). The scoring system for flights is: Above Average, Average, Below Average, and Unsatisfactory, which is a 'Down'. Two Belows equals one Down. Your NSS reflects how many Aboves and Belows you have, compared to the 200 to 300 students who went just before you, so it's all comparative. This is because the instructors come and go, and thus the grading changes a little bit; it's kind of fluid. To keep track of where I am in relation to my classmates, it's just a matter of counting up those NSS grades, and some people do that. That's not something that I obsess about. You'll drive yourself nuts if you keep comparing yourself to your buddies. The thing to do is just to go into every flight and give it your best, 100 per cent.

"I had faith in my instructors. I think they were pretty good and pretty fair, and I knew it would all work out the way it should because those people had been in aviation for years. I trusted them with the grades. I'm sure people on the outside probably think it's pretty cut-throat, but it's not. I've never known anyone who screwed a buddy to get ahead in this program. Everybody always helps everybody else. You have to cooperate to get winged. That's hard enough, and there is a huge attrition rate, even in Pre-flight, so you really can't make it without your buddies. The workload is so intense that you have to split up the work. I haven't met any Lone Rangers. You just can't do it. I've worked in groups from the beginning. The instructors encourage it. I think it's a necessity. You have to, to get it all done. And you rely on your buddies to cheer you up, to keep you stable and centered. It can be pretty stressful.

"There are no particular problems in being female in the program. There are still not that many of us, so, naturally most of my friends are guys. There hasn't been anything that has really got in my way. I think if anybody does have prejudices and stereotypes, they brought them with them from the civilian world into the Navy . . . the way they were raised or the area of the country they come from. I don't think the Navy breeds that at all. Most people just want to know, can you do your job? The percentage of women in the program was small. I think there were six or seven female students in the squadron, out of over a hundred students. There are few of us— markedly fewer of us—but at the same time we were not such an oddity anymore. There were not many female instructors. I've flown with one since I started, and that's from Primary on. I work in a pretty much all-male environment, but I'm used to it. The Academy trained me for that. It would have been a bigger adjustment had I come from a civilian school where the ratio was 50/50, so I was kind of lucky in that respect. The military is kind of inherently masculine, and a lot of women compensate by being more masculine. That's not necessary anymore. I think the situation has changed. You can just be yourself. Everything that is feminine isn't bad anymore, and it doesn't necessarily mean you are weak to be feminine.

"Again, people are interested in the bottom line. Can you fly? Can you navigate to the target? Can you get to the target on time? Are you safe? Do you know your emergency procedures? Can you make good judgement calls? Do you do thorough pre-flight planning? All that stuff is pretty gender-neutral.

"To get through the program, you really have to love it. That's what I tell people who are just starting. If you don't love it, don't bother, 'cause it only gets harder and more demanding. Your attitude has to be: 'I get to do this,' not, I have to do this. I'm really lucky to be doing this. I saw a lot of my buddies get attrited for medical problems or because they didn't have the grades for Aviation. I've been really fortunate to be in the program and I was not gonna make myself miserable just because it's hard. You have to earn something to appreciate it. I knew a long time ago that I wanted to be in the Navy for a long-term career. If you love your job, it's the biggest blessing in life. I would do this if they paid me in sand. As for the future, I'd like to command a carrier one of these days. Right now, I'm just trying to fly as much as I possibly can.

"I think the Navy is a great opportunity. Great people. I know I sound like a recruiter, but it's true. The caveat is, it's what you make of it. If you want to be miserable, you can be miserable. It's not hard to do. If you don't want to grab the opportunities, you don't have to, but they are there and, if you love your job, you'll find those opportunities. They'll find you, and you'll make the best of it and have a great career.

"The Naval Academy is a great place. It had a big part in making me who I am today. I'll always be grateful and proud that I went there."

In April 1995, the nuclear-powered *Nimitz*-class supercarrier USS *Abraham Lincoln* (CVN-72) sailed from San Diego on a six-month fleet deployment to the waters of the Persian Gulf to run reconnaissance and combat air patrols in Operation Southern Watch. Southern Watch was an American effort to enforce a United Nations no-fly zone south of the 33rd parallel in Iraq and to discourage any renewed Iraqi military activity against Kuwait or Saudi Arabia. The Iraqis challenged the no-fly zone several times after its inception in 1992, but their personnel and equipment were relatively stable until October 1994, when they began troop movements south towards Kuwait, prompting American and coalition forces to mount an intensified operation called Vigilant Sentinel. Upset about the continuing U.N. sanctions against Iraq, Saddam Hussein then deployed his mechanized infantry troops and armoured vehicles to the Kuwaiti border, causing the coalition forces to deploy additional aircraft in the region. It was into this tense environment that the *Abraham Lincoln* arrived, the first Pacific Fleet carrier to embark with female combat pilots aboard.

There were eighteen female fliers in the air wing of the *Lincoln* as the ship was being made ready for her Gulf deployment—eighteen out of the 120 aviators, a bit less than 1/6 of the aviators aboard were women. One of them was twenty-seven-year-old Lieutenant Loree Hirschman, the pilot of an S-3B Viking anti-submarine warfare aircraft. She is the daughter of Marine Corps Brigadier General Thomas Draude and the wife of Navy F/A-18 pilot Harry Hirschman. In three Vietnam War tours, General Draude could not have imagined wanting women in his units. His perspective changed, however, in the Gulf War when he observed and appreciated how well women performed in that conflict. General Draude: "Would you let your daughter fly in combat with the possibility of her becoming a POW? The answer is yes. I believe we have to send our best. If that means it is my daughter or my son, they should go."

Loree Hirschman: "I was the first female pilot to go directly from flight training into VFA-125, the squadron for new Hornet pilots at Lemoore,

[California] and the senior officers there quickly made it plain that they resented my presence and would do whatever they could to get rid of me. I certainly hadn't expected open arms and a key to the city when I arrived at Lemoore, but I wasn't prepared for the hostility, deceit, and antagonism I faced there. When I would greet any of the instructors in the hallways, they would walk by without answering or look away. Several were being investigated by the navy for their actions at the Tailhook convention [1991], and the instructors at Lemoore treated me like a disease . . . none of the IPs [Instructor Pilots] would speak to me except to communicate information required for our flights. When I walked into the ready room, the place would instantly become silent and icy. Instructors would get up and leave. They treated me like a leper, an enemy. Behind my back, they said the only reason I had been assigned to Hornets was that my dad was a marine general. Once again, the accusation was totally untrue.

"In the airplanes, the IPs were even more antagonistic. They weren't trying to teach me; they were looking for excuses to ground me. They didn't offer advice or helpful hints as my previous jet instructors had done. They just critiqued me and kept a running tally of my mistakes. Each flight was like a final exam. Everything I did or didn't do was endlessly analyzed, scrutinized, and dissected. It seemed it was up to me to teach myself how to fly the Hornet. As the weeks went by, the IPs seemed more determined than ever to make me fail. As a middle-class white girl, I had never felt discrimination before. I knew in an abstract sense that it existed, and I had come across plenty of individuals with bad attitudes. But I had never been confronted by officially sanctioned malevolence, hypocrisy, and double standards until I got to Lemoore. I tried to convince myself that I could persevere, that I could win the IPs over by working hard and proving my competency. But the more I tried, the clearer it became that the cards were stacked against me."

From a letter to Loree written by her father, General Thomas Draude: "Once you've gone through the various emotions and trials of being one of the first, you'll have to come to grips with how you go on from here. Tough as it is, you must continue to do your job. Without notice or publicity you must just fly your missions and take care of your troops."

"My chief tormentor at Lemoore was Lt. Cdr. Matthew 'Pug' Boyne, then the operations officer for VFA-125. Whenever I approached him he would grin and act as if everything was wonderful and he was my good buddy. Then he tried to get me kicked out of training and end my navy flying career. He assumed that because I was female, I was unqualified to fly fighters. Then he set it out to prove it.

". . . with only two flights remaining before the end of the Hornet instructional course, Pug pounced. A 'Human Factors Board' was convened to decide whether outside influences were interfering with my ability to learn. The four-member board was told to decide whether I should be allowed to keep flying, as I argued, or whether a Field Evaluation of Naval Aviator Board, FENAB, should be convened with the possibility of drumming me out of the navy.

The evaluation board was split, two to two and the commander of the squadron broke the tie allowing Loree to keep flying and finish her Hornet training. She insisted that the squadron commander evaluate her final flight. She wanted to show him that she could fly an F/A-18 as well as any other new pilot. She had found it odd that, although he knew how much difficulty I was having with his instructors, he had never flown with her himself to form his own opinion. He consented to fly her last flight with her, and they went out on a night hop together, in separate, single-seat jets. They flew in formation, made aerial rendezvous and instrument approaches—everything the syllabus required and more. When they landed, Loree felt that she had proved her point. The commander evidently agreed.

Loree went on to VAQ-34 and flew Hornets in simulated electronic warfare missions. The more she flew, the more at home she felt in the airplanes. Then, less than a year after she joined VAQ-34, the squadron was dissolved because of budget cuts. At the same time, however, Defense Secretary Les Aspin lifted the combat exclusion law for women. Loree hoped to go back to VFA-125 and learn to use the Hornet as a weapon. But the instructor pilots got the last laugh; they made sure that when the navy's female pilots received their 'combat transition' assignments, she was sent elsewhere to fly some other type of aircraft. Friends of hers in the navy's personnel department told her that Lemoore instructors called assignment makers and told them she was a trouble-maker and a poor pilot. Though she had no evidence that Pug was involved, she couldn't help but feel that he was part of the reason that she was sent to San Diego to fly S-3 Vikings instead of being allowed to stay in Hornets.

Loree was faced with a decision: she could fight the orders and call for an investigation into the harassment she endured at VFA-125, but that would guarantee that she would not fly for a long time while the administrative details were settled, and she would not be doing her country any service by sitting around waiting for all the paperwork to be processed. Also, by the time she had received her orders, two other women who were senior to her had started Hornet training at VFA-125, and she was afraid an investigation would agitate the instuctors and harm those women's chances for success. She chose to accept the orders to S-3s.

Shortly after arriving at VS-41 in San Diego to start S-3 Viking flight training, Loree went to talk with Captain Jansen Buckner, skipper of the training squadron. She hoped to dispel the negative rumors that had followed her from the Lemoore Hornet squadron. Before she could begin, however, Buckner said, "You're talking about the past, and that's a subject I'm not particularly interested in. You're in my squadron now, and I promise you that for better or worse, you'll be evaluated on your performance. Nothing else matters."

Aboard the USS *Abraham Lincoln* Loree Hirschman experienced wide-ranging institutional resistance to the presence of women pilots that inhibited the training and advancement of the women in naval aviation. When the carrier had returned to California after its 1995 deployment to the Gulf, one of her female aviators had been killed, another had turned in her wings, a third had been sent home for poor performance, and another would leave due to illness. Most of the others, however, progressed well in spite of the stresses, pressures and prejudices against their presence. They struggled to overcome the resentment and mistrust, and Lt Hirschman reflected on the irony of flying her jet in defence of Arab countries that would not permit women to drive cars, bare their arms and faces, or go out alone in public.

General Draude was a member of the Presidential Commission on the Assignment of Women in the Armed Forces under President George Bush in November 1992. The commission voted initially against women in air combat, greatly disappointing General Draude. Lt (jg) Harry Hirschman, Loree's then boyfriend (later her husband), was a staff member on the commission and she was able to sit in on some of the proceedings. A few of her flight training comrades, Pam Lyons and Brenda Scheufele, had appeared to provide their views and they were shocked by some of the other testimony. Scheufele: "It was the first time I've heard such open hatred and hostility from fellow aviators."

When the matter of physical capability came up in the discussion, the standard voice in opposition to women aviators in combat roles was heard . . . that these women were being allowed into flight training and were inherently less qualified to fly military aircraft than men, and were not required to actually match the men in such rudimentary fitness tests as the eight-foot "climbing wall" at Pensacola's obstacle course. Scheufele: "If you can do everything the plane asks of you, then you have passed the test. If you can pull the G's in the plane, you're strong enough." One of their instructors had expressed his apparently sincere concern that "the United States would tailor its rescue efforts to get back any captive woman, without regard for larger strategic objectives."

Some of the female aviators were of the opinion that their male counterparts could not perform (or believed they could not perform) as well in the air when there was a woman in the plane next to them. The women felt that, if the men couldn't handle that in the air, then they didn't belong in combat. Because combat is much more stressful than just having a woman on your wing. Hirschman: "Once people see that each person in the unit is carrying their load, then they won't have a claim."

Loree Hirschman's squadron skipper in VS-29 was Commander Chuck Smith. Hirschman: "Smith was a tough disciplinarian, but he had been absolutely impartial, fair, and evenhanded to me and the other women under his command. He had a reputation for demanding a lot of his junior officers, but in return he backed us to the hilt. Aboard the *Lincoln*, whenever the Air Boss summoned one of the pilots in our squadron to his office to be verbally harangued for screwing up an approach or making some other kind of mistake, our skipper walked up nine flights of ladders and absorbed the Boss's wrath himself. Later he would talk to the offending pilot and offer constructive criticism, not bombast and invective. Very few squadron commanders were willing to become human heat shields for their junior officers. Smith had worked hard behind the scenes to help me and the other female aviators during our first few months at sea. He had done his best to make the integration of women work in his squadron—and when he left, I had the sense that I would miss his quiet support."

One of Loree Hirschman's roommates on the *Lincoln* was Lt Sue McNally, an E-2C Hawkeye pilot. After experiencing a particularly frightening night landing, Lt McNally chose to turn in her wings, telling her commanding officer that she didn't want to fly anymore and preferred to give it up rather than face an evaluation board. Loree Hirschman: ". . . it was sobering and a little discouraging to realize that with what were likely going to be the toughest months of our cruise still ahead, one-fourth of the female pilots originally assigned to the *Lincoln* were gone. And with each female pilot who went home, those of us who remained felt added pressure. When one of your contemporaries throws in the towel and says, 'This isn't worth it,' it's hard not to get rattled. Such actions force a kind of mental reappraisal among those who stay behind, and I just didn't want to go through that wrenching process on the ship.

"Personally I wanted to be part of this historic cruise. I had asked for the assignment and was glad that I had gotten it. I felt I could play an important role as part of a pioneering group, and I believed I could perform my duties well and make things better for the women who would follow us. Even in my darkest times on the ship, I wouldn't have traded places with anyone. For me the novelty of being one of the first women to fly combat planes had worn off long ago. I hadn't chosen to go into aviation to draw attention to myself or break down social barriers; I just wanted to serve my country in a challenging, meaningful assignment. And once I began flying airplanes, I found that I wanted to go as far as my ability could take me. I also truly believed that my seeing the Lincoln's cruise through to a successful conclusion would benefit many others in the navy. Being around competent, mission-oriented female pilots would increase men's confidence in their female shipmates and smooth the transition for everyone. That was one of the thoughts that kept me going."

Fighter pilots in combat must be killers. It is a part of the job description. Can women be killers and enter air combat with the same 'go for it' attitude that has always been required of males in the role? History produces many examples, not least being that of the Soviet Air Force in the Second World War. During the siege of Stalingrad, Lt Lily Litvak, described as a small, charming, girlish, and deadly Yak-9 pilot flew as a 'free hunter' in many of the search-and-destroy missions against the fighter pilots of the German Luftwaffe. She chalked up a total of twelve kills in her illustrious combat career, establishing herself among the most effective of Soviet aviators in that time.

"This is not a time when women should be patient. We are in a war and we need to fight it with all our ability and every weapon possible. Women pilots, in this particular case, are a weapon waiting to be used."
—Eleanor Roosevelt, 1942

By the time Loree Hirschman went on her second Gulf deployment, women aviators in the Navy had begun to make great strides in being accepted— by the Navy in general and by their fellow pilots. One of the new female F/A-18 Hornet pilots even won the "Top Nugget" award for the highest score in qualification. Loree placed in the top ten qualifiers.

Another of the female aviators serving aboard the *Lincoln* prior to that Gulf deployment was Lieutenant Kara Spears Hultgreen, twenty-nine, of Greenwich, Connecticut. An F-14 Tomcat fighter pilot, Kara was the first female carrier-based fighter pilot. She grew up in Chicago, Toronto and San Antonio, Texas, where she attended Alamo Heights High School before receiving a congressional nomination to the U.S. Naval Academy. She did not win an appointment to the Academy and attended the University of Texas, Austin, where she majored in Aerospace Engineering.

Hultgreen earned her commission through the Aviation Officer Candidate School at Pensacola and advanced to NAS Corpus Christi, where she was designated a naval aviator flying EA-6A Prowler aircraft and assigned to VAQ-33 at NAS Key West, Florida. When the Navy began integrating women into combat roles in 1993, Kara was among the first female pilots selected for F-14 fighter training at NAS Miramar, San Diego. Assigned to Fleet Replacement Squadron VF-124 there, she failed her first attempt at carrier qualification, but successfully qualified in a second try on the USS *Constellation* (CV-64) in summer 1994. She became the first combat-qualified female navy aviator and was assigned to VF-213, the Black Lions squadron, then preparing for a six-month Persian Gulf deployment. Her call-sign was Revlon.

Kara Hultgreen died in the afternoon of 25 October 1994 when her Grumman F-14A Tomcat fighter crashed on approach to landing on the USS *Abraham Lincoln* fifty miles off the coast of San Diego after a routine mission. The Navy videotape of the incident appears to show the F-14 beginning to overshoot the centerline of the carrier deck, and the pilot attempting to correct the approach by yawing the aircraft.

Some people believe that this caused the left-hand engine to suffer a compressor stall and lose power—a low-speed deficiency known to be characteristic of the TF-30-P414A engine, as inlet air no longer flows into it.

What happened next has become the subject of much debate and conjecture. An investigation by the Navy Judge Advocate General (JAG) concluded that the primary cause of the crash was mechanical malfunction. It was the official Navy position in the matter. A separate investigation by the Naval Safety Center issued a Mishap Investigation Report (MIR) which is not normally made public. The Navy has long believed that the confidentiality of this report protects the witnesses and ensures getting at the whole truth of a mishap. The report, however, was leaked and it concluded that pilot error was the primary factor in the incident.

As the F-14 lost power asymmetrically, one report indicates that the pilot tried to compensate for the power loss by selecting full afterburner power on the remaining engine, resulting in even greater assymetry. The aircraft was entering a higher angle of attack, which caused an unrecoverable approach-turn stall and a rapid wing-drop to the left. There is a clearly audible 'wave-off' on the videotape immediately following the apparent engine failure; then a gear-up command from the Landing Signal Officer. In but a few seconds from the stall, the Radar Intercept Officer (RIO) initiated the ejection sequence from his rear seat for himself and Lt Hultgreen when it became obvious to him that the airplane was uncontrollable. He went out first in the automated ejection sequence and survived. Lt Hultgreen's seat fired 0.4s later, when the rapidly rolling plane had passed the horizontal. She was ejected downward into the water. The entire event had occurred in less than twenty seconds.

After three attempts, the Navy salvaged the Tomcat and recovered Lt Hultgreen's body, still strapped into her ejection seat, from a depth of 3,700 feet nineteen days after the crash. She was buried with full military honors in Arlington National Cemetery, Virginia.

The *New York Times* wrote of her: "One of the Navy's first female combat pilots, Kara S. Hultgreen, 29, was killed in October when her F-14 Tomcat crashed into the sea off San Diego as she was approaching an aircraft carrier for a landing. It was a controversial death: Hultgreen's pioneer position in that male bastion, the Navy, hadn't been achieved without resistance, and the accident raised questions about whether she had been adequately trained. But fellow pilots praised her performance, noting that 10 F-14 aviators have died in accidents since 1992.

"Hers was a dream denied, then deferred and finally granted, to fly with the elite in a fighter jet so fast, so complex and so advanced that its wings heave back and forth along its glinting body, shifting angles for attack, landing, takeoff and approach, a machine hurtling 35 tons of metal, raw speed and unspent ammunition toward a combat target or a floating field called home.

"To fly an F-14 has always been for the few. Kara Spears Hultgreen fought for the privilege. Again and again, the system closed its doors, but systems change. When the ban on women in combat was finally lifted, Hultgreen was prepared. She had a Navy post, about 1,000 hours of flight experience and a reputation as a pilot unfazed by the rigors of life along the thin blue line of the earth's atmosphere.

"When she was a college senior, her mother, Sally Spears, thought she would make a stunning debutante. Instead, she joined the Navy and became a stunning fighter pilot—5 foot 10, lean with silk brown hair, vivacious, with a ready smile. She also had an edge when edge was needed.

"Once, after landing on an aircraft carrier off Key West, she was striding down the deck when the flight bosses noticed her hair tumbling below her helmet. They said it was a safety hazard and she was told to cut it short. She balked: 'You don't want to keep me from exploring my feminine side, do you?' The Pentagon spent hundreds of thousands of dollars studying the problem. But Hultgreen did not wait for the result. Instead, she bought a race car helmet, which solved the problem. And that ended that."

Following the Hultgreen accident, an anonymous caller provoked controversy in the media by claiming that the Navy had lowered its standards to allow Kara to qualify for duty aboard a carrier, for the sake of political correctness. Her commanding officer and some fellow aviators spoke up in her defense, commending her as an excellent pilot and her mother released her official flight records with her score of third highest in a group of seven qualifying pilots.

The Navy investigating officer's findings were also released. "Based on witness statements, logbooks and official records, and the engineering analysis of the F-14 aircraft recovered after the accident, they concluded that Lt Hultgreen was fully qualified to fly the F-14A and Lt Klemish [her RIO] was a fully qualified F-14A radar intercept officer. The mishap occurred during the landing phase of routine carrier operations and the emergency resulting in the mishap was precipitated by a left engine malfunction at an extremely vulnerable moment as the aircraft was approaching the carrier to land. The pilot attempted to continue flying the aircraft to safety but was unable to do so."

The Commander, Naval Air Force, Pacific Fleet, Vice Admiral Robert J. Spane: "All too often we forget how narrow the margin of safety is in naval carrier aviation. This pilot did her best to keep this aircraft flying under conditions that were all but impossible."

Loree Hirschman: "I thought about how different the last six months would have been if Kara had lived. Surely there wouldn't have been as much pressure on the female aviators, and perhaps the whole controversy about whether women were qualified to fly would have remained under wraps. Kara's death had cast a shadow over the entire air wing, and we hadn't been able to shake it. The aftermath brought out the worst in a lot of people, and it strained relationships between the male and female aviators. Worst of all for our air wing, it deprived us of a strong leader who could have been successful as the navy's first female fighter pilot.

"On the next cruise I will be one of the more senior members of my squadron. I will be able to concentrate on my job without wondering whether I am regarded as a token or some kind of feminist social experiment."

The second female naval aviator to qualify as an F-14 combat pilot aboard the *Lincoln*, after Kara Hultgreen, was Lt. (J.G.) Carey Lohrenz. One of five female combat pilots assigned to Air Group 11 on the carrier, Lohrenz was a 22-year-old University of Wisconsin graduate with no illusions about the attitudes and ways of behavior sometimes displayed by the male naval aviators. The occasional arrogance, misogynist joking, and the macho posturing of some of them was understandable. She came from a family in which her father, brother and husband were all Navy or Marine pilots, and she readily accepted such behavior as their way of dealing with the fear and pressure that comes with the job.

Of concern though to the women aviators in the air group was that, as new carrier pilots, or "nuggets" in Navy jargon, they were not receiving the extra training and mentoring that is commonly given by the more experienced pilots to the newcomers to help them adjust to the hazardous business of landing jets at sea. They believed they were being left to sink or swim.

One day while the *Lincoln* was steaming towards the Persian Gulf the commanding officer of Air Group 11 invited the five women pilots for tea and cookies and told them that he wasn't sure the American people were ready to see women taken prisoners of war, explaining that he regarded women under his command the way he did his own wife—as females who needed to be protected. The women thought they were being patronized and singled out as women, rather than being treated as fellow officers. There was concern that they were being set up to fail. The normal wash-out rate out of the 120 pilots of a carrier air wing is about one or two per deployment.

A *Newsweek* magazine piece by Evan Thomas in March 1997 considered the integration of women into the ranks. "It appears that the female pilots aboard the *Abraham Lincoln* were quietly ostracized and derided. Warriors talk about 'unit cohesion,' the intricate relationships that bond fighting men together. Because soldiers die for their buddies, not out of abstract notions of patriotism, those bonds can make the difference between fighting and fleeing. The Pentagon insists that women are now being welcomed into the fleet and that their failure rate is not significantly higher than that of male pilots. But the experience of the female fliers aboard the *Abraham Lincoln*—or the 'Babe,' as it was quickly dubbed—shows that some deep prejudices will have to be overcome before women can be accepted as top guns."

The 6 foot 1 Lohrenz was only recently out of flight training when she became one of the first two women ever qualified to fly F-14s on combat missions. The F-14 was then the Navy's premier fighter plane, the best of the best, flown by the elite of naval aviators. But it was also considered unstable, with a history of mechanical malfunctions, and difficult to land on a carrier deck. Of the 632 F-14s built since 1972, —144—have crashed. The F-14 is no longer part of the Navy inventory of carrier-based aircraft.

On 25 October 1994, Lohrenz was ready to depart NAS Miramar on a flight out to the *Lincoln*, about fifty miles off San Diego, when she received a radio call to "stand down." In a few moments she learned that a pilot had crashed an F-14 while trying to land on the carrier. She guessed it was Kara Hultgreen. Evan Thomas: "When a pilot is killed, his mates often take a few days off. But Lohrenz had to make 10 'passes' at landing on the carrier the day she learned her comrade had died. True, pilots are taught to 'compartmentalize' their emotions. 'It doesn't matter if your left foot is on fire or you've just heard that your mom and dad are dead,' she says. 'You do your job.' Still, Lohrenz knew she was in trouble when she taxied out that day. 'I'm going to have some snakes in the cockpit today,' she told her RIO, the radar intercept officer who sits behind the pilot in an F-14.

"Too fast: Lohrenz did not fly well that day. Twice she 'boltered': she came in too high and too fast, and the tailhook of her plane failed to snag one of the four arresting wires on the ship's deck. She was forced to abort the landing and try again. Getting planes aboard quickly is important in wartime: a carrier steaming straight and steady into the wind to recover fighters makes a fat target for enemy submarines. Pilots are marked down for boltering by the officers who grade every landing. But Lohrenz was afraid of a worse fate: coming in too low and cracking up her plane on the fantail.

"When Lohrenz stumbled into her squadron ready room after flying that day, none of her mates criticized her. But there was little commiseration over Hultgreen's death. The ready room, with its personalized armchairs, is the squadron's frat house, the place where pilots swap war stories and nuggets are initiated into the rites of fighter jockdom with rough-and-tumble joking. The camaraderie is often raunchy. On the floor of the ready room of Lohrenz's squadron, VF-213, is the squadron symbol, a black lion with a pair of big golden testicles. When Lohrenz and Hultgreen came aboard, the lion's balls were covered over with blue tile. Meanwhile, the officers in the newly integrated squadrons grumbled that they were no longer allowed to watch porno movies in the ready room. They also resented the intense media interest in the women. Naval aviators are accustomed to being the center of attention, and the men disliked the fact that reporters were brushing by them to talk to the women on board."

The majority of aviators aboard the *Lincoln*, including Lohrenz, believed that pilot error had been a factor in Hultgreen's crash and that, as part of the suspected "double-standard" for the female aviators, the Navy was covering up. The ostracizing of Carey Lohrenz seemed to be expanding as the Navy officially blamed Hultgreen's mishap on mechanical failure. The stressful situation for her was compounded when the CO required the women aboard Lincoln to take a pregnancy test. "You trust me to fly a $40 million airplane, but you don't trust me to tell you if I'm pregnant?" Now clippings from newspapers were circulating around the ship, alleging that Hultgreen and another female F-14 pilot, identified as "Pilot B" were unqualified to fly F-14s. The article quoted a right-wing defence organization which claimed that the two women had been sent to the fleet for political reasons. Lohrenz, being the only other female F-14 pilot then, was easily identified as Pilot B.

Like many of her male counterparts, Lohrenz failed to qualify for carrier duty on her first try. On her second attempt she was rated "average", though the newspaper articles made her seem incompetent. She was horrified to realize that someone had evidently stolen her training records and leaked a highly selective and inaccurate version. Her fellow pilots began calling her "Pilot B."

She felt totally isolated. Her two roommates, female pilots who flew the COD or Carrier Onboard Delivery twin-engined prop plane, tried to keep her spirits up, but they were not fighter pilots. The two women pilots who roomed across the hall from Lohrenz were fighter pilots who flew the F/A-18 Hornet and they too were experiencing problems in the essentially male environment of the air group. One of them, Lt Pam Carel, was told by her commander not to hang around with the other junior officers. She realized that, in the aftermath of the notorious Tailhook scandal in which 83 women and 7 men claimed to have been victims of sexual assault and harassment during the 1991 annual gathering of the Tailhook Association, resulting in damaged or shortened Navy careers for 300 aviators and fourteen admirals, the male pilots of the air group were highly cautious. They didn't want to risk being seen joking or flirting with a woman officer for fear of being accused of sexual harassment.

Carel and her roommate, Lt Brenda Scheufele, seemed to keep their distance from Carey Lohrenz, which Lohrenz attributed to the "heat-transfer theory," a Navy notion that, when the heat is on, your friends don't want to

get too close in case they might get burned. Lohrenz was feeling completely alone.

At that point, the situation was affecting her flying. As the ship neared
the Gulf that spring, she began boltering again, twice missing the arresting
wires on night landings. On 27 May, she was scheduled to fly her first combat mission, a patrol in the no-fly zone over southern Iraq. She arrived in the
squadron ready room that morning to find that her name had been removed
from the flight schedule. The CO told her that she was to appear before a
panel of fellow aviators who would decide if she should be grounded for
unsafe flying. She knew that such decisions could be subjective. The panel
rated her flying "unpredictable, related to personal factors." In his own evaluation, her CO wrote "A tragic disaster is just a matter of time." Surprised
by the verdict of the panel, Lohrenz had not been told about her declining rat-
ings. The CO denied this and said that she had been given "plenty of feed-
back."

After a month in limbo, Lohrenz was officially grounded and ordered
back to San Diego. A few weeks later, Pam Carel was put on probation. The
third female pilot from the air group to be grounded—an EA-6B Prowler
pilot, Nancy Nichols, had been grounded in March, before the carrier left
for the Persian Gulf. The one remaining female combat pilot, Brenda
Scheufele, developed a stomach ailment lasting several weeks and then left
the air group to become a test pilot.

In the wake of Kara Hultgreen's accident and Carey Lohrenz's grounding, a
group called the Center for Military Readiness, headquartered in Livonia,
Michigan, headed by a woman named Elaine Donnelly, and billing itself as
an independent, non-partisan, educational organization formed to take a
leadership role in promoting sound military policies in the armed forces,
took an interest in Lohrenz, the Hultgreen mishap, and the presence of
female combat pilots in the U.S. military services. In early 1995, Donnelly
wrote to Senator Strom Thurmond, then Chairman of the Senate Armed
Services Committee, that the Navy was promoting unqualified women in "the
demanding and dangerous field of carrier aviation in the F-14 community."
In April of that year, Donnelly published a report from her organization,
which included her letter to Senator Thurmond as well as a copy of Carey
Lohrenz's confidential training record, identified as the training record of
"Pilot B", but obviously that of Lohrenz (then the only carrier-qualified
female pilot in the Navy.) The following month, Lohrenz lost her flight status. In a speech to the Army-Navy Club in Washington, DC a year later,
Donnelly again claimed that Lohrenz was an incompetent pilot.

Carey Lohrenz's training records show that she earned "first place honors"
in her primary flight training and her superior performance there entitled
her to select her preference for aircraft to fly. She chose jets. When she

completed jet training, however, she was told that there was no place for female jet pilots at that time and was given the options of serving as a flight instructor or leaving the Navy. But then the Navy policy changed and she was again given her choice—combat jets, for which she was qualified.

With the loss of her flight status and her carrier aviation career in tatters in 1995, Lohrenz sued the Navy for sexual discrimination, sued Donnelly and the CFMR for defamation and invasion of privacy. She claimed that pressure by critics had affected her flying. The Navy elected to pay a $150,000 settlement. In 2002, a U.S. federal judge dismissed the Lohrenz suit against Donnelly, ruling that Lohrenz was a public figure. Former White House counsel John W. Dean took an interest in the case and wrote: "Why was Lohrenz deemed a public figure? She held no public office, nor had she ever sought fame; she simply wanted to be a pilot—not, say, a television commentator on military issues. She hardly had the kind of media access that a true public figure has. The Court reasoned—dubiously—that when Lohrenz and Hultgreen went into 'combat status,' at a time that the issue of women in combat was very controversial, they somehow thrust themselves into the controversy in such a way as to make themselves public figures for the limited purpose of this debate. Obviously, Lohrenz did not have a clue she was giving up her privacy and the right to defend her reputation by this decision. Nevertheless, the courts claimed she had assumed the status of a limited purpose public figure voluntarily.

"Never mind that Lohrenz just wanted to do the job she was so good at: The fact that others wanted to talk about her barrier-breaking made her a 'public figure' in the courts' eyes. The idea that she has voluntarily become one is laughable—but in this case, it was the law."

After the tragic Kara Hultgreen crash, a series of anonymous faxes circulated within the Navy, impugning her flight record. The faxes claimed that, in its efforts to desegregate naval aviation, the Navy was rushing unqualified pilots into the fleet. The Navy maintained an official policy of silence about Hultgreen's flight records, stating only that she had been an "average to above average F-14 pilot." With the continuing controversy over her capability and the cause of her crash, the Navy conducted a costly salvage operation to raise Hultgreen's Tomcat fighter. A four-month investigation followed, concluding that the crash had been the result of technical malfunction, not pilot error, and that when the left engine stalled on her landing approach to the carrier, virtually no pilot would have been able to save the plane.

Francesco 'Paco' Chierici, F-14 Tomcat pilot, VF-213, Landing Signal Officer Team Leader, USS *Abraham Lincoln* [1995]: "For seventy-five years navy pilots had been men, and all the traditions and social customs were developed exclusively by and for males. For example, each squadron's ready room was the center of activity, and ready rooms could be pretty raunchy places. But suddenly female officers were a part of the ready room, and no one was quite sure how to behave anymore. Most nights we watched movies, and in the darkened room with thirty or forty people, the off-color comments would fly. Any time there was sex or nudity or violence in the movies, people would shout out jokes and comments. Some of the women tried to fit in. They did their best to be part of the crowd, but I'm sure it was difficult for them.

"On the flight deck all of the women were rookies, and there were no really strong ball fliers among them. That's not unusual, since it typically takes at least one cruise before a pilot really finds the groove. Flying on and off aircraft carriers is demanding and there's so much to learn that it's rare for someone to master all of it right away.

"Let's face it, the women were put on the *Lincoln* by congressional decree. Right or wrong, they didn't have to go through the same selection process that the men did, and everyone on the ship knew it. Joining an operational squadron is kind of like being the new player on a baseball team. Everyone has roles, everyone knows each other, and new arrivals have to learn the subtle ways each individual communicates. Some rookies try too hard to be part of the team; some are aloof. Every new person gets tested, and everything they do is scrutinized. That's the way it was with the women on the Lincoln, only more so.

"The women on the *Lincoln* seemed to fall into two categories: those who believed that the men were conspiring against them, and those who did not. In general, those who believed we were plotting against them didn't perform very well. They became bitter, they blamed others for their shortcomings, and they didn't progress. Those who concentrated on improving their skills, however, generally succeeded."

In the years since Tailhook, and the wreckage of so many careers in its wake, the progress and achievement of women aviators in the United States Navy has stabilized and advanced in considerable measure. These female pilots have wanted the chance to fly jets in the service of their country, which is their right, as Jean Zimmerman pointed out in her book, *Tailspin.* "If they die," she said, "that too is their right." Of Lt Kara Spears Hultgreen, who was killed in her F-14, Zimmerman wrote: "Hultgreen's crash rendered her concerted efforts to fly front-line jets in tragic high relief—all the days spent in congressional hearings, all the requests for transfer to combat aircraft, lobbying for her right to die. Hultgreen was, of course, after something else: the right to live her life on her own terms. What was especially bitter was that every person has to fight to be in her line of work, but nobody had to fight as hard as she did. Her death might have placed her activities in a light both ironic and cruel, but it cannot detract from the essential dignity of that effort."

THE HELICOPTER

The concept of the helicopter is at least as old as the fourth century AD when a Daoist book recorded: "Someone asked the master about the principles of mounting to dangerous heights and traveling into the vast inane. The master said, 'Some have made flying cars with wood from the inner part of the jujube tree, using ox-leather [straps] fastened to returning blades so as to set the machine in motion.'

The "machine" is a rotary aircraft whose thrust and lift result from one or more engine-driven rotors. It is capable of taking off and landing vertically, of hovering, and flying forwards, backwards, and sideways. Its advantages over conventional fixed-wing aircraft include the ability to operate in congested or isolated areas, and to hover and loiter for extended periods while its crew handle specialised tasks such as search and rescue operations. The word helicopter derives from the French helicoptére, which originated from the Greek words helik/helix (twisted or curved) and pteron (wing) and was first coined by the French inventor, Gustave de Ponton d'Amécourt in 1861. This begins to describe Leonardo da Vinci's 15th century idea for vertical flight achievable by means of what he referred to as an "aerial screw". A seemingly insignificant moment came late in the 19th century when the French toy maker Alphonse Pénaud built small, rubber-band-powered coaxial rotor model helicopter toys and one of them was given to the brothers Orville and Wilbur Wright by their father. It is believed to have influenced and inspired the Wrights in their own efforts to develop and operate a flying machine.

Enrico Forlanini invented an unmanned helicopter-like machine in 1878, powered by a steam engine. It achieved a vertical take-off and a height of 40 feet where it hovered for about twenty seconds. And in 1907, another French inventor, Paul Cornu, built a helicopter employing two twenty-foot counter-rotating rotors with power provided by a 24 hp Antoinette engine. It's initial twenty-second flight to an altitude of one foot is considered to be the first helicopter free flight with a pilot.

The technology of the helicopter was ramped up substantially in the 1920s when the Argentine inventor Raúl Pateras-Pescara success- fully experimented with and demonstrated the concepts of cyclic pitch and autorotation, and, with British government funding, produced a helicopter powered by a 250 hp radial engine, capable of flying for ten minutes.

In the years leading up to the Second World War, several other pioneering inventors advanced the development of the machine that came to be popularly known as the chopper, and in 1936, the German Focke-Wulf Fw 61 entered limited production, becoming the world's first operational helicopter.

In the United States, Igor Sikorsky designed and built the R-4, which would become the first mass-produced helicopter and would serve in the Second World War, mainly in the rescue role. Sikorsky produced more than 400 R-4s, R-5s, and R-6s by the end of the war. Meanwhile, the American manufacturer Bell Aircraft was building the more sophisticated Model 30, which would become the Bell 47, the first helicopter certified for civilian use and the most popular helicopter for the next three decades.

The varied uses for the helicopter, with its extended hovering capability, its vertical take-off and landing capability, and its stable handling characteristics at low airspeeds, quickly developed both military and civilian markets for it. They included transportation, tourism, fire-fighting, construction, and, in the navy, anti-submarine warfare, search and rescue, replenishment, and a variety of other jobs of importance.

To achieve its amazing flight capabilities, a helicopter is equipped with four flight control inputs: a cyclic, a collective, anti-torque pedals, and a throttle. The cyclic control is commonly positioned between the pilot's legs and is sometimes called the cyclic stick, and is similar to the control stick in a fighter aircraft. The cyclic is called that because it alters the pitch of the rotor blades cyclically, tilting the rotor disk in a particular direction. Thus, pushing the cyclic forward tilts the rotor disk forward, causing the rotor to produce forward thrust. Pushing the cyclic to one side tilts the rotor disk to that side producing thrust in that direction, making the helicopter hover in that direction.

The collective (collective pitch control) is to the left of the pilot's seat. It has a friction control that may be set to prevent inadvertent movement. Using the collective alters the pitch angle of the main rotor blades—collectively—to increase or decrease the altitude of the helicopter. The anti-torque pedals function similarly to the rudder pedals in a fixed-wing aircraft, controlling the direction of the nose of the aircraft, by changing the pitch of the tail rotor blades to increase or decrease the thrust of the tail rotor

In 1957, the Sikorsky Aircraft Corporation of Stratford, Connecticut, received a U.S. Navy contract to design and develop an amphibious anti-submarine warfare helicopter capable of detecting and attacking submarines. Less than two years later the Sea King prototype flew and in 1961, production deliveries of the new helicopter began. The Sea King served the Navy for forty-five years, finally being retired in 2006, to be succeeded by the Sikorsky SH-60 Seahawk.

The Sea King was innovative as the first anti-submarine helicopter powered by turbo-shaft engines. It proved superb in the anti-submarine and hunter-killer roles, which had previously been handled by two separate helicopter types. Intended for shipboard operations, Sea King's five main rotor blades could be folded back for stowage. The reliable workhorse helicopter had the added safety factor of being able to fly safely on only one of its two engines, and with its design incorporating an amphibious hull, it was able to land on water if necessary. The Sea King excelled in various capacities including, but not limited to, anti-submarine warfare, search and rescue, transport, airborne early warning, and anti-shipping, as well as acting as a plane guard responding when another aircraft crashed during carrier take-off or landing.

The Sikorsky SH-60 multi-role shipboard helicopter has been represented in the U.S. Navy fleet in three distinct versions. The B is an anti-submarine warfare version. With its radar, magnetic anomaly detector, electronic surveillance measures, infra-red and sonobuoy sensors, the SH-60B Seahawk is able to detect and track submarines and surface ships, and attack them with missiles and torpedoes. The SH-60F Ocean Hawk is the supercarrier-embarked version whose primary job is to provide an anti-submarine warfare capability for the inner-zone defence of the carrier strike group. Additionally, the F operates in rescue, plane guard, and logistics roles, as well as combat search and rescue, and the insertion and extraction of special warfare forces. An advanced model, the SH-60R Strikehawk, has replaced both the B and F models, minus the magnetic anomaly detector. The R brings many improvements to the Navy: additional stores stations, improved computer and cockpit displays, the AQS-22 dipping sonar, the UYS-2 acoustic processor, a multi-mode radar, improved infra-red sensor, and an improved electronic surveillance system, along with an integrated self-defence system. It began service with the Navy in 2002. The B and F versions are also operated by Australia, Greece, Japan, Spain, Thailand, and Turkey.

Another form of seaborne utilization of the helicopter is the amphibious assault ship, or landing platform—helicopter. The Royal Navy's HMS *Ocean* was designed and built in the 1990s to support amphibious landing operations, deploying an embarked force of Royal Marine Commandos, and operating as a support base for counter-terrorism activity, supported by aviation and landing craft. *Ocean* is further capable of limited anti-submarine warfare.

Launched in 1995, *Ocean* was homeported in Devonport, Plymouth, England. With a cruise speed of fifteen knots, she has an 8,000-mile range. She operates with a ship's complement of 285 officers and crew, together with 180 Fleet Air Arm personnel. She has capacity for 830 Royal Marines, their equipment and forty vehicles. Her armament is four 20mm cannon and three Phalanx anti-missile defence close-in weapons.

Ocean's Air Group was equipped with up to six HC-4 Sea King helicopters, and six AH-7 Lynx light-lift/anti-tank helicopters, and the
Commando Helicopter Force provides up to six AH-1 Apache helicopters
operated by the Army Air Corps.

Among her assignments, Ocean participated, together with the carrier
HMS *Illustrious*, in the 2000 suppression of rebel activity in Sierra
Leone; a UK task force deployment in the 2003 Iraq war; in various
Allied joint exercises; in humanitarian operations relating to the 2010
eruption of the Eyjafjallajokull volcano in Iceland; and in 2011, she was
deployed as part of the Response Force Task Group in aid of operations
in Libya. She is assigned to participate in security operations for the
2012 London Olympic Games.

In 1950, helicopter training for the U.S. Navy was shifted from NAS Lakehurst,
New Jersey (site of the tragic destruction of the airship *Hindenburg* on 6
May 1937), to Ellyson Field, Pensacola, Florida, the cradle of naval avi-
ation. The field was named in honour of the Navy's first aviator,
Commander Theodore G. Ellyson.

The Pensacola/Milton, Florida area is home to NAS Whiting Field, one
of the Navy's two primary pilot training bases (the other is NAS Corpus
Christi, Texas). Whiting also provides training for Coast Guard, Air Force,
and U.S. Marine Corps student pilots. Whiting is split into two training
fields; one for students learning to fly the fixed-wing Beechcraft T-6
Texan II trainer, and the other for trainees on the Bell TH-57 Sea Ranger
helicopter. The TH-57 became operational with the Navy in 1968 and has
since trained several hundred student pilots a year.

In 1983, helicopter training at Whiting moved from use of the
Vietnam-era TH-1 Huey, to the advanced TH-57C Sea Ranger. It is on
the Sea Ranger that the student naval aviator is taught that his or her
instrument, stability, and control systems are to be believed in and trusted. And at Whiting, they must learn their job and sharpen their skills in
the context of the difficult turbulence and thermals that are regularly
part of the Gulf Coast weather. Beyond learning to fly the helicopter, the
training stresses the manoeuvres used in the fleet helicopter operations of
the Navy, Marine Corps, and Coast Guard in relation to external loads,
night landing zone, low-level navigation, climbs, descents, crossovers,
break-ups, rendezvous, and emergency procedures. All of this leads to
carrier qualification after more than 200 flight time hours of extremely
demanding training as the student naval aviator makes his or her way
through the rotary-wing pipeline to the fleet.

In 2000, Claire Donegan flew Sea King Mk 6 helicopters with 820 Squadron,
Royal Navy, from HMS *Illustrious*: "We have to do the dunker every

two years. As aircrew, you have to do six runs. The first one, you go to Yeovilton where the dunker is. They strap you in the seat in the front. Then you go down in the water to the bottom of the pool and, when the thing has come to rest on the bottom, you make your escape. Then they do a series of runs that get more and more difficult. In the final one, they don't even really give you a chance to strap in. It's a sort of uncontrolled situation where they turn the lights off around the pool so it's pitch black. Then they drop the dunker into the water and spin it around a few times so you end up upside-down. They also fix it that some of the exits that you would normally use to get out of are blocked; the windows have buckled or whatever. You actually have to use the little oxygen supply, which is almost like a little aqualung, that we carry on our survival vests. You practice getting that into your mouth, controlling your breathing using it, and then finding your way through the aircraft to an alternative exit.

"We also do Culdrose every six months, where we jump in the pool and inflate our life jacket, get in our little personal survival pack which we clip to our life vest and sit on throughout the whole of the sortie and which, in the event of a ditching, should come with us. Abandon Aircraft drills . . . we do wet-winching, so we'll be thrown into the sea and picked up by a search-and-rescue helicopter from our squadron. That's done every two years. We have a naval swimming test which is to swim about fifty metres in overalls. You have to do that at Dartmouth or in your basic training as soon as you join the Navy. If you don't pass, then you have to go into remedial swimming lessons."

Jason Phillips was an Observer Instructor and Warfare Instructor in Sea King helicopters with 820 Squadron aboard HMS *Illustrious*: "Our primary role on the squadron is to hunt submarines. We do that using sonar and there are two sonars on board. The active sonar is like a big microphone, a long bit of electric string that we lower into the water. We press a button and it sends out a pulse of noise. If there is anything out there, the pulse bounces off it, comes back and is displayed on the computer's green waterfall display. Because we put out a 'ping' when using active sonar, that lets the submariner know that we are there. Ideally, we like to sneak up on him, to give our weapon the best chance. We also use a passive sonar: a smaller microphone on a thinner bit of electric string. It goes down in the water and just listens. It floats to the surface and has a little radio antenna. Everything it hears is up-linked to the aircraft and displayed on the same screens. No noise, no ping, it just listens. A trained air crewman with super-sensitive hearing will pick out the contact and pass the information across to the observer who is the tactical coordinator. We can be the tactical nerve centre when we get a contact with a submarine. I would then take over as the scene-of-action commander. No matter the seniority of the ships in the area, we can tell them to move out of the way while we deal with the submarine. We control the weapons and carry up to four torpedoes on board. The weapon we use is a Stingray, a highly intelligent weapon. Another bit of equipment we have is the MAD or magnetic anomaly detector, which detects magnetic disruptions in the earth's field. It's a big bar magnet and if we fly over something like a submarine, a big lump of metal, it causes a disturbance. We have a sensor which a crewman operates, and the contact is also painted on an old-fashioned chart recorder. If we think there is a target down there, we can fly over it just to corroborate our information."

TO THE FLEET

Their training standards are among the highest in the world. They have to be. Naval aviators must be capable of operating safely and efficiently in the most adverse circumstances. When the pilots of a carrier air wing come out to the boat for a refresher carrier qualification (part of the ship's work-up prior to a six-month deployment), they normally practice their landing approaches when the ship is within a reasonably short distance of the beach. They know that if they have to, chances are that they will be able to divert and land safely on a nearby airfield. The practice is good for perfecting their skills and helps build their confidence for doing what is probably the most important and demanding part of the job: bringing their multi-million dollar airplanes, and themselves, safely back aboard the carrier. Once deployed, however, they can no longer rely on that safe proximity to a friendly airfield ashore should they need it. For them, it's the boat or nothing. They need to have worked out any kinks in their approach and landing technique before they can perform safely and confidently in the blue water environment, out of reach of the beach.

A pilot who gets too many bolters (failed carrier landing attempts), or has a tendency to be a bit low in the approach, for example, must cure himself of such habits and achieve consistency in his traps (carrier landings), both day and night, to become truly blue water-competent. Key in the final weeks of the pre-deployment work-up is the identification of any such flaws. If these habits cannot be overcome, both mechanically and psychologically, the pilot will be deemed not up to scratch, and unsuitable for operational deployment.

Who are these men and women who fly the warplanes of the Navy? Where do they come from, these pilots and aircrew who don flight suits, g-suits, survival gear, helmets, oxygen masks and more, and shoehorn themselves into tight-fitting cockpits so they can sling-shot from the relative security of their carrier to whatever may await them on their missions? How did they get to the fleet, these people who, in all weathers and the blackest of nights, must return from their missions and somehow locate their ship, often with no visual ques, and come aboard, no matter what, because there is no other place to land? They are the best of the best, drawn, like moths to light, to the greatest challenge in aviation.

Jeff Mulkey flew with Helicopter Anti-Submarine Squadron 8 aboard the carrier USS *John C. Stennis* [CVN-74]. A 1993 graduate of the U.S. Naval Academy, he describes the path taken by those who want to fly with the U.S. Navy. A typical American naval aviator comes to NAS Pensacola, the cradle of naval aviation, from either the Naval Academy or a college ROTC program, or from Officer Candidate School. "It all starts in Pensacola with API—Aviation Preflight Indoctrination, which lasts for about six weeks. Then you go on to a Primary Flight Training squadron, known as a VT, at either Pensacola or Corpus Christi, Texas. All naval aviators—regardless of whether they become jet pilots, fixed-wing propeller pilots, helicopter pilots, or Naval Flight Officers—start primary training in fixed-wing and the basic training is all the same no matter what type of aviator you are in the Navy.

"From Primary training it branches out, based on the needs of the Navy in the week that you are graduated. The grades that you receive during that training also affect the Navy's decision about which aircraft community you will be sent to. It will send you to one of several pipelines, the biggest ones being Propeller, in which you would end up flying P3s, C-130s or some other prop type; Helicopter, which can branch out to any of the types of helicopters we fly; and Jets, which could be F-18s, S-3s, EA6Bs, etc. If you go into the helicopter pipeline, you stay there at Pensacola and train in the TH-57 at Whiting Field. The pipelines then branch out to Advanced training. For advanced in Jets, you go on to either Meridian, Mississippi, or Kingsville, Texas; for Advanced Propeller, it's Corpus Christi, Texas. At the completion of Advanced training, pilots are 'winged' and officially become naval aviators. Then you go to the Fleet Replacement Squadron (FRS), also known as the RAG or Replacement Air Group. At the FRS or RAG, you learn to fly the particular type of aircraft that you will fly permanently in the fleet. That is where a jet pilot may become an F-18 pilot, or a helicopter pilot may become an HH-60 pilot. There you are sent to your community within the communities at the FRS.

"In terms of elapsed time before you get to the fleet, it depends on the particular pipeline and how smoothly things are running for you, but if all goes well, you can get to the FRS in a year-and-a-half to two years. On completion at the FRS, you head to your first sea tour or fleet squadron. The flow of the pipelines works pretty much the same for all naval aviators, whether helicopter, jet or prop. On average the total process these days takes you about three years to get to your first fleet squadron—a pretty long time. But they are making an effort to weed out some of the 'pools' that have built up in the past, and the demand is certainly high for pilots in the Navy, so they are beginning to move more quickly through the pipelines. The primary reason for the increased demand is the number of mid-grade pilots that are electing to leave the service. The Navy is losing a lot of the more senior folks; the mid-career officers who have finished their initial commitments and have opted to get out and pursue other interests, whether they be commercial aviation or some other type of job. The senior leadership is still there. The new guys are still coming in, but the middle is eroding a bit. It's the same across the board . . . fixed-wing, rotary and jets.

"Everyone in naval aviation is aware of their obligation. No one enters into it without realizing how much time they're gonna owe. But life changes. Most people are not married and do not have children when they start flight training. If you do get married and have children, suddenly you are five years into it and your outlook may be quite a bit different from what it was when you were single. It's talked about—separation—but until you have actually done it, until you have gone through a carrier work-up cycle, until you have been away from home for six months or more and gone through a cruise and experienced what it's like, only then can you know.

"Everyone thinks at the outset that they are ready to accept the life and the obligation, but they don't really know until they have been there. The Navy sets the commitment that both it and the individual agree to and accept. It's a contract and all sides understand that. Certain people deal with it better than others; some enjoy it more than others, but the contract is always honored, whether for personal reasons or because the Navy says you will, or out of a sense of honor and obligation, or because of monetary reasons. A whole lot of money is spent training a person to do what we do and the Navy has every right to expect to get our services for a number of years, for training us to do this."

Dale Dean, Director of the Aviation Training School at NAS Pensacola: "We give you a test to see how smart you are and how good you are at problem-solving. If I were to define the perfect person for us, it would be someone who scored well on the test and is about 5 feet 8 inches tall. That's important because we have anthropometric concerns. When you are sitting in the aircraft, you have to be able to see over the glare shield, to reach all the switches, to fully throw the controls in out-of-control flight, maybe negative g, and you have to be able to reach the rudder pedals, and, if you have to eject, not tear your legs off. If you are 5 feet 2 inches tall and have little T-Rex arms, you're probably not going to qualify. If you are 6 feet 7 inches tall and your legs go under the glare shield, you are probably not going to qualify, at least not for jets. We want that academic profile and we're looking for a fairly athletic, medium-build person. And then there is the part that is hard to
define . . . motivation. You have to really want to be here. You're not just coming to get your ticket punched, spend a couple of years flying here and then go on to the airlines. How badly do you want to be here? Are you willing to gut it out and put up with the inconveniences to get to fly?

"So, it's a three-part requirement. You have to be able to do the job, fit in the plane, and really want to be here. The people who do best . . . are not necessarily the ones who have engineering degrees; it's the ones who really want to fly, they just want to fly. They are really smart, have good eyesight, good hand-eye coordination, a quick mind, able to quickly grasp detail. In general, most successful naval pilots or NFOs are successful naval officers as well. They do pretty well with their ground jobs, are multifaceted and able to handle more than one detail at a time. A lot of it is attitude. You have to want to be here. You have to enjoy it. You have to want to be in charge, to take control of the situation. That's where success comes from."

What sort of person flies the F/A-18 Hornet front-line fighter in the U.S. Navy today? One example is David Tarry of VFA-147 on the USS *John C. Stennis*: "I've been flying the F-18 for about fourteen months. Ten months getting through the initial training and four months with the squadron. The primary purpose of the airplane is to cover both the fighter and attack roles. We have different master modes for our computer that let us fight our way in, drop our ordnance and then fight our way out, without dedicated fighter support. The Navy is moving towards a multi-role airplane and away from the dedicated fighter and the dedicated attack plane. The F-14 has been phased out and the Super Hornet is our next front-line, followed eventually by the Joint Strike Fighter (JSF). The Super Hornet is also taking over the tanking, which the A-6 used to do, and is the future of naval aviation until we can get the JSF on line.

"When we launch from the cat, the F-18 pilot grabs the 'towel rack', a grab-handle on the canopy frame, prior to and during the launch. The aircraft rotates on its own with the trim that we set, but right after you come off the front end, you grab the stick immediately. They just don't want you to put in any stick control because it would disturb the trim. You can do the same taking off at the field. It's pretty much hands-off. As you get the airspeed and wind over the wing, it just naturally rotates and takes off. It's a very user-friendly plane. The computer systems we have allow us to go from a two-seat cockpit, like the F-14 or the A-6, dedicated fighter or dedicated attack, to where we can do all of that with a single-seat plane because it is so user-friendly, with the hands-on throttle and stick system (HOTAS). You can run your computer and all your displays, and almost never take your hands off the stick and throttle. It takes most of the work out of flying and actually lets you concentrate on working the weapons systems and flying the plane as a weapon. Higher level guys who have at least a few hundred hours in the plane are very comfortable working their way in and working their way out, and not having a backseater to help them. The computer is really your backseater, taking care of a lot of the administrative tasks.

"To land an F-18 on a carrier, you are coming in at somewhere between

130 and 140 knots and trying to hit that little piece of ground and stop that quick. Lots of my friends can't believe I do it. They can't see how you can do something that precise. But really, with the training you have, you just start off and everything is just baby steps. They never have you take a big step. You start out in a small turboprop, just learning basic flying and how to land at the field. You go to an Intermediate jet trainer where you start working with higher speed manoeuvres, but still just working at the field. You get into Advanced training and start learning more tactical things. You start doing some bombing, some air-to-air fighting. Then you do a long period of field carrier qualifications, using the lens to land at the field. They work you up and work you up, and then you go to the boat in Advanced during the day. Then you go to the FRS, the RAG, where you learn how to fly the F-18. You learn how to do the bombing, how to do the air-to-air fighting, and then you do day and night field carrier work, and, finally, eventually, the carrier qualification. But everything is done in baby steps. By the time you get to the fleet, it's not an unfamiliar environment. That's a big step. Seeing the sight picture; looking down from 16,000 feet while holding overhead and thinking, 'I'm gonna land on that postage stamp down there', sure gets your heart rate going. But they baby-step you along so much that it's really not a huge leap of faith to be able to do it.

"When you learn to land at night on a carrier, it's basically the same pattern that you fly during the day. So when you make the transition to night, you're doing the same thing you do in the day. You just don't have the visual reference, but if you do everything at night the way you are supposed to do it during the day, you should roll out in exactly the same spot. Again, it's a little step. Take away the visual reference. But you do it enough at the field, and you start flying extended patterns, or holding in a marshal stack and then flying straight in to pick up the Instrument Landing System (ILS) or the Automatic Carrier Landing System (ACLS). I find that night landing is actually a little easier, because you are doing a straight-in. You aren't doing the approach, hitting specific numbers and having to roll out. Rolling out, making the transition from the turn to wings level, is a pretty big power correction. With the small, stubby wing that we have, you're pretty high up on the power in that approach turn, so when you roll out you get all that lift back under your wings You've got to come quite a bit off the power, keep the rate of descent, and then get back on the power so you can find the middle happy place. But if you're coming in on a straight-in approach, you are three miles out and making the transition from straight and level flight to about three degrees glide slope down, a little power off, a little power back on, adjustments here and there to establish yourself on glide slope, and then, for three miles you're just fine-tuning. By the time you are flying the ball, it's just little corrections and maybe a little power on as you fly through the burble, depending on how the winds are across the deck.

"Once you get used to flying at night, and get over the mental aspect, which is really what the problem with night is . . . it's more of a mental thing . . . that you don't have the horizon and the visual reference, but once you get over that it's really not bad at all. You use the same rules that the Landing Signal Officers (LSO) teach us all the time. If you're a little high, lead it and step it down. If you're low, get it back up where it's supposed to be. There is no life below the datums. You don't want to be caught just hanging around down there, so get it back up. Ball flying is ball flying, whether it's dark or light out. You do so much of it at the field that it becomes more muscle-memory than anything. 'OK, the ball is down. I've got to get it back up.' It becomes subconscious. The talk about the zen of ball flying. It's an art, it's a religion to have that touch, that feel. I don't know that I have it yet. I'm still working on it.

"The F-18 is fun to fly. It's the greatest job in the world. Every day I fly, I can't believe that I'm doing it. I can't believe that anybody would let somebody do it. We're no different from anybody else; there's nothing that sets us apart from everybody else except, maybe, that we have the eyesight to get in. That's the big thing with carrier aviation. It keeps out a huge percentage of people who would love to do this and are more than smart enough to be able to go through the training and do it. But the Navy has such rigorous eyesight standards, mostly because of night landing. You have to have really good eyesight.

"The Hornet is a great airplane; a great ball-flying airplane. It's easy to put the ball where you want it, easier than the F-14 or the Prowler, whose systems are more manual and take a lot more work to fly. The F-18 has a great system that helps us to be safe and get aboard safely. Taking off the front and landing on the back is more admin than anything else, and you just want to be able to do it safely. The LSOs are always pushing: 'Just be safe.' You don't want to be low on approach because it's not safe. If you are high you can always go around and try again. If you do that four times and you have to tank, we have tankers. Go get some more gas, but always be safe. Never drag the ball in low just to get aboard, taking the risk of settling right at the back end of the boat. Our bosses tell us that our job is to go downtown and drop bombs, or fight our way, or defend the strike package that's going in. Getting back on the boat is just admin, but it's one of the prime spots where you can get in trouble."

"Usually a student is kept free of trouble by instructors, and the student tries to keep himself out of trouble because he wants to succeed alongside his peers. But stupidity appears to many of us at the very time we are happiest. In 1954, during Primary Training at Pensacola after I had soloed, I thought I had mastered the SNJ trainer, and one day over Perdido Bay I was practicing aerobatics for my next check ride. I did a slow roll and hadn't

got the nose high enough on the entry.When I was upside down I let the nose fall through, and, rather than roll out, I split-essed. I blacked out from g during the pull-out and awakened to see the Indicated Air Speed needle exceeding the red line, and expected to see the wings tear off, but the airplane held together. It shook me up but I got over it."
—Paul Ludwig, former U.S. Navy attack pilot

Royal Navy pilot Danny Stembridge flew FA2 Sea Harriers with 801 Squadron from HMS *Illustrious*: "I went through flying training to fly the Lynx maritime attack helicopter. I had a fantastic time doing it and part of me actually still misses it. It wasn't as satisfying as flying a fast jet, but I think it was more enjoyable. When you are flying a fighter there is very little time to think, 'Wow, this is fun.' That's more in retrospect. Now I think that the satisfaction I got from flying Sea Harriers outweighed the fun I had flying helicopters. The Sea Harrier was very demanding. It wasn't hugely ergonomic inside, and you were working hard because of that. The air defence environment is a busy one, and you're on your own. Then you have to come back and land on a ship in a VSTOL fighter. Bringing the Sea Harrier alongside, with its lack of systems to help you and its inherent lack of thrust, and therefore the amount of fuel that you require to come aboard . . . it takes a lot of brain power and piloting ability. You're working, from the minute you start preparing for a sortie 'til the minute you finish debriefing it, and afterwards, if it's gone right, it's immensely satisfying. It's a job that has to be done, when you're airborne, whether you are training or not, and the satisfaction comes afterward.

"If you mishandle the Sea Harrier in any way, particularly in the VSTOL regime, it will bite you hard. It will really punish you if you make a basic error in VSTOL regime. But the training is pretty intense and pretty long as well. Because of my rotary flying background, I had a slightly different pipeline, but the Sea Harrier training is a very long course and a lot of it is spent in learning to tame the plane in the VSTOL regime, just flying it. With other fighters, once you've learned, they are similar to other types, but with the Harrier, you are always learning how to fly it and how to operate it in the role for which it was designed.

"Coming from flying helicopters, I have found it easier and a lot more comfortable around the ship than other people do, because of my experience of about 1,200 deck landings on very small ships in a helicopter, many of them at night. Ship-borne operations are unique, and to have that to fall back on when everything is looking horrible . . . you're coming down the glide slope, you're in cloud and wondering if the ship is actually gonnabe there at the end . . . I'm used to seeing the ship pop out of the gloop at the bottom. Other people may not be. I also think that the hovering experience has helped me immensely.

"As for the danger involved in the flying, it doesn't keep me awake at night. In the past, when I've done what could be construed as scary things, that hasn't kept me awake. Maybe in six months my view will have changed. But I think if you're the kind of person to do this, then it's very unlikely to worry you. Otherwise you wouldn't be doing it."

Michelle Vorce graduated from the U.S. Naval Academy in May 1997: "As I went through the Academy, I wanted to go into the Medical Corps. Aviation wasn't my first choice. I'm unusual in that, for about 95 per cent of the people at Pensacola/ Whiting Field, Aviation was their first choice. I had been selected for med school and by the time we had to turn in our final selection sheets, I hadn't heard back from the medical schools where I had been interviewed, and I had to make a selection. I had done a one-month cruise on the carrier *Kittyhawk* and was able to fly all sorts of aircraft, so I decided to give aviation a shot and see how I liked it. I chose it as my first choice and got it. I went through API at Pensacola and then did my Primary at Whiting. After four-and-a-half months I selected jets and went to Kingsville, and was there for six months before they realized that what they called my anthropometrics, my height measurement, didn't fit the fleet. I was sent back to Whiting to fly helicopters and was winged on 17 December 1999.

"I went through the Academy from '93 to '97, which was after all the problems with sexual harassment. I never once experienced a problem. I got high leadership positions without a problem and I think I was generally respected by both male and female counterparts. I fit in real well and was accepted and respected. In training it was on a par or even better, especially in the helicopter community. We females are still a definite minority, especially in this field, but it's getting better. The instructors are very respectful, never surprised or shocked at our ability or competency. If you study hard and perform well, and you show that you've earned the right to be there, just like your male counterpart, you are accepted right off."

One who came late to flying is Nick Walker of 801 Squadron, Royal Navy. Nick was a ship driver until July 1994, when he entered flying training: "I hit the front line on Sea Harriers in July '99. The Sea Harrier is unique. It's not the fastest or the most modern aeroplane. It's got a great radar, a great weapon, which makes it very formidable as an air defence fighter. And it's got these nozzles which make it unique. Learning to fly it was . . . very different. You get used to learning how to fly aircraft faster and faster and lower and lower, and then you get to the Sea Harrier and they teach you how to stop in flight. From about 100 knots downward, its wing is not very efficient and produces very little lift, so once through 100 knots in a decelerating phase, you have to progressively put more and more power on to keep the aircraft in the air. Coordination. It certainly concentrates the mind, recovering to the ship. Half the time we land conventionally, going forward at speed. But on the boat it's vertical landings every time; recovering to a moving airfield that is going up and down as well as forward, is a challenge.

"Coming back to the ship is very well controlled. We have a certain time to be landing on deck. It's called a Charlie time and it is given to us to fit in with the rest of the ship's programmes. Once airborne we are managing our fuel, both to achieve the mission aims, do our training or whatever, and also so that we can arrive back in the vicinity of the ship with the correct amount of fuel, so we are not too heavy for the vertical landing. You have to be quite critical and careful about how you manage your fuel. If you are going to start dumping it, which you have to do on most sorties to make your weight back at the boat, you need to dump down at the correct time, generally about fifteen minutes before your recovery so you can properly slot into the boat.

"Assuming it's a nice day, it's then up to us to come back to the boat on our own. We might get some assistance from the air directors in the Ops room who can pick us up on radar and give us steers back to the overhead. We then set up a holding pattern 1,000 feet over the ship. The pattern is about two-and-a-half minutes long. You go around in a circle above the ship and, two-and-a-half minutes prior to your landing, or Charlie time, you fly past the ship at 600 feet and slightly on the starboard side of it. That's called the slot, and once you have slotted, you then turn in front of the boat so that you are effectively on a cross-wind leg and you roll out going down wind . . . the opposite way to the boat. As you approach the back of the boat, with all your checks complete and your landing gear down, you tip into the finals turn and it's around that turn that you start to wash off your speed by using some of the nozzles. You are playing the nozzles to keep your speed and angle of attack under control around the turn. As you approach, you roll out behind the boat and start in towards it. You then judge when to take the hover stop, to move the nozzles all the way downward to allow the aircraft to hover. This means that there is no thrust going out the back of the aircraft, so it starts to slow down a bit more rapidly. The idea is to arrive alongside the boat in a steady hover next to the landing area you have been allocated, at about 80 feet above the sea level and just off to the left side of the boat. Once you have steadied yourself into a nice position and are happy with your references next to the boat, you transition across by moving sideways about thirty feet to line up just over the mark you have picked. You reduce power just a bit and the aircraft starts to sink. It's quite a firm landing because on a wet or pitching deck, if the wheels don't make a good contact, it would be easy to slide about.

"You think about the danger, although not all the time. You're very aware that the Sea Harrier is a difficult machine to fly; that if you don't keep on top of it, if you don't concentrate during decelerations and accelerations into and out of the hover, it can go wrong very quickly. There is a higher chance in this aeroplane that you may have an accident or crash or have to eject, or even be killed. It's something that you do think about now and then. I don't think about it when I strap into an aeroplane, when I go flying. The training you get is very good, and there is no way they are going to send someone out to fly the aeroplane if they don't think they can do it. When something happens to someone you know, that brings it home to you. It is a dangerous occupation, but I don't think it would stop me doing it. I don't think it would ever make me so scared that I wouldn't want to do it."

Once told by his flying instructor, "You will never solo. You are the dumbest cadet I have ever laid eyes on." U.S. Marine night-fighter ace Bruce Porter became one of the great fighter pilots of the Second World War: "As I stood watching my first night carrier ops, the feeling that crept over me was as eerie as any I had ever had. All I could hear was two high-performance engines. All I could see were two sets of landing lights. There was absolutely no moon to light the wake or give a hint of the ship's whereabouts. There was a slight breeze over the bow.

"Suddenly, one set of lights was over the wake. The approach was textbook perfect, right up to the wake at precisely the correct speed, attitude and altitude. I heard the engine drone lower as the pilot took the cut and I watched the outline of the night-fighter arrest on the first of second wire. As the first Hellcat taxied forward to just beneath my perch, the second one set down in a textbook landing.

"For all the hours of training and instruction I had received, I had not really believed it possible before seeing it with my own eyes.

"We gathered around the two Navy veterans and asked a set of rapid-fire, nervous final questions. Then someone with a bullhorn blared: 'Fly One, Marines, man your airplanes.'

"It had been decided that only one of us would launch and recover at a time, until everyone had completed one landing. I was the senior one in the group, so I would launch first. I did my best to hide my terror, and I think the only reason I was not found out was that everyone else was too deeply involved in masking their own fright to notice mine. My flight gear was still in the cockpit of my Hellcat, so I climbed aboard and quickly snapped snaps and pulled straps. I recalled my first real moment of truth in an airplane, my qualifying solo at the elimination base at Long Beach, California in 1940. I had been eager to fly then and had remained eager as I passed every milestone to this moment, when I found myself unforgivably apprehensive for the first time in my flying career. The prospect of first

combat had not come as close to terrorizing me as this flight. I turned up
the engine and allowed myself to be guided to the catapult. Before giving
the catapult officer the 'ready' signal, I nervously checked and rechecked
my harness, pulling the straps again for good measure. Then I ran through
my pre-flight checklist; screw the men in the island who were moaning
about how long I was taking: canopy back and locked, engine at full rpm,
prop at full low pitch, flaps all the way down for maximum lift, right foot
hovering above right rudder pedal ready to overcome the left torque of the
spinning prop, stick held loosely
in my right hand, throttle grasped loosely in my left hand, head resting
against the headrest to take up the shock of the catapult.

"I looked to my left and saluted. Ready! In response a dimly-perceived
deckhand standing over the catapult crew's catwalk whirled a flashlight.
Go! I turned my eyes front, loosened my grip on the stick, set my jaw and
leaned back into my seat.

"WHACK. My conscious mind was aeons behind my senses, as it had
been on all previous catapult launches. I had a very busy couple of seconds
as I kicked right rudder pedal and yanked the stick into the pit of my stomach. I had no time to dwell on how dark it was out there.

"My equilibrium returned. The Hellcat was climbing away to the left. I
got the wheels and flaps up in one motion. I had that familiar short sinking
sensation as the flaps went up and the Hellcat dropped slightly. Then my
mind kicked in: 'needle—ball—airspeed, you dumb cluck.' A destroyer
passed beneath my left wing. I had just enough time to notice two blinking
navigation lights before the inky black of the perfectly dark night enfolded
me.

"All my training and experience saw me through a climb to 3,000 feet.
While my mind reeled off a thousand facts about my flying, my voice
talked to the ship in calm tones, reporting on routine matters the air officer
would want to hear about. I was neither here nor there.

"I was cleared to land, which was both relief and concern. I wanted to
get down but first I had to find the carrier.

"I coaxed the Hellcat into one full circuit of the area in which I was
pretty sure I had left the Tripoli and her escorts. I saw the two navigation
lights on the forward destroyer I had overflown after launch. Then I saw
two more which had to be the plane guard destroyer deployed a few thousand yards directly astern of the carrier, to pick up downed 'zoomies', as
we carrier pilots were known.

"Now I knew exactly where the flight deck lay. I also knew that, in the
event of extreme danger, the carrier flight deck lights would be flicked on
to help me find a safe roost. But that would mean failure, and there
were too many people watching to let that happen.

"After reassuring myself that I was flying on a heading opposite that of the ship, I flew down the carrier's port side and approached the plane guard from ahead, keeping it just off my port wing. I could not help ruminating about how useless a night search for a bilged aviator must be.

"I flicked on my radio altimeter, a brand new instrument that had been installed in my cockpit just before we left San Diego. I had set it for 150 feet. If I flew above that altitude, I'd get a white signal light. If I flew below 150 feet, I'd get a red danger light, and if I was flying right at 150 feet, I'd get a comforting green light. The light was green when I turned on the altimeter.

"I flew upwind the length of the tiny destroyer and sighted her deck lights, which could only be seen from the air. This was the only concession to a pilot's natural tendency to become disoriented across even the briefest interval of night space.

I had been timing my flight ever since passing the carrier and spotting the plane guard's lights. At what I judged to be the best moment, I turned 90 degrees port, dropped my wheels and flaps, enriched the fuel mixture, partly opened the cowl flaps, put the prop in low pitch, and turned another 90 degrees to arrive at a downwind position dead astern of the carrier.

"My night vision was, by then, as good as it would become. I had been training myself to find dim objects with my peripheral vision, which was the preferred method. Thus, I was able to pick out the dim shape of the totally darkened carrier as I floated up the wake.

"I was committed to the approach. All my attention was focused on sighting the LSO's luminous paddles. I momentarily panicked and said, or thought I might have said, 'Where the hell are you?'

"First, I sensed the colored paddles; then I knew I saw them. The LSO's arms were both out straight. Roger! My ragged confidence was restored, though I was a good deal less cocky. I checked my airspeed, which was down to the required 90 knots. Before I knew it, I saw the cut. The tail-hook caught a wire and I was stopped.

"I taxied past the barrier, came to a rest beside the island and cut my engine. As had been the case after my first combat mission, my flight suit was reeking of sweat.

"During the rest of the night, my eight fellow fledglings each made one night landing. My subordinates accounted for more than a few wave-offs, but that was partly my doing. I had asked the LSO to be particularly unforgiving of minor gaffes. We all knew how important it was to get this exercise 100 per cent perfect."

Paul Ludwig: "It has been said that those who stand and wait also serve. I didn't fly combat because there was no war. Like countless others, I was there if they needed me. I had to be content with peacetime operations, and I was. It excited me to fly the meatball or make paddle passes, to launch from a deck run over the bow or, once in a while, get a cat shot, and fly the downwind leg, judge the 180 degree turn in a stiff tailwind and come aboard smartly in a prop-tailwheel type aircraft, like my heroes in F6Fs and F4Us did in World War II. I was a kid, hoping to follow in their footsteps if there had been a war. Few are eager for a war, yet every kid joining the fleet thinks he is bullet-proof and that, if war comes, he'll just follow his leader and do whatever he does.

"Everyone remembers his solo flight, his first emergency, his first girl, first car and so on. I ate up six months of peacetime carrier flying as though nothing else in the world mattered. In some ways, nothing has ever topped that, other than the love of a wife and the births of healthy children. Thank God there wasn't a war on when I served, but when you're in uniform, you serve. I am damned proud of what I did."

Willam Hannan was a jet engine mechanic aboard the carrier USS *Kearsarge* during the Korean War. "It would be difficult to imagine a more hazardous place to live than an aircraft carrier. Apart from the airplanes landing (and sometimes crashing) on our roof, the ship carried millions of gallons of flammables, including fuel oil, high-octane gasoline, paints, thinner, as well as tons of bombs, rockets and assorted ammunition. And scuttlebutt had it that we were being shadowed by submarines.

"Although much of our maintenance work was performed on the hangar deck, some of it was topside, under incredibly harrowing conditions. Imagine working on a wintry night, on a frosty deck in rough seas, close to the edge of the ship. Only dim, red-lens flashlights could be employed under blackout conditions. If a man happened to slip over the side into the ocean, about eighty feet below, there was little chance of him being missed, let alone rescued. Being assigned to plane-pushing meant long hours of physically hard work in particularly dangerous circumstances. Once during my turn on this dreaded duty, I was well forward on the wet flight deck during a launch operation when I was suddenly blown to the deck. I went sliding rapidly towards the propeller planes poised aft with their engines running. I was desperately clawing at the wooden deck, hoping to grab on to one of the numerous metal tie-down strips, when a huge bruiser of a fellow spotted my predicament and, at considerable risk to himself, literally tackled me and dragged me over the edge of the deck into a catwalk. Probably no one else had even seen me. I was speechless, and didn't even have a chance to thank him before he rushed back to his post . . . a hero in my view, but probably all in a day's work on the flight deck for him.

"Oral communication was often difficult on the flight deck, even without aircraft engines running. With jet and prop plane run-ups, it was almost impossible. The ship's powerful 'bull horn' public address system could sometimes be heard over the din, but, even in the absence of noise, the bull horn messages were sometimes garbled or distorted like old-time railroad station announcements. So an elaborate system of hand-signals evolved that usually worked to make a point.

"The *Kearsarge* converted sea water into fresh quite efficiently, but it had to serve many purposes, the first of which was feeding the ship's thirsty boilers. Conservation measures had to be strictly observed. The shower protocol, for example, was to wet down, turn off the water, soap up, turn on the water, rinse, and turn off the water. Once, I had just finished soaping up and was covered with suds, when 'general quarters' was sounded (loud horns over the intercom system, meaning 'get to your duty station immediately!') I grabbed a pair of shower sandals and my jockey shorts and rushed up to the hangar deck. A 'red alert' was in effect and we could not leave our stations for any reason until the all-clear was sounded. Still covered in soapsuds, I was very cold and beginning to itch all over. But it could have been worse. At least I wasn't up on the flight deck.

"Field days were clean-up times, and meant hard work to anyone involved. The worst thing about them was the closure of the heads (toilet facilities) for cleaning. Time on the ship for 'pit stops' was at a premium there, and often there was little margin for delay in attending to such bodily functions. How frustrating then, after climbing down a deck or two, to find a HEAD SECURED FOR CLEANING sign on the entrance, and, either by coincidence or design, any nearby heads were also frequently out of service.

"We headed home at a leisurely pace, probably to reduce wear and tear on the ship's machinery. As keeping idel hands out of mischief was a foremost consideration in the Navy, all sorts of chores, such as chipping paint from decks and then repainting them, were assigned to anyone who appeared to be unoccupied. In our squadron, the most unsavory of our F9F Panthers was selected to have its paint manually stripped, a dirty, tedious job at best, especially when it was freely admitted that the job really didn't need doing."

Among the many wonderful aircraft of the Duxford, England-based Fighter Collection is, arguably, the ultimate piston-engined air superiority fighter of the World War Two era: the Grumman F8F Bearcat. Stephen Grey is the man behind The Fighter Collection and he flies the Bearcat, as well as several other splendid fighter types, in air shows every year, the greatest being Flying Legends each summer at Duxford. Grey probably knows the Bearcat at least as well as anyone who has ever had anything to do with it. "One approaches the Bear with care. On the deck, it looks exactly as it was intended—the smallest airframe that could be mated to the Pratt & Whitney 2800 engine, whilst swinging that huge Aeroproducts propeller, 12' 7" in diameter, with the broadest blades you ever did see and just six inches ground clearance, without the oleos depressed. The whole thing is achieved by sitting it on extraordinarily long mainwheel legs. They have, of necessity, been attached to the extremities of the wing centre section and an ingenious double hinge system is adopted to fold the upper portion outwards as the main portion folds in. Difficult to describe but, believe me, an amazing amount of ironmongery folds away into a small hole (as the actress said to the Bishop). Somehow, they also found space for a 150-gallon centreline drop tank.

"The span is only 35' 6", the length an exceptionally short 27' 8" but it sits 13' 8" high. A mean, muscular-looking Bulldog. The cockpit is tiny, European style, with controls well placed but with canopy rails so tight against my shoulders that I have to be helped in—damn that apple pie.

"I am in it, so fly it. Those early days were quite educational. The only piston engined fighter I had then flown was the Mustang. Whilst the 51 has bags of torque, no one would complain that it was overpowered—rather, slightly overweight, like certain pilots I know. The briefing was pretty exhaustive: 'Do not exceed 54" and get the gear up before 140 knots.'

"Having been used to the long throttle travel on the 51 and needing all of it on take-off, I was surprised that an inch of throttle movement gave me 50" and a very rapid view of the side of the runway. I pulled up the nose to avoid exceeding the gear speed and the runway lights, to find myself in what seemed like the vertical. Finally cleaned up, I looked down to see this major Florida airfield as a tiny model, thousands of feet below. Out over the Everglades, even back at 1900 r.p.m. and 29.5", I was still several miles behind the aircraft. Within a few more minutes I had a sensation of familiarity and increasing exhilaration. The Bearcat is a joy to throw around. Harmony of control, aided by its spring tab ailerons, is outstanding; the controls delightfully light and very responsive. It demonstrates all the hallmarks of a great day fighter in that it has poor stability, which translates into rapid divergence and, with its high power/thrust to weight ratio, outstanding agility. The manual says this is not an instrument aeroplane. Believe it.

"Clean stalls are under the book figure of 100 knots, as the Fighter Collection aircraft is unarmed and lighter. The onset has little warning, excepting a very brief stick shudder prior to an immediate wing drop. With everything down, the stall comes at 70 knots, the nose dropping hard and violently off to the left after the same brief shudder. A rapid application of power will torque you around the prop. Potentially disastrous on the approach.

"Accelerated stalls are straightforward, until you try them whilst reducing or, still worse, adding coarse power. The resulting snap rolls have to be experienced to be believed. The aircraft is so short coupled, you need the draught over the tail at any time you go for high Alphas.

"Another cute trick, which took me some time to work out, is aileron reversal. Induced by simultaneously pulling hard and rolling at very high speeds at low altitude, I first put in hard left aileron and found myself rolling right. Then, just as you have considered what the hell is happening and the speed is backing off, the Bear rolls hard left. We went right through the geometry, the rigging, the spring tabs, the lot, before I flew it again.

"Subsequent, deep examination of the manual showed a max deflection aileron limit of 4.5g. An experienced old salt confirmed that the wing was first twisting unloaded, then the ailerons work. This was, apparently, a 'design feature' of all Bearcats. Whoever said wing warping was ineffective? Needless to say, we now do no barrel-like manoeuvres at high speed in the Fighter Collection Bearcat.

Another part of the early education was during practice for the first air show. I pulled up for the first Cuban and whilst inverted looked for the rollout target on the airfield, only to find it twice as small as the same in a 51. Yippee, I will do a one-and-a-half downward instead of a half. Through 360 degrees and back to inverted, the Bear was oscillating longitudinally and beginning to tuck under. A quick glance at the ASI showed I had hit the Candy bar, 435 knots and still accelerating. Fortunately I was unladen and still rolling (the correct way) when I hit the compressibility dive brakes. The oscillation stopped and I now had the problem of avoiding the increasingly large airfield. We thoroughly inspected the airframe and my underwear after that one.

"I do not wish to leave you with the impression of an impossible roaring monster. The aeroplane is a beautiful, well domesticated 'Pussycat' (but still with teeth and claws) when flown well within its envelope—as we have done since those early 'hooligan' days.

"The Bearcat was the end of an Era, the end of a technology. The ultimate piston engined air superiority fighter? The Spitfire XIV or the Sea Fury could give it a run but different fun."

When Hellcat pilot Larry Cauble left the west coast of the United States aboard the jeep aircraft carrier USS *Barnes* in February 1944, he could not have imagined the adventure that awaited him in the south-western Pacific. "The jeep carrier was built on a merchant ship hull and was smaller and slower than the fleet carriers. It was built utilizing the Kaiser shipyard assembly-line method, which took only about one-fifth of the time needed to build a fleet carrier. The ship was packed from stem to stern and the hangar deck was full of aircraft being transported to the combat area to replace losses. There were about thirty of us Ensigns going out as replacement pilots to squadrons in action. The number of additional officers made things very crowded on a ship of that size. We were travelling through the tropics and, of course, in those days there was no air conditioning. Such niceties as sleeping spaces, cool ventilation, and water for showers, were in short supply.

"It can be a little awkward, joining a squadron already in combat and replacing a pilot who has been killed or lost in action. The squadron members may tend to compare you with their missing friend and squadron mate. I have to say though that in both of the squadrons I joined and flew combat with, I was readily accepted and, after a few days of flying, was treated as a fully-fledged member.

"I was assigned to Fighting Squadron Five (VF-5) aboard the USS *Yorktown*

(CV-10) when we arrived at Espiritu Santos in the New Hebrides. After a brief familiarization with the squadron, my first combat flight was to be an attack on airfields on the island of Peleliu. It was 30 March 1944, and I was so nervous and keyed-up that I didn't see a lot of what was going on, including where my own .50 calibre rounds were hitting.

"As we circled back after strafing and sinking a small enemy freighter about five miles off the coast, we saw life boats in the water with uniformed soldiers in them. We knew that the Japanese were shipping replacement ground troops down from the home islands, so we attacked the life boats. The .50 calibre machine guns really tear up wooden boats and human bodies. Between my section leader and myself, we were firing twelve .50s. Pieces of life boats and bodies were flying everywhere. What we didn't know when we opened fire was that, in addition to the soldiers, there were women in the boats. What they were doing there, in an active combat area, I had no idea. Although it was an unpleasant and very graphic sight, if I had it to do over, I would not do the mission differently. We had, of course, read of terrible atrocities committed by the Japanese; Nanking, where some 300,000 Chinese civilians were raped and slaughtered, being just one example, and our squadron had lost three pilots the day before this mission, so revenge was undoubtedly a factor too. Our Marines were then having a difficult time in the ground fighting on Palau, and they certainly didn't need to face fresh enemy reinforcements. War is a messy business of killing people and breaking things. There is no nice way to do it. Obviously, I would have preferred that there had been no women in those life boats, but they were there so they were going to get the same treatment as the combat troops in that situation.

"I had only been with the squadron two months when it was ordered to return to the US to be reformed and readied for another combat tour. I persuaded the CO to let me transfer to a training squadron so I would be sent out again as a replacement pilot. I was ordered to VF-1 and flew a brand new F6F Hellcat aboard the *Yorktown*. On my first day aboard, the commanding officer invited the eleven of us who had just reported in, to his stateroom. He told us that he didn't know why we were aboard, and that he didn't need us. He then chastised several officers for having non-regulation belts or other uniform infractions. That was the last time I had any direct contact with him. VF-1 had been out in the combat area for about five months when I joined them, and had been shore-based on the island of Tarawa before being transferred to the *Yorktown*. After our greeting from the skipper I had no desire to stay with VF-1, so when we got back to Hawaii I requested transfer to the replacement squadron at Barber's Point.

"The replacement squadron felt that our squadron had been out in combat for such a long time that we needed a rest, so they sent us to spend two weeks in a mansion right on Waikiki Beach for a little R and R. It was delightful . . . private beach, surf boards, food prepared by a Navy staff, and a hostess who mothered us and chaperoned when young ladies were brought out from town.

"After that pleasant interlude I returned to the war, this time with VF-19 aboard the USS *Lexington*, and a great commanding officer. My fellow pilots there were most welcoming. Friendships and comeraderie develop quickly under combat conditions, not just between contemporaries, but between seniors and juniors, because each is dependent on the other in a tactical situation for protection from attack by enemy aircraft, and other mutual assistance.

"I was assigned as wingman to Lieutenant Bruce Williams. Lieutenant JG Paul Gartland was the second section leader. I flew many combat flights with this tactical division. The first five flights were combat air patrol over the fleet. These flights were in defense of the task group and we generally flew in thirty to forty mile circles at 20,000 to 25,000 feet, waiting for the ship's fighter director to send us to intercept incoming enemy attack aircraft.

"On 21 September 1944 I participated in the very first attack of the war on Manila. We were part of a fighter sweep sent to get control of the air. It was to be the first time that I had been fired at by another airplane. Tracer shells going by your wing can get your adrenaline going very quickly. Some pilots lose control of one bodily function or another in such circumstances. It is a very frightening experience. Fortunately, another pilot behind our division shot the attacking plane down before its pilot had a chance to correct his aim. Over Manila one of our planes was badly shot up and the pilot had to bail out. We saw his parachute open, but as he was descending he was strafed by an enemy fighter. The bullets appeared to saw him in half. It was a gruesome sight and made us realize that there was no chivalry in this air war. That particular enemy fighter was then shot down by one of our squadron pilots.

"On 14 October I shot down a Zeke, my second kill. I shared it with 'Willy' Williams since we had both fired at it simultaneously. The task force then headed south. Being so close to Japan, the Navy was concerned that the enemy could fly replacement aircraft down to reinforce its units on Formosa, and for the next three days I flew combat air patrol over the fleet as we headed for an area to the east of the southern Philippines.

"Our division was sent out on 21 October to fly west across the Philippines and look for targets of opportunity. We found a wooden barge tied up at the island of San Isadore, and there was no anti-aircraft fire so Willy told us to get ready by sections for a strafing run. As Willy and I made our run in from 5,000 feet, we were scoring a lot of hits when the barge suddenly erupted in one massive explosion. Willy's plane was slightly ahead and about fifty feet lower than mine, and he caught the full force of the blast from what had obviously been an ammunition barge.

"Willy's canopy was shattered. His face was cut in so many places that blood was getting in his eyes. He thought he was losing his eyesight. We had been at full power for the strafing run and Willy was still at full power and heading west, away from our ship. We were now 250 miles from the *Lexington* and were concerned about having enough fuel to get back to the ship. We had been out about two-and-a-half hours. Leading the second section, Paul radioed for me to get Willy; that he [Paul] was heading back to the carrier. There was no response to my radio calls asking Willy to reduce power and turn back towards the ship. Finally, I caught up with him and could see that there were big chunks of wood protruding from his wings, pieces of flap and tail section were missing, and his canopy was broken.

"We were using fuel at an alarming rate and heading the wrong way. It took three or four minutes and seemed like an eternity until, with the use of hand signals, I was able to get him to give me the lead. I started reducing power to economic cruise and got us turned around and headed towards the *Lex*. We had a two-and-a-half hour flight ahead of us, so we exchanged hand signals every few minutes as I wanted to keep Willy alert and informed about fuel management, the distance to go, and other flight information. Many of his instruments were shattered, so he could not navigate. When we were thirty miles out from the carrier, I contacted them about our situation. They instructed me to land first. They were concerned that Willy might crash-land and foul the deck if he landed first, leaving me no possibility of coming aboard. Willy seemed to understand my hand signals that he was to land last, but when he saw the carrier he headed straight in without flying a pattern, landed and immediately ran out of fuel. I circled once while they pushed him out of the landing area. Then I landed and ran out of fuel. We had been in the air five hours and thirty-six minutes, a long flight for the Hellcat.

"On 28 October *Lexington* was ordered to the fleet anchorage at Majuro in preparation for her return to Hawaii and the US. As we were leaving the combat area, we were told to transfer some of our best airplanes to the USS *Franklin*. I was one of the pilots selected to fly a Hellcat over to the *Franklin*. We were to fly there, land and be returned by breeches buoy transfer to a destroyer, and then transfer back to the *Lexington*. We expected to be back aboard the *Lex* in two to three hours. It was late in the day and, as there was a slight chance that we might not be able to get back before dark, I decided to take a shaving kit and a khaki uniform with me. We no sooner landed aboard *Franklin* when the fleet was attacked by Betty bombers out from Manila. Our transfer was cancelled, of course. The *Lexington* was hit by a kamikaze which did great damage to the island structure. The *Lex* was ordered to leave the task force and proceed to the fleet anchorage at Majuro for emergency repairs. There I was on the *Franklin*, with no way to get back to my clothes and possessions, my squadron mates and my ticket back to the States. Then things got worse.

"The next day the *Franklin* was hit by a kamikaze. Many people were killed, there was a lot of fire and the damage was considerable. I had no general quarters station so I joined one of the pilots from VF-13 in manning a fire hose on the flight deck. I knew several of the pilots there from training and replacement squadron days, and they helped me get a place to bunk. Owing to the extensive damage, there were to be no hot meals for the duration of my stay on board.

"*Franklin* survived (just) to return to Majuro for emergency repairs, so she could get back to the Pearl Harbor shipyard for a more complete repair. Luckily, Air Group 19 was being transferred from the *Lexington* to the *Enterprise*, for transportation back to Hawaii and on to the US, and I was able to get back to the *Lex* to pack my things and leave the war zone for the last time."

George Wallace, as Royal Navy Fleet Air Arm Commander (Air) headed the Air Department aboard HMS *Illustrious* in 2000, and was responsible for all aspects of flying on board the carrier. Known in *Illustrious* as "Wings", his role was equivalent to the Air Boss on an American carrier. The Air Department in the British carrier was made up of two parts. One, the ship's company, are with the ship permanently; the other is comprised of the squadrons, which were not always with the ship. When the squadrons were embarked, they fell within the Air Department, and when they were disembarked—which could be for months at a time—they went back to their air stations, such as RNAS Yeovilton in Somerset. While they were disembarked it was the responsibility of the air stations to be sure that they delivered the squadrons back to the ship ready to do their jobs and be operationally capable. Wallace: "I talked with the air stations so that they had a good understanding of the requirement on board the carrier. When the guys came to the ship with their aeroplanes, they had been properly trained and were fit for purpose. We then got them on board and went off to do what we needed to do.

"Normally, we had on board a squadron of Sea Harriers, six or seven aircraft, a squadron of anti-submarine warfare Sea King helicopter, seven aircraft, and a flight of electronic warfare Sea Kings. Recently, [in 2000] we had a flight of RAF Harrier GR7s. These embarked from time to time for training and for operations in the Gulf and the Adriatic in recent years. That is the way of the future, a joint package of capability which can be delivered from the sea, to combine the fighter sweep, escort, and combat air patrol, with the GR7's air-to-ground capability.

"I think the RAF came to the ship with a bit of trepidation, not quite knowing what they were letting themselves in for, but it worked very well and they went away thinking 'we can do this.' There was a lot of work needed before embarkation to make sure that any difficulties or problems, either from our perspective or theirs, were ironed out before they got here so they were comfortable with coming on board. We needed to work quite carefully together so that when we deployed that capability for real, it was not something that was new. It was something we were all comfortable with, that we had worked towards and that was going to be a continuing process. It was carefully linked into Joint Force 2000, a coherent organisation putting RAF Harriers and Navy

Harriers together with Nimrods and search-and-rescue Sea Kings. Joint Force 2000 would enable a joint view towards how we were going to deliver capability at sea and from ashore. Putting the Harrier force together, was to be the first step in a joint expeditionary-style operation.

"Most RAF guys didn't join that service to go to sea. The crucial thing, though, was to be able to deliver that capability. That means a properly planned sequence of training events to build that capability and maintain it. The special needs of operating aircraft at sea are such that you can't just expect to have them fly aboard and, five minutes later it all works. It doesn't. It needs a lot of hard work to bring it all together. We knew the size and shape of the task and could apply the right sort of effort to be sure that the end product was useful and efficient.

"We had to fly at a certain level or standard to maintain the skills, and practice them daily, weekly, or whatever. The ship's programme was really the driver in putting together a programme of activity to maintain or work up skills for a particular operation.

"My job fell into two main parts. One was planning what we were going to be doing, and the other was doing it, on a day-by-day or week-by-week basis.

"The integration of the RAF GR7s brought with it a degree of uncertainty about what was going to happen. These were guys who hadn't flown to the deck before, so that was an interesting, heartbeat-raising period. When we were doing an exercise, it got really busy. For example, using the Harrier FA2s to generate a two-over-two combat air patrol on a continuous basis . . . that was quite a drain. On the fixed-wing side alone we ended up launching and recovering aircraft every hour-and-a-quarter throughout the day. There were peaks of activity punctuating the day, and on top of all that you had the helicopter flying, which was going on throughout. All that was quite challenging, but we had watchkeepers in the Air Department so we could keep that sort of thing going twenty-four hours a day. The thing I had difficulty with, there was only one of me, and keeping it going twenty-four hours a day relied on me being around when the plans were coming together and when potentially tricky events were happening. That was quite tiring. Generally, in an exercise, I was up and working from five in the morning until midnight the next day. Once you got into that sort of routine, it was OK, but making the transition from a more normal working regime to that regime takes a few days. My principal job, in terms of the day-to-day conduct of flying, was maintaining the wide picture so we didn't forget things . . . so that the things that happened at short notice could be picked up while all the other things were going on all around us.

Understanding the nuances of fixed- and rotary-wing aircraft can be tricky. Commander Wallace came from a helicopter background and he understood the Sea King. His previous job, prior to coming to *Illustrious*, was at RNAS Yeovilton, where he was responsible for delivering the Sea Harrier jet "product" to the front line, a job he held for two-and-a-half years. "I had that much understanding of the Sea Harrier force, but the Sea Harrier was a single-seat fighter and unless you're a single-seat fighter pilot you never really know what it's like. I had a feeling and interpretation of what it was like, but in this job I had to rely heavily on the fixed-wing expertise of our Harrier pilots, the guys who *do* know. You can't, of course, be skilled in every aspect of flying, and it's the mix of the team that's important.

"Certainly, the fixed-wing stuff was the most interesting flying we conducted. Generally, the helicopters went about their business and, once we had the plan together, that was fine. With the fixed-wing side there were always going to be peaks of activity. The perceived or actual pressure to get the jets launched on time to meet their operational target . . . if it was during an exercise, there was not quite so much pressure. In an operation though, where you had, say, four FA2 Sea Harriers and four GR7s launching at the same time to go rendezvous with a much bigger package at a particular time, getting them off the deck was quite a challenge. If it was at night or in dodgy weather, or both, it was more of a challenge. The most difficult and stressful time was when you had everything on the margins: marginal weather, aeroplanes with marginal performance and marginal fuel states, all coming back at the same time, and you have get them on the deck because there is nowhere else for them to go. That was, perhaps, the most testing of times, but it could be done and was done regularly. The more we practiced the more comfortable we were that it could be done safely and efficiently—and getting things done safely was what it was all about. Whether in peacetime or in support of an operational mission, it's got to be done safely.

"When I went through flying training a number of years ago, I suspect there was a degree of latitude that individuals had which I don't think is the case today. I think the standards today are very rigorous and they are applied absolutely. I know the standards and am very happy when a guy comes and joins a squadron here. I know that he is capable. There is less latitude these days and that is perfectly right. We have complicated aeroplanes and complicated missions to be done, and we need the highest standards for the guys that we are inviting to go off and do these missions. It's tighter these days and I'm glad it is. Not to say that we were getting it wrong twenty years ago, but it was different. The aircraft were older and we didn't have quite so much reliance on technology and switchology which every aeroplane brings these days. People today have to be extremely capable of making it all work because if it doesn't, the mission is not going to work. It's better today, but we do demand a huge amount from our people and they do come and provide the goods. It's a management challenge to try to keep that motivation and enthusiasm going so that we can sustain."

The author is grateful to the following people for their kind, generous assistance in the research, preparation, and development of this book, and for the use of their published and unpublished texts: John Bolt, Eric Brown, Shannon Callahan, Francesco Chierici, John W. Dean, James H. Doolittle, Thomas Draude, Claire Donegan, Frank Furbish, George Gay, Tess Gay, Paul Gillcrist, Ross Greening, Loree Hirschman, John Keegan, Paul Ludwig, Ted Mason, Richard McCutcheon, Jeff Mulkey, Jason Phillips, Bruce Porter, Eleanor Roosevelt, Saburo Sakai, Kazuo Sakamaki, David Tarry, Michelle Vorce, John Waldron, Nick Walker, Nigel Ward, John Wellham,

BIBLIOGRAPHY
Bennett, Christopher, *Supercarrier*, Motorbooks International, 1996.
Brown, Captain Eric, *Wings of the Navy*, Airlife Publishing Ltd., 1987.
Caidin, Martin, *Golden Wings*, Bramhall House, 1960.
Clancy, Tom, *Carrier*, Berkley Books, 1999.
Eliot-Morison, Samuel, *The Two-Ocean War*, Atlantic-Little Brown, 1963.
Farmer, James H., *Celluloid Wings*, Tab Books, 1984.
Garrison, Peter & Hall, George, *Carrier Aviation*, Presidio Press, 1980.
Harrison, W.A., *Swordfish Special*, Ian Allen, 1977.
Humble, Richard, *Aircraft Carriers*, Michael Joseph Ltd., 1982.
Ireland, Bernard, *The Rise and Fall of the Aircraft Carrier*, Marshall Cavendish, 1979.
Jackson, Robert, *Air War Korea 1950-1953*, Airlife Publishing Ltd,, 1998.
Johnston, Stanley, *Queen of the Flattops*, E.P. Dutton & Co., 1942.
Kelly, Orr, *Hornet*, Airlife Publishing Ltd., 1990.
Lawson, Robert & Tillman, Barrett, *Carrier Air War*, Motorbooks Int'l., 1996
Loomis, Robert D., *Great American Fighter Pilots of World War II*, Random House, 1961.
Lowry, Thomas P. & Wellham, John, *The Attack on Taranto*, Stackpole Books, 1995.
McManners, Hugh, *Top Guns*, Network Books, 1996.
Mercer, Neil, *The Sharp End*, Airlife Publishing Ltd., 1995.
Poolman, Kenneth, *Escort Carrier 1941-1945*, Ian Allen, 1972.
Shores, Christoper, *Air Aces*, Bison Books Ltd., 1983.
Smithers, A.J., *Taranto 1940*, Leo Cooper, 1995.
Sweetman, Bill, *Joint Strike Fighter*, MBI Publishing Company, 1999.
Wellham, John, *With Naval Wings*, Spellmount, 1995.
Wrynn, V. Dennis, *Forge of Freedom*, Motorbooks International, 1996.